CIMA

PRACTICE & REVISION KIT

Stage 1 Paper 3

Economic Environment

BPP Publishing
January 2000

First edition 1995
Sixth edition January 2000

ISBN 0 7517 3488 8 (previous edition 0 7517 3847 6)

British Library Cataloguing-in-Publication Data
A catalogue record for this book
is available from the British Library

Published by

BPP Publishing Limited
Aldine House, Aldine Place
London W12 8AW

www.bpp.com

Printed in England by
DACOSTA PRINT
35/37 Queensland Road
London N7 7AH
(0171) 700 1000

We are grateful to the Chartered Institute of Management Accountants for permission to reproduce past examination questions. The suggested solutions to both the specimen paper questions and past examination questions have been prepared by BPP Publishing Limited.

CONTENTS

 BPP Publishing

Question and answer checklist/index

The headings indicate the main topics of questions, but questions often cover several different topics.

Tutorial questions, listed in italics, are followed by advice on how to **approach the question,** thus easing the transition from study to examination practice.

A date alone (11/96, say) or 'specimen paper' after the question title refers to a current syllabus paper.

Questions preceded by * are **key questions** which we think you must attempt in order to pass the exam. Tick them off on this list as you complete them.

REVISION

This is a very important time as you approach the exam. You must remember three things.

> **Use time sensibly**
> **Set realistic goals**
> **Believe in yourself**

Use time sensibly

1 **How much study time do you have?** Remember that you must EAT, SLEEP, and of course, RELAX.

2 **How will you split that available time between each subject?** What are your weaker subjects? They need more time.

3 **What is your learning style?** AM/PM? Little and often/long sessions? Evenings/ weekends?

4 **Are you taking regular breaks?** Most people absorb more if they do not attempt to study for long uninterrupted periods of time. A five minute break every hour (to make coffee, watch the news headlines) can make all the difference.

5 **Do you have quality study time?** Unplug the phone. Let everybody know that you're studying and shouldn't be disturbed.

Set realistic goals

1 Have you set a **clearly defined objective** for each study period?

2 Is the objective **achievable?**

3 Will you **stick to your plan?** Will you make up for any **lost time?**

4 Are you **rewarding yourself** for your hard work?

5 Are you leading a **healthy lifestyle?**

Believe in yourself

Are you cultivating the right attitude of mind? There is absolutely no reason why you should not pass this exam if you adopt the correct approach.

- **Be confident** - you've passed exams before, you can pass them again
- **Be calm** - plenty of adrenaline but no panicking
- **Be focused** - commit yourself to passing the exam

QUESTION PRACTICE

There is little point in simply opening this Kit and, beginning with question 1, attempting all of the questions. You need to ask yourself three questions.

> **Am I ready to answer questions?**
> **Do I know which questions to do first?**
> **How should I use this Kit?**

> **Am I ready to answer questions?**

1   Try to fill in the blanks on the **Do you know? checklist** for a particular syllabus area. Compare your answers with the corresponding **Did you know? checklist**.

2   If you are happy with what you have written, you can go ahead and start answering questions. **Do not attempt questions if you could not fill in any of the blanks**. Go back to your BPP Study Text and revise first.

> **Do I know which questions to do first?**

1   **Start with tutorial questions**. They warm you up for key and difficult areas of the syllabus. Try to produce at least a plan for these questions, using the guidance notes following the question to ensure your answer is structured so as to gain a good pass mark.

2   Don't worry about the time it takes to answer these questions. Concentrate on producing good answers. There are 10 tutorial questions in this Kit.

> **How should I use this Kit?**

1   Once you are confident with the Do you know? checklists and the tutorial questions, you should try as many as possible of the exam-standard questions; at the very least you should attempt the **key questions,** which are highlighted in the **question and answer checklist/index** at the front of the Kit.

2   Try to **produce full answers under timed conditions**; you are practising exam technique as much as knowledge recall here. Don't look at the answer, your BPP Study Text or your notes for any help at all.

3   **Mark your answers to the non-tutorial questions as if you were the examiner.** Only give yourself marks for what you have written, not for what you meant to put down, or would have put down if you had had more time. If you did badly, try another question.

4   Read the **Pass marks** in the answers carefully and take note of the advice given and any **comments by the examiner.**

5   When you have practised the whole syllabus, go back to the areas you had problems with and **practise further questions**.

6   Finally, when you think you really understand the entire subject, **attempt the mock exam** at the end of the Kit. Sit the paper under strict exam conditions, so that you gain experience of selecting and sequencing your questions, and managing your time, as well as of writing answers.

EXAM TECHNIQUE

Passing professional examinations is half about having the knowledge, and half about doing yourself full justice in the examination. You must have the right approach to two things.

> **The day of the exam**
> **Your time in the exam hall**

The day of the exam

1   Set at least one **alarm** (or get an alarm call) for a morning exam.

2   Have **something to eat** but beware of eating too much; you may feel sleepy if your system is digesting a large meal.

3   Allow plenty of **time to get to the exam hall**; have your route worked out in advance and listen to news bulletins to check for potential travel problems.

4   **Don't forget** pens, pencils, rulers, erasers, calculator.

5   **Avoid discussion** about the exam with other candidates outside the exam hall.

Your time in the exam hall

1   *Read the instructions (the 'rubric') on the front of the exam paper carefully*

Check that the exam format hasn't changed. It is surprising how often examiners' reports remark on the number of students who attempt too few - or too many - questions, or who attempt the wrong number of questions from different parts of the paper. Make sure that you are planning to answer the **right number of questions**.

2   *Select questions carefully*

Read through the paper once, then quickly jot down key points against each question in a second read through. Select those questions where you could latch on to 'what the question is about' - but remember to check carefully that you have got the right end of the stick before putting pen to paper.

3   *Plan your attack carefully*

Consider the **order** in which you are going to tackle questions. It is a good idea to start with your best question to boost your morale and get some easy marks 'in the bag'.

4   *Check the time allocation for each question*

Each mark carries with it a **time allocation** of 1.8 minutes (including time for selecting and reading questions). A 24 mark question therefore should be completed in 43 minutes. When time is up, you *must* go on to the next question or part. Going even one minute over the time allowed brings you a lot closer to failure.

5   *Read the question carefully and plan your answer*

Read through the question again very carefully when you come to answer it. Plan your answer to ensure that you **keep to the point**. Two minutes of planning plus eight minutes of writing is virtually certain to earn you more marks than ten minutes of writing.

6   *Produce relevant answers*

Particularly with written answers, make sure you **answer the question set**, and not the question you would have preferred to have been set.

7   *Gain the easy marks*

Include the obvious if it answers the question and don't try to produce the perfect answer.

Don't get bogged down in small parts of questions. If you find a part of a question difficult, get on with the rest of the question. If you are having problems with something, the chances are that everyone else is too.

8   *Produce an answer in the correct format*

The examiner will **state in the requirements** the format in which the question should be answered, for example in a report or memorandum.

9   *Follow the examiner's instructions*

You will annoy the examiner if you ignore him or her. The **examiner will state** whether he or she wishes you to 'discuss', 'comment', 'evaluate' or 'recommend' (see the section on examiners' instructions on page (xxii)).

10   *Lay out your numerical computations and use workings correctly*

Make sure the layout fits the **type of question**.

11   *Present a tidy paper*

You are a professional, and it should show in the **presentation of your work**. Students are penalised for poor presentation and so you should make sure that you write legibly, label diagrams clearly and lay out your work neatly. Markers of scripts each have hundreds of papers to mark; a badly written scrawl is unlikely to receive the same attention as a neat and well laid out paper.

12   *Stay until the end of the exam*

Use any spare time **checking and rechecking** your script.

13   *Don't worry if you feel you have performed badly in the exam*

It is more than likely that the other candidates will have found the exam difficult too. Don't forget that there is a competitive element in these exams. As soon as you get up to leave the exam hall, *forget* that exam and think about the next - or, if it is the last one, celebrate!

14   *Don't discuss an exam with other candidates*

This is particularly the case if you **still have other exams to sit**. Even if you have finished, you should put it out of your mind until the day of the results. Forget about exams and relax!

THE EXAM PAPER

Format of the Year 2000 exams

A new exam format was introduced in 1999.

		Number of marks
Section A	one compulsory question composed of 14 multiple choice sub-questions	28
Section B	data response question - one from a choice of two	24
Section C	essay questions - two from a choice of five	48
		100

Time allowed : 3 hours

Recent pass rates

The UK pass rate for the May 1999 exam was 47.2%, which was the lowest of the Stage 1 papers.

Analysis of past papers 1995-1999

The analysis below shows the topics which have been examined in the ten sittings of the syllabus and the CIMA Specimen paper for *Economic Environment*.

November 1999

Section A

1   Fourteen multiple choice questions

Section B (Data response questions)

2   Economies of scale, competition
3   Trade cycle, inflation

Section C (Essay questions)

4   Price mechanism, public and merit goods, indirect taxes and subsidies
5   Financial intermediation, share prices
6   Monetary policy
7   Unemployment and fiscal policy
8   Exchange rates, currency unions

This paper forms the mock exam at the end of the Kit, and so only an outline of its contents is given here.

May 1999		*Question number in this Kit*

Section A

1	Fourteen multiple choice questions	69

Section B (Data response questions)

2	Oligopoly, barriers to entry, vertical and horizontal integration	20
3	Structure of UK trade and comparative advantage	64

Section C (Essay questions)

4	Profit and other objectives in a market economy	6
5	Functions of money and control of the money supply	36
6	The money and capital markets and their use by business and government	32
7	Aggregate demand and macroeconomic policy	45
8	Persistent inflation, its effects and controlling it	53

November 1998

May 1998

Examiner's comments

Performance was disappointing after the improvement in the previous examination. Many candidates seemed to be poorly prepared and made basic and fundamental errors.

The most common weaknesses were:

- Failure to grasp fundamental concepts such as price and income elasticity, the distinction between financing and correcting a financial deficit, and the concept of barriers to entry.

- Lack of knowledge of the basic terminology relating to the economy, eg the term 'public sector'.

- Poor examination technique, especially in section C where too many candidates failed to answer the question and many did not balance their effort in relation to the distribution of marks.

Despite this, some high marks were achieved in all questions, especially question 2.

November 1997

Section A

1	Ten multiple choice questions	71

Section B (Data response questions)

2	Output determination for the firm; price elasticity of demand; the demand curve	7
3	The money supply, the rate of inflation and the quantity theory of money	37

Section C (Essay questions)

4	Vertical and horizontal integration; MMC investigations	-
5	Interest rate determination; effects of interest rate changes on business investment and exchange rates	26
6	Role of the central bank; supervision of the banking system	-
7	Injections and withdrawals in the circular flow of income, effect of a rise in savings rate on the business sector	43
8	Causes, financing and correction of a balance of payments current account deficit	65

Examiner's comments

There was a modest improvement in overall performance. Although there are still weaknesses in many scripts, most candidates are making a good attempt at the paper.

The best scripts demonstrated a sound understanding of economic principles and their application, and good examination technique. The most common weaknesses were:

- A poor understanding of some of the elementary ideas in the subject. A small majority of candidates struggled with very basic elasticity concepts in Question 2.

- A continued weakness in questions relating to syllabus section (e), *The International Environment*. While the relevant multiple choice questions were answered quite well, Question 8 was the least well answered of the narrative questions.

- Poor examination technique, especially in section C. Essays were often poorly constructed and candidates frequently failed to allocate their effort in proportion to the marks available for each part.

Examiner's comments

The best scripts showed an excellent grasp of the relevant economic concepts and theories and candidates displayed an ability to use these to explain the particular issues in hand. However, many scripts showed a lack of knowledge and understanding and indicated poor preparation for the examination. The main weaknesses were:

- A poor grasp of some of the fundamentals of the subject, especially in the data response questions (2 and 3).

- An inability to use diagrams appropriately even when these were of the most basic kind.

- A continued weakness in relation to Section (e) of the syllabus (Question 3).

Overall, candidates need to concentrate on acquiring a firm grasp of the central concepts and ideas of the subject; this and an appropriate allocation of time and effort to Section (e) of the syllabus would ensure a significant improvement in examination performance.

Examiner's comments

Overall performance was below that of the May examination. This somewhat poorer performance was partly the result of poor preparation, and partly the result of poor examination technique. Three points in particular should be noted.

- In essay questions, a list of possibly relevant points will secure fewer marks than a clear and structured argument.

- The examination paper is an invitation to candidates to display their knowledge of economic principles and concepts, not to depend on 'general knowledge' to answer questions.

- Candidates should not ignore elements of the syllabus: the examination again revealed that candidates had a relatively poor knowledge of Section (e) of the syllabus, *The International Environment* (Question 8).

May 1996

Section A

1	Ten multiple choice questions	74

Section B (Data response questions)

2	Security/liquidity/ profitability and structure of assets of commercial banks	34
3	Sources of taxation; direct and indirect taxation; taxation, incentives and income distribution	57

Section C (Essay questions)

4	Location of industries; problems with regional specialisation	15
5	Privatisation; regulation of privatised utilities	51
6	Sources of long-term finance for companies; relative merits of equity and debt	31
7	Effects of inflation; anti-inflation policies	53
8	Currency devaluation and its effects on domestic companies	63

Examiner's comments

An improvement in overall performance was noticeable in the data response and essay sections while performance in the multiple choice section was comparable to that of recent examinations. There was general improvement in the understanding of basic economic concepts, suggesting that candidates are coming to the examination better prepared than previously.

The following key weaknesses can be identified.

- Poor examination technique, including poor time allocation between questions and between sections of questions, and answering the wrong number of questions.

- A tendency to resort to using general knowledge instead of economic concepts. As with previous papers this can be seen in parts (b) of Section C questions but was also a problem with the whole of Question 4.

- Candidates need to identify, explain and use the appropriate economic concepts in order to obtain the highest marks.

- Poor performance in questions relating to the International Environment section of the syllabus was evident in both Section A and Section C of the paper, suggesting poor preparation in this area on the part of many candidates.

November 1995

Examiner's comments

The best scripts showed a broad range of knowledge of economic theory and concepts and an ability to use economic theory to explain real economic issues and problems. For many scripts however, the weaknesses that have characterised previous examinations remain, including the following.

- Poor examination techniques. Some candidates answered an incorrect number of questions or failed to complete the paper. Too many candidates failed to allocate time and effort in line with the marks available.

- A problem of application of economic theory. Many candidates scored quite high marks in those sections of questions requiring an explanation of some economic theory or concept, but did very poorly when it came to applying the theory. The mere acquisition of knowledge of economic concepts without the ability to apply them will be of little use to the management accountant.

- Lack of basic knowledge. This reflects insufficient reading of textbooks and of the financial and business press.

May 1995

Examiner's comments

A significant number of candidates failed to follow the instructions given, and answered both data response questions.

Knowledge of basic concepts is essential: even Question 4 on elasticity was poorly answered by many. If students can develop their ability to use economic ideas to explain real world problems, the recent improvement in marks will continue.

Low marks are still being scored on elements of questions which require application or expansion of economic concepts.

Specimen paper

Economic environment: ten common errors, **The Chief Examiner, CIMA Student, August 1995**

The Chief Examiner has found that although most Paper 3 candidates have a good grasp of quite complex economic theory and can use it to explain real-world issues, many repeat errors and misunderstandings about economic concepts.

This article identifies ten errors which you should take care to avoid.

- *Do not confuse a stock and a flow.* In particular, do not use the term 'money' when 'income' is meant. Income is a flow of purchasing power over a period of time; money is a stock of liquid financial assets held at any one time.

- *Understand the implication of price elasticity of demand for total revenue.* Candidates' understanding often stops at the argument that elasticity measures the relationship between a change in the price of a good and the volume of demand for it. For pricing decisions by firms, the critical issue is the effect of a price change on total revenue gained from sales. If the price elasticity of demand exceeds –1, a price reduction will raise total revenue, and a price rise will reduce total revenue.

- *Do not confuse the determinants of short-run costs (the law of diminishing returns to a fixed factor) with those of the long run (returns to scale).*

- *Be clear about the difference between the demand for labour and the supply of labour.* The demand curve for labour shows the willingness of employers to employ workers at different wage rates. The supply curve of labour shows the number of workers willing and able to work in that industry/company at different wage rates.

- *Distinguish clearly between output and productivity.* Output refers to the volume of output (a flow) over a given period of time, for a single company, an industry or the economy as a whole. Productivity refers to output per unit of input over a given period of time, whether of labour or of capital or of some combination of inputs ('total factor productivity'). If output rises (economic growth), productivity has not necessarily increased: it may be simply that more resources are being employed.

- *Be clear about the difference between growth in output and growth in output capacity.* Long-term economic growth is about raising the economy's long-term capacity to produce output and may require a different set of policies from a short-term rise in output. Keynesian reflation may raise output where the economy is operating below full capacity but has nothing to do with raising output capacity.

- *Be clear about the meanings of 'savings' and 'investment' in economics.* 'Savings' refer to that part of the flow of income which is not consumed, and may take the form of acquiring larger money balances or increasing the stock of financial assets held. 'Investment' is a different process by which capital goods (buildings, machines etc) are acquired. Investment must be financed by savings or by borrowing the savings of others via financial intermediaries. The possibility that the volume of intended saving may be different from the volume of intended investment is at the heart of important macroeconomic debates about the stability of market economies.

- *Do not confuse trade deficits and budget deficits.* If the flow of visible and invisible exports is less than the flow of visible and invisible imports, a country is said to have a deficit on the current account of the balance of payments (trade deficit). If a government has a level of taxation income which is less than its expenditure, it is said to have a budget deficit.

- *Understand that financing of a deficit is distinct from correcting a deficit.* A budget deficit can be *financed* by borrowing. A balance of payments deficit can be *financed* by overseas borrowing, selling assets overseas or running down reserves. A budget deficit can be *corrected* either by raising taxation or by reducing public expenditure. A balance of payments deficit can be *corrected* by reducing imports and/or raising exports, for example by devaluation.

* *Do not confuse the balance of trade and the terms of trade*. The current account includes trade in goods and services. The balance of import and exports of visible goods is called the balance of trade. The phrase 'terms of trade' refers not to the total value of imports and exports but to the average price of imports compared to the average price of exports, usually measured as an index of relative prices.

The analysis below shows which topics have been explained in data response and essay questions.

	11/99	5/99	11/98	5/98	11/97	5/97	11/96	5/96	11/95	5/95	Specimen
(a) Economic concepts											
Central issues of economics						✓	✓				
Scarce resources and costs			✓								
Labour and capital technology			✓								
Entrepreneurship and profit								✓			
Demand and supply; elasticity	✓		✓	✓	✓	✓			✓		
Cost, revenue and profits						✓		✓			
Costs and scale of output; growth						✓		✓			
Industry: specialisation and taxation							✓				✓
Business motivation: profit/not-for-profit		✓						✓			
(b) The market environment											
Market structure and competition	✓			✓			✓		✓		✓
Monopoly; oligopoly; monopolistic competition	✓	✓	✓			✓	✓			✓	✓
Public policy on competition					✓			✓			
Competition, efficiency and welfare						✓	✓	✓			
(c) The financial environment											
Financial needs of business/government		✓		✓		✓		✓	✓		
Money; credit; banking	✓	✓	✓		✓		✓	✓	✓	✓	✓
Money demand/supply; interest rates			✓	✓	✓	✓	✓		✓	✓	✓
Capital market institutions								✓			
Share price indices		✓									
(d) Government and the macroeconomic environment											
National income; its calculation				✓					✓	✓	
National income determination		✓				✓	✓	✓			✓
Employment and inflation	✓	✓	✓				✓	✓	✓		
Government policy objectives	✓							✓		✓	
Fiscal policy			✓	✓		✓	✓	✓		✓	✓
Monetary policy						✓	✓	✓			
(e) The international environment											
Trade and the balance of payments			✓		✓	✓			✓	✓	
Foreign exchange	✓		✓	✓				✓			
Trade; its determinants		✓			✓		✓		✓	✓	
Exchange rate systems	✓		✓								✓

(The full syllabus is on pages (xxiii) to (xxv).)

CURRENT ISSUES

Summary of recent articles

The content of any relevant articles published before July 1998 are reflected in the BPP Study Text for *Economic Environment*. Articles published since then have been noted briefly below.

Supply and demand, Steve Adams, CIMA Student, September 1999, pp 78-79

To EMU or not to EMU, Glenn Haldane, CIMA Student, October 1999, p81

EXAMINERS' INSTRUCTIONS

The examinations department of the CIMA has asked the Institute's examiners to be precise when drafting questions. In particular, examiners have been asked to use precise instruction words. It will probably help you to know what instruction words may be used, and what they mean. With the Institute's permission, their list of recommended requirement words, and their meaning, is shown below.

Recommended requirement words

Advise/recommend	Present information, opinions or recommendations to someone to enable that recipient to take action
Amplify	Expand or enlarge upon the meaning of (a statement or quotation)
Analyse	Determine and explain the constituent parts of
Appraise/assess/evaluate	Judge the importance or value of
Assess	See 'appraise'
Clarify	Explain more clearly the meaning of
Comment (critically)	Explain
Compare (with)	Explain similarities and differences between
Contrast	Place in opposition to bring out difference(s)
Criticise	Present the faults in a theory or policy or opinion
Demonstrate	Show by reasoning the truth of
Describe	Present the details and characteristics of
Discuss	Explain the opposing arguments
Distinguish	Specify the differences between
Evaluate	See 'appraise'
Explain/interpret	Set out in detail the meaning of
Illustrate	Use an example - chart, diagram, graph or figure as appropriate - to explain something
Interpret	See 'explain'
Justify	State adequate grounds for
List (and explain)	Itemise (and detail meaning of)
Prove	Show by testing the accuracy of
Recommend	See 'advise'
Reconcile	Make compatible apparently conflicting statements or theories
Relate	Show connections between separate matters
State	Express
Summarise	State briefly the essential points (dispensing with examples and details)
Tabulate	Set out facts or figures in a table

Requirement words which will be avoided

Examiners have been asked to avoid instructions which are imprecise or which may not specifically elicit an answer. The following words will not be used.

Consider	As candidates could do this without writing a word
Define	In the sense of stating exactly what a thing is, as CIMA wishes to avoid requiring evidence of rote learning
Examine	As this is what the examiner is doing, not the examinee
Enumerate	'List' is preferred
Identify	
Justify	When the requirement is not 'to state adequate grounds for' but 'to state the advantage of'
List	On its own, without an additional requirement such as 'list and explain'
Outline	As its meaning is imprecise. The addition of the word 'briefly' to any of the suggested action words is more satisfactory
Review	
Specify	
Trace	

SYLLABUS

The syllabus contains a weighting for each syllabus area, and a ranking of the level of ability required in each topic. The Institute has published the following explanatory notes on these points.

'Study weightings

A percentage weighting is shown against each topic in the syllabus; this is intended as a guide to the amount of study time each topic requires.

All topics in a syllabus must be studied, as a question may examine more than one topic, or carry a higher proportion of marks than the percentage study time suggested.

The weightings do not specify the number of marks which will be allocated to topics in the examination.

Abilities required in the examination

Each examination paper contains a number of topics. Each topic has been given a number to indicate the level of ability required of the candidate.

The numbers range from 1 to 4 and represent the following ability levels:

Appreciation (1)
To understand a knowledge area at an early stage of learning, or outside the core of management accounting, at a level which enables the accountant to communicate and work with other members of the management team.

Knowledge (2)
To have detailed knowledge of such matters as laws, standards, facts and techniques so as to advise at a level appropriate to a management accounting specialist.

Skill (3)
To apply theoretical knowledge, concepts and techniques to the solutions of problems where it is clear what technique has to be used and the information needed is clearly indicated.

Application (4)
To apply knowledge and skills where candidates have to determine from a number of techniques which is the most appropriate and select the information required from a fairly wide range of data, some of which might not be relevant; to exercise professional judgement and to communicate and work with members of the management team and other recipients of financial reports.'

Syllabus overview

This syllabus gives students an understanding of how individual businesses operate within the constraints of the broader economy. It calls for an understanding of the market environment, financial environment, government policy and international trade. Also required is an awareness of resource utilisation, efficiency and productivity, the relationships between cost and price, and supply and demand in domestic and world markets. It is intended as a grounding in economic literacy, and students working through this subject should acquire an ability to read and comprehend much of the information in the financial press about the economy, its systems, markets and institutions.

 BPP Publishing

Syllabus

Aims

To test the candidate's ability to:

- describe the economic and financial environment within which businesses and government organisations operate

- explain how market systems operate and the role of specialist institutions within the markets

- appreciate reports in the financial press about economic developments, the financial markets and their implications for industry and commerce

Content and ability required

		Ability required
3(a)	**Economic concepts** *(study weighting 20%)*	
(i)	Central issues of economics: scarce resources and their allocation	2
(ii)	Scarce resources and costs: land and natural resources, capital, labour and enterprise	1
(iii)	Labour: demand and supply; labour productivity and the role of capital technology	2
(iv)	Entrepreneurship and the nature of profit	2
(v)	Demand, supply and the determination of price; the concept of elasticity	2
(vi)	Costs, revenue and profits; profit maximisation	2
(vii)	Costs and the scale of output, problems of growth	2
(viii)	Industry: specialisation and location	2
(ix)	Business motivation: profit-making and not-for-profit organisations	2
3(b)	**The market environment** *(study weighting 15%)*	
(i)	Forms of market structure and competition	2
(ii)	Monopoly, oligopoly and monopolistic competition: output, prices and efficiency	2
(iii)	Public policy towards competition and business behaviour	2
(iv)	The private and public sectors: competition, efficiency and economic welfare	2
3(c)	**The financial environment** *(study weighting 25%)*	
(i)	Financial needs of business and government; the role of the money and capital markets	2
(ii)	Money and credit; the banking system and its institutions; central, commercial and offshore banking; capital adequacy; money market instruments	1
(iii)	The demand for and supply of money. Credit creation, interest rates and banking activity; yield curve; benchmark interest rates and their significance	2
(iv)	Capital: the capital market and its institutions: stock markets and government bond markets, institutional investors; venture capital; capital market instruments	1
(v)	Share price indices	2

3(d)	**Government and the macroeconomic environment** *(study weighting 25%)*	
(i)	National income and its calculation: income, output and expenditure	2
(ii)	The determination of national income; consumption and investment, accelerator and multiplier effects; government expenditure and taxation and the trade sector	2
(iii)	National income, employment and inflation; measurement of inflation and price indices	2
(iv)	Government policy objectives: growth, price stability, employment, balance of payments	2
(v)	Fiscal policy: direct and indirect taxation; principles, methods and forms of taxation (income tax, National Insurance Contributions, value added tax, corporation tax, capital gains tax, inheritance tax and other taxes and duties)	2
(vi)	Monetary policy: the supply of money and interest rate policy	2

3(e)	**The international environment** *(study weighting 15%)*	
(i)	Trade and the balance of payments	2
(ii)	Foreign exchange; exchange rates: their nature, function and determination; the foreign exchange markets	2
(iii)	Trade and its determinants: prices, exchange rates and demand for imports and exports	2
(iv)	Exchange rate systems: floating and fixed exchange rates	2

CIMA SYLLABUS GUIDANCE NOTES 1999-2000

Syllabus Guidance Notes published by the CIMA in the August 1999 edition of CIMA Student *are reproduced below.*

The following guidelines have been drafted by the Chief Examiner. They are intended to inform candidates and lecturers about the scope of the syllabus, the emphasis that should be placed on various topics and the approach which the examination paper will adopt.

Chartered Management Accountants operate within a wide variety of business organisations, all of which function within the broader economic environment.

The purpose of this syllabus is to enable students to acquire an understanding of how businesses operate within the constraints of that broader economic environment. This calls for an understanding of the economic aspects of the business itself, especially the determination of costs and revenue, and of the wider economy in which the business operates. The latter involves a consideration of the nature of the markets in which businesses operate and of the national and international economy in which those markets are located. The overall intention is to provide a grounding in economic literacy, so that Chartered Management Accountants can use economic principles to explain and understand the economic environment. Students working through the subject should acquire an ability to read and comprehend much of the information in the financial press about developments in the economy, its systems, markets, institutions and performance.

Economic concepts	*Syllabus reference 3 (a)*
	Study weighting 20%

Candidates must have a firm understanding of the basic concepts which underlie much of economic theory. This is important not only because the basic concepts may be directly examined (eg in questions about the price system and resource allocation), but also because they may appear as underlying principles in virtually any question (eg the notion of elasticity). Moreover, questions in Section C will normally require candidates to explain some important principles and to demonstrate an ability to use these principles to explain, or illustrate, an economic issue or problem.

In the examination, candidates may be required to:

- demonstrate an understanding of the significance and origins of the concept of opportunity cost and how it differs from financial cost

- distinguish between the conditions that determine the position of the demand curve (eg consumer preferences and consumer incomes) and the factors that influence the elasticity of demand (eg availability of substitutes and the relative importance of the price of the item in the consumer budget)

- measure price elasticity from given price and demand data using either the point or arc elasticity approach

- draw appropriate conclusions from such information, in particular demonstrating an understanding of the implications for the total revenue of the producer of changes in the price of the product

- demonstrate an understanding of the concepts of fixed and variable costs and their relationship to average and marginal costs, and of the relationship between price, average revenue and marginal revenue. Also calculate such variables from limited cost and revenue data and use the variables to draw conclusions about the business in question

- demonstrate a sound knowledge of the sources of economies and diseconomies of scale and their impact on the structure of costs. Also an appreciation of the general motives for growth and the means by which business growth is achieved, including integration of various kinds

- demonstrate an awareness of the three categories of industry (primary, secondary and tertiary) and an appreciation of the characteristics of each sector including growth and employment patterns, and the degree of involvement in international trade

- demonstrate an awareness of the reasons for government intervention in location decisions and the means by which such intervention is implemented

- demonstrate knowledge of basic theory concerning the nature of the markets for factors of production, in particular the labour market. Also candidates may need to show understanding of wage determination including the marginal productivity theory of wages

The following items are *not* examinable:

- indifference curve analysis

- detailed knowledge of particular industries

- detailed knowledge of the historical development of regional policy in the UK or elsewhere

- detailed knowledge of the institutional arrangements for wage bargaining

The market environment

Syllabus reference 3 (b)

Study weighting 15%

Candidates will be required to display a sound grasp of the relevant economic models of markets and firms. Questions will often involve the application of these models to the explanation of real world market structures and processes.

In the examination, candidates may be required to:

- demonstrate a full understanding of each of the models of market structure: perfect competition, monopolistic competition, oligopoly and monopoly. This includes the importance of the number of firms, the nature of the product and the ease of entry and exit in the industry. Candidates may be required to use the appropriate diagrams of cost and revenue to illustrate their arguments and to demonstrate the concepts of equilibrium and efficiency in each market structure

- apply an understanding of market structures in discussing of issues of public policy towards competition. Prior knowledge of particular cases of government intervention will not be required, but candidates should have a general awareness of the issues involved and the role of the Monopolies and Mergers Commission (MMC) and the Office of Fair Trading (OFT)

- demonstrate an understanding of the public goods, merit goods and natural monopoly arguments for public ownership of productive assets; also of the limitations of public ownership, particularly with respect to productive and allocative efficiency

- explain the benefits and the limitations of a policy of privatisation

The following items are *not* examinable:

- detailed knowledge of the MMC and its relationships with the OFT and the Department of Trade and Industry (DTI)

- detailed knowledge of particular industries in either the public or private sector, although candidates should be able to use examples to illustrate more general arguments

The financial environment

Syllabus reference 3 (c)

Study weighting 25%

Candidates will be expected to have a sound appreciation (ability level 1) of the institutional features of the money and capital markets and a knowledge (ability level 2) of how these markets function. Candidates will also need a basic understanding of offshore banking (the Eurocurrency market), capital adequacy, yield curves and venture capital, but these topics will not form the basis of questions in Sections B and C.

In the examination, candidates may be required to:

- demonstrate an understanding of the financial environment with particular emphasis on the role of money and financial intermediation and the current and capital funding needs of business and government

- demonstrate more than a simple descriptive knowledge of financial institutions. The use of economic theory to explain their roles, functions and relationships will also normally be required

- explain both the determination of interest rates and the supply of credit as well as the impact which changes in these have on business. Candidates will therefore be expected to display a knowledge of the underlying economic theory behind the demand for and supply of money

The following items are *not* examinable:

- detailed knowledge of the operation of particular institutions in the money and capital markets. However, candidates must have a sound knowledge of the main features and functions of commercial banks, stock markets and the central bank. Questions in this area will refer, as far as possible, to generic types (eg central banks) and not to particular national institutions

- theories of share price behaviour; however, candidates should be aware of the possible factors influencing share prices, notably changes in the level of interest rates

Government and the macroeconomic environment

Syllabus reference 3 (d)

Study weighting 25%

Government and the macroeconomic environment

Candidates will be expected to display a sound grasp of economic theories about the economy as a whole and to be able to use simple models to explain such phenomena as unemployment and inflation. They should also be able to demonstrate an awareness of recent and current events in the economy and the development of government economic policy. The examination will often contain questions relating to recent macroeconomic issues and problems.

In the examination, candidates may be required to:

- answer questions about the concept, measurement and interpretation of national income, including questions in which the interpretation of real national income data is required

- explain the basic macroeconomic model. Such questions may deal with the model as a whole or with some part of the model; most questions will require the use of appropriate diagrams (such as the Keynesian 'cross' diagram). Many questions will require the use of the model to deal with applied issues such as the impact of changes in national income on the business sector. Both the income/expenditure model and the aggregate demand and supply model are acceptable as a general model; it is likely that questions requiring specification of a model will focus on the former. Nonetheless, candidates will need a basic grasp of the concepts of aggregate demand and supply, eg for answering questions about inflation

- answer questions relating to the nature of government policy objectives, their attainability and their impact on the economy. This involves the use of economic theory to discuss and explain the issues involved. Candidates will, therefore, need an awareness of the main differences between Keynesian and Monetarist approaches to economic theory and policy. This will include an understanding of the original Phillips curve and an awareness of its limitations and the possibility of a vertical Phillips curve (NAIRU)

- answer questions about fiscal policy as a whole and about the nature of particular taxation systems. In both cases, candidates will be expected to use economic theory to answer questions and to use their knowledge of recent developments in, and discussions about, fiscal and taxation policy to illustrate their arguments

- use economic theory and knowledge of recent developments in the operation of monetary policy (such as the impact of the UK's departure from the ERM) to answer questions about monetary policy. Typically, such questions will also require candidates to consider the impact of monetary policy on the business sector. For this, candidates will need an understanding of: the nature of the demand for money, the relationship between the supply of money and the level of interest rates, and the conduct of monetary policy (especially the importance of the PSBR, open market operations and control of the money base). Candidates should be aware of the difference between narrow and broad money and be able to discuss the importance of the monetary aggregates

The following items are *not* examinable:

- detailed statistical knowledge of taxation and expenditure, nor will questions involve numerical calculations of the effects of particular taxes on business concerns

- the ability to reproduce the details of the different monetary aggregates

The international environment

Syllabus reference 3 (e)

Study weighting 15%

Candidates must understand the importance of the flow of goods and services between countries and the flow of financial capital. They must also have a knowledge of the factors which influence the size, direction and nature of such flows including the importance of competitiveness and the role of the exchange rate.

Questions will require candidates to display an appreciation of the relevant concepts involved in international economics such as the balance of payments, and may often require a demonstration of an understanding of the relevant economic theory underlying these concepts. Questions will not be restricted to theoretical issues and normally candidates will be required to explain the impact of the international environment on businesses. As with other sections of the syllabus, candidates must expect current and recent issues to be reflected in the examination paper.

In the examination, candidates may be required to:

- analyse the determination of the state of the balance of payments, the financing of surpluses/deficits and policy to correct such disequilibria. Candidates may be asked to interpret balance of payments data and to draw conclusions based on that data and on their knowledge of the relevant economic theory

- distinguish between, and explain the importance of, the terms of trade and the balance of trade

- explain the determination of exchange rates and their influence on businesses and on the economy as a whole. Candidates may be required to discuss policy towards exchange rates and the effect of exchange rate changes on businesses and on the economy as a whole

- demonstrate an awareness of the debates concerning the relative merits of alternative exchange rate systems and an understanding of the economic theory on which they are based; also a knowledge of recent developments in this area, especially in relation to the European Monetary System

The following item is *not* examinable:

- detailed knowledge of the nature and functions of international institutions such as the World Bank and the IMF. However, candidates should have a basic awareness of the World Bank and the IMF and their functions since this may be relevant to other questions on the financing of current account deficits and the conduct of domestic economic policy under differing international monetary arrangements

Question bank

DO YOU KNOW? - RESOURCE ALLOCATION AND THE MARKET

- *Check that you can fill in the blanks in the statements below before you attempt any questions. If in doubt, you should go back to your BPP Study Text and revise first.*

- Economics is about .... production and distribution, and efficiency of economic systems.

- Economists assume that decision making (whether by ...., ..., ..., or ....) is rational.

  o Rational decision making is seen as seeking to maximise something (eg ...., ...).

  o If maximisation is achieved, an .... is reached.

  o Decision makers will choose an action whose benefit (utility) outweighs its .... (the utility of an alternative action forgone).

- Production brings together different types of resource (.....................), classified as natural resources (.....................),....................................,..................... (eg equipment), and ..../ ....

- A production possibility curve shows the most which can be produced (eg by a country, or by a firm).

- Advanced economies are characterised by .... and the .... of labour.

- Alternative economic systems are the .... economy and the .... economy, each of which have advantages and disadvantages.

  o In a .... economy, the allocation of resources, distribution of income and so on are determined by market forces and the price mechanism.

  o In a .... economy, these are determined by a central body (the state).

  o A .... economy contains elements of planning as well as free markets.

- A demand .... is an estimate of demand for a good per time period (per day, per month etc) at any given price level. A demand .... is a graph of a demand ....

- Factors influencing demand for a good are:

  o ....
  o ....
  o ....
  o ....
  o ....
  o ....

- In a stable free market, demand equals supply at the .... price.

- A .... schedule shows how much will be produced at different prices.

  TRY QUESTIONS 1 AND 2

- Elasticity of demand (eg price elasticity) measures the change in quantity demanded in response to a change in one of the factors (eg price) influencing demand. *Other elasticity measures* are the .... and the ....

- .... is a situation in which the market mechanism fails to result in economic efficiency, and therefore the outcome is sub-optimal.

- Positive or negative external effects on third parties resulting from production and consumption activities are called ....

  TRY QUESTIONS 3-6

- *Possible pitfalls*

  Write down the mistakes you know you should avoid.

DID YOU KNOW? - RESOURCE ALLOCATION AND THE MARKET

- *Could you fill in the blanks? The answers are in bold. Use this page for revision purposes as you approach the exam.*

- Economics is about **allocation of resources**, production and distribution, and efficiency of economic systems.

- Economists assume that decision making (whether by **producers/firms**, **consumers/ households** or **governments**) is rational.

  o Rational decision making is seen as seeking to maximise something (eg profits, utility).

  o If maximisation is achieved, an **optimum** is reached.

  o Decision makers will choose an action whose benefit (utility) outweighs its **opportunity cost** (the utility of an alternative action forgone).

- Production brings together different types of resource (**factors of production**), classified as natural resources ('**land**'), **labour**, **capital** (eg equipment), and **enterprise/entrepreneurship**.

- A **production possibility curve** shows the most which can be produced (eg by a country, or by a firm).

- Advanced economies are characterised by **specialisation** and the **division** of labour.

- Alternative economic systems are the **market** economy and the **planned/command** economy, each of which have advantages and disadvantages.

  o In a **market** economy, the allocation of resources, distribution of income and so on are determined by market forces and the price mechanism.

  o In a **planned** economy, these are determined by a central body (the state).

  o A **mixed** economy contains elements of planning as well as free markets.

- A demand **schedule** is an estimate of demand for a good per time period (per day, per month etc) at any given price level. A demand **curve** is a graph of a demand **schedule**.

- Factors influencing demand for a good are:

  o **the price of the good**

  o **the price and availability of substitute goods**

  o **the price and availability of complements**

  o **the size of household income and the distribution of income among the population**

  o **tastes, fashions, attitudes towards a good**

  o **consumer expectations about future market conditions (eg expected price rises or supply shortages).**

- In a stable free market, demand equals supply at the **market clearing/equilibrium** price.

- A **supply** schedule shows how much will be produced at different prices.

TRY QUESTIONS 1 AND 2

- Elasticity of demand (eg price elasticity) measures the change in quantity demanded in response to a change in one of the factors (eg price) influencing demand. Other elasticity measures are the **elasticity of supply** and the **cross elasticity of demand**.

- **Market failure** is a situation in which the market mechanism fails to result in economic efficiency, and therefore the outcome is sub-optimal.

- Positive or negative external effects on third parties resulting from production and consumption activities are called **externalities**.

TRY QUESTIONS 3-6

- *Possible pitfalls*

  o **Misunderstanding the implication of price elasticity of demand**

  o **Omitting diagrams**

1   TUTORIAL QUESTION: NEW PRODUCT

Does the introduction of a new product affect only the demand for close substitutes or can it also affect the demand for all other products?

Approaching the question

1   Under examination pressure it is tempting, having spotted the word 'substitutes', to see the question as an opportunity to write all one knows about substitutes and complementary goods. But the question is looking for a more analytical approach. Your answer needs to examine the effect of introducing the new product on demand for substitutes *and* all other products.

2   Explain how, on introduction of a new product, the consumer will adjust his or her pattern of consumption so that the condition still holds between all available goods and services.

3   The question could alternatively be answered using indifference curve analysis. But note that you will not be set questions which necessarily *require* the use of indifference curve analysis.

2   TUTORIAL QUESTION: ELASTICITY OF SUPPLY

How is the elasticity of supply influenced by (a) time, and (b) costs?

Approaching the question

1   As with any exam question, you need to plan what you are going to say before starting to write out your answer.

2   Your plan might be along the following lines.

  (a)   Define elasticity of supply, and explain its measurement.

  (b)   Explain the effect of time, as measured in market, short and long periods, emphasising the possibility of changing factors of production, thus altering costs.

  (c)   Explain how the cost structure is important for supply. What is the effect of raising output on the level and structure of costs in both the short and long run?

3   DATA RESPONSE QUESTION: EUROTUNNEL (11/94, amended)   *43 mins*

Read the following extract concerning the operations of the Eurotunnel company which runs the rail tunnel link between the United Kingdom and the European continent. Eurotunnel opened for business in 1994, providing new competition for the existing ferry companies.

'Eurotunnel is risking bankruptcy by setting its initial prices for travelling through the Channel Tunnel too high, according to a report published today.

Dr Stefan Szymanski, economics lecturer at London University's Imperial College, concludes that pricing too high is more of a threat to Eurotunnel's financial future than pricing too low.

Lower prices could double the profitability of the £10 billion project, he says, claiming that Eurotunnel could feasibly halve its prices once the tunnel is running at full capacity.

The report sets out various scenarios detailing the impact on revenue of varying levels of consumer enthusiasm and price sensitivity which show that, given Eurotunnel's £8 billion debt burden, 'in most cases failure to implement optimal prices (to maximise profits) significantly reduces revenue and may even lead to bankruptcy.'

But more competitive pricing would inevitably kill off ferry services on the key Dover-Calais route. 'Under most plausible scenarios Eurotunnel will find it profitable to offer considerably lower prices and take a dominant share of the market,' Dr Szymanski says.

'In response, the ferry companies will find it hard to offer prices which can compete and still cover their overhead costs.'   (*The Guardian*, 19 January 1994)

(a) Explain the concept of price elasticity of demand and the factors which determine its value for different goods.   **6 Marks**

(b) Applying both your knowledge of economic theory and material contained in the extract:

  (i)   use the concept of price elasticity of demand to discuss the conclusions reached by the report concerning the appropriate pricing policy for Eurotunnel;   **7 Marks**

  (ii) explain the concept of the cross elasticity of demand, and use it to discuss the possible problems, highlighted in the report, facing the ferry companies;   **7 Marks**

  (iii) assess the possible benefits to consumers in both the short and long run of competition between Eurotunnel and the ferry companies.   **4 Marks**

Total Marks = 24

4   **DATA RESPONSE QUESTION: ELASTICITIES** (5/98)   *36 mins*

The following data refer to the UK economy.

Estimates of price elasticities of demand for goods and services

Broad category		Narrow category	
Fuel & light	−0.47	Dairy produce	−0.05
Food	−0.52	Bread & cereals	−0.22
Alcohol	−0.83	Entertainment	−1.40
Durable goods	−0.89	Travel abroad	−1.63
Services	−1.02	Catering	−2.61

Estimates of income elasticities of demand for goods and services

Broad category		Narrow category	
Fuel & light	0.30	Coal	−2.02
Food	0.45	Bread & cereals	−0.50
Alcohol	1.14	Vegetables	0.87
Durable goods	1.47	Travel abroad	1.14
Services	1.75	Wines & spirits	2.60

Required

Using both your knowledge of economic theory and the data above:

(a) explain what is meant by 'price elasticity of demand' and show how it is measured;   **3 Marks**

(b) from the data, identify those goods with 'price elastic' and 'price inelastic' demand and give *two* reasons for the variations in price elasticity;   **3 Marks**

(c) explain what is meant by 'income elasticity of demand' and show how it is measured;   **3 Marks**

(d) from the data, identify the 'inferior goods' and give *two* reasons for the variations in income elasticity of different goods in the UK;   **3 Marks**

(e) explain the importance for businesses of a knowledge of the price and income elasticities of demand for their product.   **8 Marks**

Total Marks = 20

5   **PRICE SYSTEM (11/96)**   *36 mins*

(a) Explain how the price system works to allocate resources in a market economy.
                                                               10 Marks

(b) Describe the main reasons why markets do not always allocate resources in an efficient manner.   **10 Marks**

                                                      Total Marks = 20

6   **NORMAL PROFIT (5/99)**   *43 mins*

(a) Distinguish between normal profit and abnormal (excess) profit and explain the functions of profit in a market economy.   **8 Marks**

(b) Using a simple demand and supply model, explain, with appropriate diagrams, what would happen to output and prices in a market if

   (i)   profits elsewhere in the economy rose;

   (ii)   profits elsewhere in the economy fell.

                                                               10 Marks

(c) Describe the objectives, other than profit maximisation, that business organisations might have.   **6 Marks**

                                                      Total Marks = 24

DO YOU KNOW? - PRODUCTION AND COSTS

- *Check that you can fill in the blanks in the statements below before you attempt any questions. If in doubt, you should go back to your BPP Study Text and revise first.*

- Production costs are what a firm must pay for the resources (.................... of production) that it uses.

  o   Total production costs = Total fixed costs + ...

- Average cost (AC) = total cost ÷ ....

- Marginal cost (MC) is the cost of ....

- An important point is that when AC reaches its minimum value, it is equal to MC.

  o   When AC is falling in value, ... > ....
  o   When AC is rising in value, ... < ....

- The firm's average cost curve has a U shape in the short run, the period in which at least one factor of production is in fixed supply, in accordance with the law of .... to the fixed factor.

- Economies of .... are concerned with long-run output decisions when all factor inputs are variable.

- A firm is in equilibrium when it is maximising its .... and cannot make bigger .... by altering the price and output level for its product or service.

- An industry is in equilibrium when:

  o   .... and .... are equal at a certain price and output level;
  o   there are no firms trying to ....

TRY QUESTIONS 7-9

- The entrepreneur organises the other factors of production (...................., ..., ...) and bears risks.

- The .... paid to labour, ... paid to capital, ... paid for land and .... earned by entrepreneurs are factor rewards, which are the opportunity costs to firms of their input resources.

- The opportunity cost of entrepreneurship is more precisely called .... - the entrepreneur's reward for risk-taking. Actual profit is what is left over after the costs of labour, capital and land have been deducted from revenue.

TRY QUESTIONS 10-13

- Economies whose industries are mainly agricultural (.................... sector) will have different economic characteristics from a largely manufacturing economy (.................... sector) or an economy based on service industries (.................... sector).

- Types of business enterprise in the mixed economy include:

  o   ....
  o   ....
  o   ....
  o   ....
  o   ....

- Major factors affecting a firm's location decision will be ...., ..., ..., ..., and ....

TRY QUESTIONS 14-16

- *Possible pitfalls*

  Write down the mistakes you know you should avoid.

DID YOU KNOW? - PRODUCTION AND COSTS

- *Could you fill in the blanks? The answers are in bold. Use this page for revision purposes as you approach the exam.*

- Production costs are what a firm must pay for the resources (**factors** of production) that it uses.

   o   Total production costs = Total fixed costs + **Total variable costs**.

- Average cost (AC) = total cost ÷ **number of units of output produced**

- Marginal cost (MC) is the cost of **producing one extra unit of output.**

- An important point is that when AC reaches its minimum value, it is equal to MC.

   o   When AC is falling in value, **AC > MC**
   o   When AC is rising in value, **AC < MC**

- The firm's average cost curve has a U shape in the short run, the period in which at least one factor of production is in fixed supply, in accordance with the law of **diminishing returns** to the fixed factor.

- Economies of **scale** are concerned with long-run output decisions when all factor inputs are variable.

- A firm is in equilibrium when it is maximising its **profits** and cannot make bigger **profits** by altering the price and output level for its product or service.

- An industry is in equilibrium when:

   o   **supply** and **demand** are equal at a certain price and output level;
   o   there are no firms trying to **enter or leave the market**.

TRY QUESTIONS 7-9

- The entrepreneur organises the other factors of production (**labour**, **land**, **capital**) and bears risks.

- The **wages** paid to labour, **interest** paid to capital, **rent** paid for land and profit earned by entrepreneurs are factor rewards, which are the opportunity costs to firms of their input resources.

- The opportunity cost of entrepreneurship is more precisely called **normal profit** - the entrepreneur's reward for risk-taking. Actual profit is what is left over after the costs of labour, capital and land have been deducted from revenue.

TRY QUESTIONS 10-13

- Economies whose industries are mainly agricultural (**primary** sector) will have different economic characteristics from a largely manufacturing economy (**secondary** sector) or an economy based on service industries (**tertiary** sector).

- Types of business enterprise in the mixed economy include:
   o   **sole traders**
   o   **partnerships**
   o   **companies**
   o   **cooperatives**
   o   **state-owned industries**

- Major factors affecting a firm's location decision will be **transport costs, resource costs at the location, customer location, economics of scale** and **regional policy.**

TRY QUESTIONS 14-16

- *Possible pitfalls*

   o   **Confusing the short run (law of diminishing returns) and the long run (returns to scale)**

   o   **confusing the demand for labour and the supply of labour**

7   **TUTORIAL QUESTION: COMPETITION AND ECONOMIES OF SCALE**

Can an explanation in terms of economies and diseconomies of scale account for variations in the number of firms in an industry and the degree of competition between them?

Approaching the question

1   A short answer is 'In general, yes'. As with most economies essay questions, your answer needs to explain the economic concepts involved in some detail.

2   Explain how economies of scale can arise, using a diagram to illustrate the points you make, and giving a brief indication of different types of economy of scale.

3   Introduce the concept of 'minimum efficient scale', and explain how diseconomies of scale can arise.

4   Explain how these principles account for industrial concentration in many industries, with implications for competition.

8   **DATA RESPONSE QUESTION: REVENUE AND COSTS (11/97)**   *36 mins*

The following data refer to the costs of a firm and the demand for its product.

Quantity sold	Price £	Total cost £
1	34	12
2	30	20
3	27	34
4	25	53
5	23	75
6	21	102
7	19	131

Required

Using both your knowledge of economic theory and the data above:

(a)   calculate for each level of output

    (i)   the marginal cost;   **2 Marks**
    (ii)   the marginal revenue;   **2 Marks**

(b)   calculate the level of profit at each level of output and identify the profit-maximising level of output;   **2 Marks**

(c)   calculate the price elasticity of demand for the good for a price fall from £25 to £23;
                                                                            4 Marks

(d)   identify the factors which might explain the value of the elasticity of demand for this good;   **5 Marks**

(e)   explain how you would expect the demand curve for this firm to vary if the number of firms in the industry were to rise.   **5 Marks**

                                                                    Total Marks = 20

9   **FALLING COSTS (11/95)**   *36 mins*

(a)   Describe the main reasons why a business may experience falling long-run average costs.   **12 Marks**

(b)   Explain how the structure of an industry and the competitive process might be affected as long-run average costs fall.   **8 Marks**

                                                                    Total Marks = 20

10   TUTORIAL QUESTION: DIVISION OF LABOUR

Identify the advantages and the disadvantages of specialisation and the division of labour.

Approaching the question

1   Specialisation, which Adam Smith wrote about in 1776, and the division of labour are fundamental features of the modern economy.

2   Your solution to this question can easily be tabulated. This helps the examiner to see how many separate points you are making. Specialisation and the division of labour are closely linked, so it is a good idea to look first at the advantages of both and then at the disadvantages of both.

3   Advantages and disadvantages are often different sides of the same coin. For example, an advantage is the better training of workers to perform specialised tasks; a disadvantage is the possible boredom and lack of job satisfaction which may result from this.

11   FACTORS OF PRODUCTION (11/98)   *36 mins*

(a)   Identify the four factors of production and their prices, and explain the meaning of the statement 'costs occur because resources are scarce and therefore command a price'.   **6 Marks**

(b)   Discuss the consequences of a sharp rise in wage rates on the cost of a business and on its employment of labour:

   (i)   in the short run   **8 Marks**
   (ii)   in the long run.   **6 Marks**

Total Marks = 20

12   LABOUR MOBILITY (5/94, amended)   *43 mins*

(a)   Distinguish between the occupational and geographical (regional) mobility of labour and explain the principal determinants of each.   **12 Marks**

(b)   Explain the effects that the imposition of a statutory minimum wage would be likely to have on prices and the level of employment.   **12 Marks**

Total Marks = 24

13   LABOUR PRODUCTIVITY (11/93)   *36 mins*

(a)   Explain the term 'labour productivity' and describe the main factors that influence its level.   **12 Marks**

(b)   How might government taxation policy influence the level of labour productivity?
8 Marks

Total Marks = 20

14   DATA RESPONSE QUESTION: SIZE OF FIRMS (11/94)   *36 mins*

The following data refer to the size distribution of firms in the UK manufacturing sector. Consider the data and answer the questions below.

Size of enterprise (numbers of employees)	1978		1989	
	Number of enterprises in each group size	*Percentage of manufacturing labour force employed*	*Number of enterprises in each group size*	*Percentage of manufacturing labour force employed*
1 - 99	84,518	22.8	142,905	28.2
100 - 499	4,228	12.8	7,159	30.4
500 - 999	619	6.5	943	13.0
1,000 - 4,999	590	18.8	536	19.7
over - 5,000	179	39.1	41	8.7
	90,134	100.0	151,584	100.0

(Source: *Prest and Coppock's The UK Economy*, M J Artis (ed),1992)

Required

(a) Describe the main features of the size distribution of firms as shown in the data, and to identify any changes between 1978 and 1989.   **6 Marks**

(b) Explain the possible reasons for the features you have identified and for any changes that have occurred between 1978 and 1989.   **10 Marks**

(c) Assess the possible effects on the competitive process of the changes in the size distribution of firms since 1978.   **4 Marks**

Total Marks = 20

15 **PROFIT (11/95)**   *36 mins*

(a) State what is meant by *profit* and explain the functions of profit in a free enterprise economy.   **12 Marks**

(b) Explain the role played by profit in influencing the number of companies in a perfectly competitive industry.   **8 Marks**

Total Marks = 20

16 **REGIONAL SPECIALISATION (5/96)**   *36 mins*

(a) Describe the main factors which influence the location of industries.   **8 Marks**

(b) Explain why companies may choose to locate their businesses close to other companies in the same industry.   **6 Marks**

(c) What economic problems may arise from a high degree of regional specialisation of industry?   **6 Marks**

Total Marks = 20

DO YOU KNOW? - THE MARKET ENVIRONMENT

- *Check that you can fill in the blanks in the statements below before you attempt any questions. If in doubt, you should go back to your BPP Study Text and revise first.*

- Equilibrium in a market is likely to differ between the short term and the long term.

    o   In the short term a loss-making firm might stay in the market, hoping that in the longer term, prices will go up or costs will fall.

    o   In the short term, a firm might earn supernormal ...., even in a competitive market.

    o   In the short term, a firm might be protected from competition by barriers to ....

- Firms in perfect competition are price -....................: an individual firm cannot influence the market price.

- In imperfect competition, including monopoly, firms are price -....................: an individual firm faces a downward-sloping demand curve and can exert some influence over the price at which it sells.

- A monopolist earns supernormal profits since, when marginal .... = marginal ...., average revenue > average cost.

- In conditions of ...., a large number of competing firms each sell a differentiated product. In the long run, supernormal profits fall to zero for such firms, but price is higher and output lower than in perfect competition.

- An .... is a market dominated by a small number of suppliers.

- To preserve their position as price ...., firms in monopolistic competition and oligopoly often use non-price competition. This can take several forms.

    o   ....
    o   ....
    o   ....
    o   ....

    TRY QUESTIONS 17-21

- A government might try to protect the consumer from the 'producer sovereignty' of the monopolist, for example by:

    o   preventing monopolies from building up

    o   regulating mergers and takeovers

    o   where there is a 'natural monopoly' through economies of scale, subjecting the firms to .... (eg using 'consumer watchdog bodies')

    o   in some countries, nationalising natural monopolies.

- Privatisation takes various forms:

    o   ....
    o   ....
    o   ....

    TRY QUESTIONS 22-24

- *Possible pitfalls*

    Write down the mistakes you know you should avoid.

DID YOU KNOW? - THE MARKET ENVIRONMENT

- *Could you fill in the blanks? The answers are in bold. Use this page for revision purposes as you approach the exam.*

- Equilibrium in a market is likely to differ between the short term and the long term.

  - In the short term a loss-making firm might stay in the market, hoping that in the longer term, prices will go up or costs will fall.

  - In the short term, a firm might earn supernormal **profits**, even in a competitive market.

  - In the short term, a firm might be protected from competition by barriers to **entry**.

- Firms in perfect competition are price-**takers**: an individual firm cannot influence the market price.

- In imperfect competition, including monopoly, firms are price-**makers**: an individual firm faces a downward-sloping demand curve and can exert some influence over the price at which it sells.

- A monopolist earns supernormal profits since, when marginal **costs** = marginal **revenue**, average revenue > average cost.

- In conditions of **monopolistic competition**, a large number of competing firms each sells a differentiated product. In the long run, supernormal profits fall to zero for such firms, but price is higher and output lower than in perfect competition.

- An **oligopoly** is a market dominated by a small number of suppliers.

- To preserve their position as price **makers**, firms in monopolistic competition and oligopoly often use non-price competition. This can take several forms.

  - **Product differentiation (eg design differences)**
  - **Branding**
  - **Advertising and sales promotion**
  - **Creating 'add-on' services**

TRY QUESTIONS 17-21

- A government might try to protect the consumer from the 'producer sovereignty' of the monopolist, for example by:

  - preventing monopolies from building up

  - regulating mergers and takeovers

  - where there is a 'natural monopoly' through economies of scale, subjecting the firms to **regulation/control** (eg using 'consumer watchdog bodies')

  - in some countries, nationalising natural monopolies.

- Privatisation takes various forms:

  - **selling off nationalised industries to the private sector;**

  - **allowing private firms to compete with state-run firms, by removing the state-run firm's legal monopoly;**

  - **allowing private firms to take over work done previously by government employees.**

TRY QUESTIONS 22-24

- *Possible pitfalls*

  - **Omitting to state assumptions underlying market structures**
  - **Omitting diagrams**

17 TUTORIAL QUESTION: PERFECT MARKET

What is a market? State the conditions necessary for a perfect market and describe the factors which cause imperfections.

Approaching the question

1   This is a wide-ranging question, and it is important not to deviate or 'wander' from the question asked.

2   First define a market, in the sense in which the term is used by economists.

3   Then, set out each of the characteristics of a 'perfect' market. The perfect market, remember, is an idealised concept - a useful assumption on which much economic theory is based.

4   Monopoly influences can be important in causing imperfections, but you should not spend time describing imperfect market types such as duopoly or oligopoly.

18 BARRIERS TO ENTRY (5/98)   *36 mins*

(a) Explain what is meant by 'barriers to entry' to an industry *and* describe the main barriers that may exist.   **12 Marks**

(b) How would the existence of effective barriers to entry influence the structure of an industry and the level of profits earned?   **8 Marks**

Total Marks = 20

19 PUBLIC INTEREST (5/97)   *36 mins*

(a) Explain how prices and output are determined under conditions of monopoly, illustrating your answer with an appropriate diagram.   **10 Marks**

(b) Evaluate the argument that monopolies are always against the public interest.

10 Marks

Total Marks = 20

20 OLIGOPOLY MARKETS (11/98)   *36 mins*

(a) Using an appropriate model, describe the main features of an oligopolistic market with particular emphasis on the concepts of uncertainty and interdependence.

14 Marks

(b) Explain why oligopolistic industries are often characterised by heavy expenditure on advertising.   **6 Marks**

Total Marks = 20

21 MONOPOLISTIC COMPETITION (11/87)   *36 mins*

Show, with the aid of diagrams, how an individual firm, in conditions of monopolistic competition, will determine the size of its output both in the short and in the long run. Indicate clearly the measure of its profit.

20 Marks

22   DATA RESPONSE QUESTION: BREWING INDUSTRY (5/99)   *43 mins*

The following passage is based on a newspaper reports.

At first sight, the UK brewing industry might seem to be very competitive, with numerous brands of beer and lager on sale in many pubs and bars. In fact, most pubs and bars are owned by the major brewing companies and generally sell only a limited range of beers. The oligopolistic nature of the brewing industry can be seen from the data on the market shares of the main companies:

Market shares of the major UK brewing companies

	1985		1996
Bass	22%	Bass	38%
Carlsberg-Tetley	13%	Scottish Courage	32%
Grand Met	12%	Whitbread	15%
Scottish & Newcastle	10%	Guinness Brewing	6%
Courage	9%	Others	9%
Others	23%		

The increasing concentration in the industry is reflected in the decline of small, independent brewers, in the face of the market power of the large brewing companies, which are vertically integrated, combining brewing with retailing. Also, horizontal integration has occurred as a result of mergers and take-overs. For example, in 1996, Bass announced the take-over of Carlsberg-Tetley: the combined company now produces many of the famous brands of beer and lager – Bass, Carling, Tennents, Worthington, Tetley, Carlsberg and Skol.

The Monopolies and Mergers Commission investigated the brewing industry and recommended that brewers should be allowed to own a maximum of 2,000 pubs and bars each. Following pressure from the major brewers, the government agreed to modify the recommendation and allow the brewers to retain more retail outlets, particularly pubs and bars. Even so, it was expected that as brewers were required to sell pubs and bars, competition would be increased. This hope was ill-founded since the brewers sold off the less popular and least profitable of their pubs and bars.

Thus, smaller brewers face two barriers to increased market share: the hold which large brewers have over the retail sector and the dominance of established brands of beer and lager. Heavy advertising of these brands makes entry of new brewers into the industry very difficult. The results of this limited competition have been to contribute to the rise in the real price of beer and lager and to reduce choice for consumers.

Required

Using both your knowledge of economic theory and information contained in the passage:

(a) explain the term barrier to entry and describe the nature of barriers to entry in the brewing industry;   **4 Marks**

(b) explain what is meant by oligopoly and describe the typical features of an oligopolistic industry;   **6 Marks**

(c) using an appropriate diagram, explain the kinked demand curve model of oligopoly, and use it to explain the features of the brewing industry;   **8 Marks**

(d) distinguish between vertical and horizontal integration, and explain the benefits the brewing companies may gain from each.   **6 Marks**

Total Marks = 24

Tutorial note: The Monopolies and Mergers Commission is now known as the Competition Commission. This is simply a change of name.

---

23   DATA RESPONSE QUESTION: OPEC (5/97)   *36 mins*

The following passage discusses changes in the price of oil.

'Between December 1973 and June 1974, the Organisation of Petroleum Exporting Countries (OPEC) put up the price of oil from $3 to $12 per barrel. The price was raised to $30 in 1979. In the 1980s the price fluctuated, but the trend was downward. By 1993 the price was $16 per barrel: in real terms (ie after correcting for inflation) the price was back to its pre-1973 level.

The initial rise in price was achieved by OPEC members restricting their output of oil by agreed amounts. The amount by which output had to be restricted in order to achieve the rise in price was relatively small because in the short run the demand for oil was highly price inelastic.

In the long run it was more difficult for OPEC to maintain the price of oil. In the long run the demand for oil was much more price elastic than in the short run. Consumers could begin to economise on the use of oil and to find substitute sources of power. Thus, the long-run demand curve would be much more elastic than the short-run curve. Moreover, income growth in the main industrial economies was slowing down under the impact of serious recessions and this affected the demand for oil.

To make matters worse for the OPEC producers, there was also a long-run supply response to their initial raising of the price of oil. The higher price of oil made oil production much more profitable and there was thus an incentive for non-OPEC producers to increase their output. An obvious example of this is North Sea oil. Moreover, OPEC members themselves were tempted to break their agreed "quotas" and sell more oil. Thus, the supply curve for oil shifted, with each new supply curve representing an increased number of oil fields in operation.'

Required

Using both your knowledge of economic theory and material contained in the passage:

(a) explain the *short-run* effect of OPEC actions on the price of oil and draw a supply and demand diagram to illustrate your explanation;   **5 Marks**

(b) explain how changes in demand affected the price of oil in the *long run* and draw a supply and demand diagram to illustrate your explanation;   **5 Marks**

(c) explain how changes in supply affected the price of oil in the *long run* and draw a supply and demand diagram to illustrate your explanation;   **5 Marks**

(d) explain how the concept of the income elasticity of demand might be relevant to understanding the *long-run* trend in the price of oil.   **5 Marks**

Total Marks = 20

24   DATA RESPONSE QUESTION: COMPACT DISCS (5/94)   *36 mins*

Read the following extract.

'British and European buyers of compact discs (CDs) get a raw deal by comparison with music lovers on the other side of the Atlantic. Prices in Europe are about 40% higher than in North America. The Director-General of Fair Trading is considering referring the matter to the Monopolies and Mergers Commission. So far the industry has failed to give a convincing explanation of why CD prices are so high. The industry's argument that the costs of supplying CDs in the UK are higher than in the US does not ring true. On the other hand, no evidence has emerged of a cartel among either record companies or retailers.

A price-fixing cartel is not necessary to achieve this because one company's music cannot normally be substituted for another's. Each title is effectively a mini-monopoly, at least where protected by copyright. Copyright law also supports market segmentation by allowing record companies to ban retailers from buying CDs at cheaper wholesale prices in other countries. This enables the industry to maintain wide differentials in wholesale prices between the US and the UK, which are then reflected in retail prices.

Market segmentation and price discrimination are not in themselves always against the public interest. Record companies have a high proportion of fixed costs. To recoup these fixed costs the industry has to charge a mark-up on top of marginal costs. Rather than charging the same mark-up for each customer, it may be more efficient to charge a higher mark-up for those who receive more value from the product, hence the higher price of the better quality CDs compared to tape cassettes.

But a similar argument cannot justify price discrimination between Europe and America. Market segmentation in this case works against consumer interests and the competition authorities should act to remove it.'   (*Financial Times, 4 May 1992*)

You are required, using both your knowledge of economic theory and material contained in the extract:

(a) to explain the conditions necessary for firms to be able to operate a policy of price discrimination;   **7 Marks**

(b) to discuss the extent of price discrimination in the market for CDs, and to identify the factors that enable record companies to practise such discrimination;   **7 Marks**

(c) to assess whether or not the Monopolies and Mergers Commission should intervene to prevent price discrimination in the CD market and to suggest the best form that such intervention could take.   **6 Marks**

Total Marks = 20

Tutorial note: The Monopolies and Mergers Commission is now known as the Competition Commission. This is simply a change of name.

DO YOU KNOW? - THE FINANCIAL ENVIRONMENT

- *Check that you can fill in the blanks in the statements below before you attempt any questions. If in doubt, you should go back to your BPP Study Text and revise first.*

- Money acts as

  - ....
  - ....
  - ....
  - ....

- Interest is the reward for .... (Contrast with microeconomics definition - the cost of capital.) Banks can create new money (with money defined broadly).

- Narrow money is money defined more narrowly as a means of exchange - eg comprising ...., ...

- Broad money is money defined more widely to include financial assets which are primarily used as a ...., but which are also fairly liquid.

- The debate between .... and .... is rooted in different theories of the money supply.

  - .... argued that the supply of money can be fixed by the government. The demand for money stems from the transactions motive, the precautionary motive and the speculative motive. Some demand for money (speculative motive) varies with the interest rate. Changes in money demand or supply will lead to interest rate changes, but there will not be direct implications for spending.

  - .... disagreed, arguing that excess money will be spent on physical goods - not just 'bonds' (as Keynes believed) basing their argument on the 'classical' quantity theory ($MV = PT$). They consider that the velocity of circulation is more or less constant, and any increase in the money supply M will result directly in an increase in expenditure in the economy (PT). If the economy is unable to produce extra output (T), prices (P) will go up. Thus, increases in the money supply result in inflation.

  .... argued that if M grew, V might become lower, leaving PT unaffected.

- Interest rates are effectively the price of .... The .... curve shows the relationship between interest rates for similar assets with different periods to maturity.

TRY QUESTIONS 25-27

- Banks try to balance the need for:

  - .... - to meet customer demand for cash withdrawals:
  - .... - by re-lending money deposited with them, banks make a profit;
  - .... - banks can charge very high interest to more risky customers, but there is a risk of bad debts. A line must be drawn somewhere.

- In the UK, the .... (central bank) has various functions. It can set the level of interest rates through open market operations; other important functions include acting as lender of last resort to banks.

- Largely short-term lending and borrowing by banks takes place in the .... markets.

- Stock markets are the main .... markets and bring companies and investors together.

  - A company comes to a stock market for the first time in a flotation.
  - The existence of a secondhand market makes shares more attractive to investors.

- There are various share price .... against which the performance of a company's share price can be judged. Such .... also act like 'barometers' of market sentiment.

TRY QUESTIONS 28-39

- *Possible pitfalls*

  Write down the mistakes you know you should avoid.

DID YOU KNOW? - THE FINANCIAL ENVIRONMENT

- *Could you fill in the blanks? The answers are in bold. Use this page for revision purposes as you approach the exam.*

- Money acts as
  - **a means of exchange**
  - **a unit of account**
  - **a standard of deferred payment**
  - **a store of value**

- Interest is the reward for **depositing or lending money**. (Contrast with microeconomics definition - the cost of capital.) Banks can create new money (with money defined broadly).

- Narrow money is money defined more narrowly as a means of exchange - eg comprising **cash**, **money in a current bank account**.

- Broad money is money defined more widely to include financial assets which are primarily used as a **store of value**, but which are also fairly liquid.

- The debate between **Keynesians** and **monetarists** is rooted in different theories of the money supply.

  - **Keynes** argued that the supply of money can be fixed by the government. The demand for money stems from the transactions motive, the precautionary motive and the speculative motive. Some demand for money (speculative motive) varies with the interest rate. Changes in money demand or supply will lead to interest rate changes, but there will not be direct implications for spending.

  - **Monetarists** disagreed, arguing that excess money will be spent on physical goods - not just 'bonds' (as Keynes believed) basing their argument on the 'classical' quantity theory (MV = PT). They consider that the velocity of circulation is more or less constant, and any increase in the money supply M will result directly in an increase in expenditure in the economy (PT). If the economy is unable to produce extra output (T), prices (P) will go up. Thus, increases in the money supply result in inflation.

  Keynesians argued that if M grew, V might become lower, leaving PT unaffected.

- Interest rates are effectively the price of **money**. The **yield** curve shows the relationship between interest rates for similar assets with different periods to maturity.

TRY QUESTIONS 25-27

- Banks try to balance the need for:

  - **liquidity** - to meet customer demand for cash withdrawals:

  - **profitability** - by re-lending money deposited with them, banks make a profit;

  - **security** - banks can charge very high interest to more risky customers, but there is a risk of bad debts. A line must be drawn somewhere.

- In the UK, the **Bank of England** (central bank) has various functions. It can set the level of interest rates through open market operations; other important functions include acting as lender of last resort to banks.

- Largely short-term lending and borrowing by banks takes place in the **money** markets.

- Stock markets are the main **capital** markets and bring companies and investors together.

  - A company comes to a stock market for the first time in a flotation.
  - The existence of a secondhand market makes shares more attractive to investors.

- There are various share price **indices** against which the performance of a company's share price can be judged. Such **indices** also act like 'barometers' of market sentiment.

TRY QUESTIONS 28-39

- *Possible pitfalls*

  - **Confusing a stock with a flow: distinguish 'money' and 'income'**
  - **Failing to distinguish the Keynesian and monetarist theories**
  - **Neglecting the topic: sources of company finance**

25   TUTORIAL QUESTION: TOO LITTLE MONEY

Can there ever be too little money in an economy?

Approaching the question

1   When confronted by a very brief question like this, it may be useful to translate it into what you think the examiner is getting at in economic terms. In this case, such a 'translation' is: 'What are the consequences in economic terms of a limited supply of money?'

2   It is not enough to propose that because the quantity of money is controlled by the monetary authorities, there can never be too little of it. Note also that details of the means by which authorities seek to control the quantity of money are not relevant to the question.

3   The quantity theory of money provides a useful starting point for your analysis.

26   INTEREST RATES (11/97)   *36 mins*

(a)   Explain how the general level of interest rates is determined in a market economy.

10 Marks

(b)   How might a change of interest rates affect:

   (i)   the level of business investment?   **5 Marks**
   (ii)   the rate of exchange for the currency?   **5 Marks**

Total Marks = 20

27   TUTORIAL QUESTION: BUSINESS CREDIT

Describe the forms of credit which are available to businesses. Why are these important?

Approaching the question

1   In discussing the importance of forms of credit, you should try to consider the issue both from a broader economic viewpoint and from the point of view of the business itself.

2   Don't confuse credit with finance. Bear in mind that various ways of financing a business would not be defined as credit.

3   You should comment in your answer on the importance of the period (short, medium or long term) over which the form of credit is required.

28   DATA RESPONSE QUESTION: CORPORATE SECTOR (11/95)   *36 mins*

The following data refer to the overall financial position of UK industrial and commercial companies from 1989 to 1993. During this period, the UK entered a severe recession and recovery only commenced in 1993.

	1989 £bn	1990 £bn	1991 £bn	1992 £bn	1993 £bn
Appropriation account					
Income					
Gross trading profits	80	79	75	75	86
Other income	31	34	30	28	28
Total	111	113	105	103	114
Allocation					
Dividends	16	17	19	21	23
Interest payments	26	32	30	27	21
Taxation	19	19	15	13	13
Other	9	7	5	5	5
Balance unallocated	41	38	36	37	52
Capital account					
Undistributed income	41	38	36	37	52
Expenditure					
Capital investment	60	55	50	48	49
Stock increases	9	(2)	(5)	(2)	0
Other	2	6	2	1	2
Financial surplus or (deficit)	(30)	(21)	(11)	(10)	1

(Source: *HMSO Economic Trends*)

Required

Using both your knowledge of economic theory and material contained in the extract:

(a) on the appropriation account, explain the principal uses to which income may be put;   **4 Marks**

(b) list and explain *three* features of the above data that would indicate the period was one of severe recession;   **9 Marks**

(c) explain what is meant by *financial intermediation* and show its relevance to the financial position of UK companies as shown above.   **7 Marks**

Total Marks = 20

29   **FINANCIAL INTERMEDIATION (5/97, amended)**   *43 mins*

(a) Explain what is meant by the term 'financial intermediation' *and* outline the roles played by the main financial institutions engaged in this activity.   **8 Marks**

(b) What arc the main advantages of financial intermediation for individuals and the business sector?   **11 Marks**

(c) Describe briefly the main features of the Financial Times Ordinary Share Index and compare it with the Financial Times - Actuaries All-Share Index.   **5 Marks**

Total Marks = 24

30   **FINANCE NEEDS (5/98)**   *36 mins*

(a) Distinguish between the 'short-term' and 'long-term' financing needs of businesses.
                                                                                6 Marks

(b) Identify and explain the principal sources of long-term finance for businesses.
                                                                                8 Marks

(c) Explain what is meant by the 'gearing ratio' *and* discuss its significance for businesses.   **6 Marks**

Total Marks = 20

31   **FINANCE SOURCES (5/96)**   *36 mins*

     (a)   Describe the principal sources of long-term finance available to companies.

                 12 Marks

     (b)   Compare the relative merits of equity capital and debt capital as a source of long-term finance for companies.   **8 Marks**

                 Total Marks = 20

32   **CAPITAL MARKETS (5/99)**   *43 mins*

     (a)   Distinguish between the money market and the capital market, and identify the main institutions which operate in each market.   **8 Marks**

     (b)   Using examples, show how a business might need to use both the money and capital markets.   **10 Marks**

     (c)   Explain the circumstances under which the government might need to use the capital market.   **6 Marks**

                 Total Marks = 24

33   **COMMERCIAL BANKS (11/98)**   *36 mins*

     (a)   Describe the functions of commercial banks and show how these meet the needs of business customers.   **10 Marks**

     (b)   With reference to the process of credit creation, explain briefly

         (i)   how commercial banks can 'create credit'   **5 Marks**

         (ii)   how the central bank can restrict the ability of commercial banks to create credit.   *Gilts + Bonds*   **5 Marks**

                 Total Marks = 20

34   **DATA RESPONSE QUESTION: BANK ASSETS (5/96)**   *36 mins*

The following data and extract refer to the structure of assets of United Kingdom commercial banks.

Distribution of commercial banks' main assets (May 1993)

Cash	0.5%
Balances with Bank of England	0.2%
Market loans	24.0%
Bills of exchange	1.8%
Investments	6.7%
Advances	62.0%
Miscellaneous	4.8%

Creating deposits enables a bank to lend money and make profits. However, this involves risks. The obvious risk is non-payment by the borrower - the risk of bad debts. In addition, there is the risk that depositors may withdraw their funds in cash; if the bank could not meet all these cash demands, customer confidence would collapse and there may be a 'run on the bank'. Therefore, the bank must retain some liquid assets - a reserve of cash, plus other assets which can be converted into cash quickly and easily. A bank which kept all of its assets in long-term loans and advances would be acting most unwisely.

However, highly liquid assets earn relatively low rates of interest: cash held by banks earns no interest at all. Thus, these assets are relatively unprofitable for the bank. Banks will, therefore, aim to maintain the minimum level of liquid assets that is consistent with the needs of liquidity.

Moreover, banks will attempt to ensure that the risks involved in lending are minimised. Banks will avoid lending if there is a possibility of non-repayment. Banks will also often require collateral in order to ensure repayment of loans. This may take the form of physical assets (eg houses) but is more likely to be other financial assets since these are more liquid.

Liquidity and profitability operate against each other: short-term loans are more liquid than long-term loans, but the rate of interest charged is lower. Thus, banks must compromise and maintain a portfolio of different assets.

Required

Using both your knowledge of economic theory and material contained in the extract:

(a) explain the importance of each of the following for the structure of bank assets:

    (i)   security   **3 Marks**
    (ii)   liquidity   **3 Marks**
    (iii) profitability;   **3 Marks**

(b) identify the principal sources of risk for commercial banks and show how these may be minimised;   **6 Marks**

(c) using examples from the table, explain the relationship between the liquidity of an asset and its profitability.   **5 Marks**

Total Marks = 20

35   CENTRAL BANK ROLE (5/95)   *36 mins*

(a) Explain the role of the central bank in a mixed economy.   **12 Marks**

(b) What would be the advantages and disadvantages of the central bank being completely independent of the government?   **8 Marks**

Total Marks = 20

36   MONEY SUPPLY (5/99)   *43 mins*

(a) Describe the functions of money in a market economy.   **8 Marks**

(b) Explain what is meant by the money supply and discuss why governments might wish to control the growth of the money supply   **8 Marks**

(a) Explain the effect on a business making and selling consumer durable goods, of a reduction in the supply of money in the economy.   **8 Marks**

Total Marks = 24

37   DATA RESPONSE QUESTION: MONEY SUPPLY AND INFLATION (11/97)

36 mins

The following data for the UK refer to the rate of inflation, as measured by the retail price index (RPI), and the growth of the money supply (M0).

	Growth of money supply (% rise in M0)	Rate of inflation (% rise in RPI)
1976	11.2	12.9
1977	13.1	17.6
1978	13.7	7.8
1979	11.9	15.6
1980	5.8	16.9
1981	2.4	10.9
1982	3.2	8.7
1983	6.0	4.2
1984	5.4	4.5
1985	3.8	6.9
1986	5.3	2.4
1987	4.3	4.4
1988	7.7	4.8
1989	5.7	8.2
1990	2.7	9.8
1991	3.1	5.5
1992	2.8	3.7
1993	6.0	1.4
1994	6.9	2.3
1995	6.1	3.5

(Source: Economic Trends, HMSO)

Required

Using both your knowledge of economic theory and material contained in the table,

(a) describe the apparent relationship between the money supply (M0) and the rate of inflation;   **4 Marks**

(b) explain the quantity theory of money;   **6 Marks**

(c) describe the extent to which the data given are in line with the predictions of the quantity theory of money;   **6 Marks**

(d) explain how the effects of a change in the money supply might differ between the short run and the long run.   **4 Marks**

Total Marks = 20

38   **CONTROL** (5/97)   *36 mins*

(a) Explain what is meant by the term 'the money supply'.   **4 Marks**

(b) Why do governments believe that it is important to control the growth of the money supply?   **8 Marks**

(c) Describe the methods by which the government can attempt to control the money supply.   **8 Marks**

Total Marks = 20

39   **DATA RESPONSE QUESTION: MONETARY THEORY** (5/95)   *36 mins*

Read the following summary of the role of monetary policy.

'The purpose of monetary policy is to influence monetary variables in the economy such as the rate of interest and the supply of money. The intention is to achieve the targets set for the government's main policy objectives.

Economic theory suggests that *the rate of interest* is important because for firms it is the cost of both their short-term borrowing for cash flow purposes and of long-term borrowing to finance investment. Also, consumer spending on durable goods may be influenced by the rate of interest since it affects the cost of hire-purchase finance. Household decisions on the portfolio of assets that they hold may be affected by the rate of interest; low interest rates may discourage savings and encourage consumption. Changes in interest rates may also have implications for the balance of payments since international movements of capital reflect differences in interest rates between countries.

Both monetarist and Keynesian economists recognise the importance of *the money supply*. In the Keynesian approach, changes in the money supply affect output and unemployment. However, for monetarists, the main impact, especially in the long run, is on the level of prices. Thus, for governments, measuring and controlling the money supply has been an important policy instrument.'

Required

Using both your knowledge of economic theory and material contained in the summary:

(a) explain the mechanisms mentioned in the summary by which changes in interest rates can influence:

    (i)   expenditure by firms,   **5 Marks**

    (ii)   expenditure by consumers;   **5 Marks**

(b) explain the monetarist theory that changes in the money supply affect mainly prices;   **6 Marks**

(c) show how a change in interest rates might affect the exchange rate for a country's currency.   **4 Marks**

Tutorial note. You may wish to postpone answering section (c) of this question until after you have studied the final section of the syllabus, *The international environment.*

Total Marks = 20

DO YOU KNOW? - NATIONAL INCOME ANALYSIS

- *Check that you can fill in the blanks in the statements below before you attempt any questions. If in doubt, you should go back to your BPP Study Text and revise first.*

- .... is the sum of all the incomes obtained from the production of goods and services by a country's economy over a period of time, usually one year. It is the value of a flow of economic activity, and is *not* the value of a country's stock of wealth.

- The usual starting point for macroeconomic theory is a four sector economy (households + ... + ... + ...), with various income flows between these sectors.

  o National income can be measured in three ways. This is because economic activity can be seen as two related circular flows - a circular flow of .... and .... and a related circular flow of ....).

  o Remember the basic equation: $Y = C + I + G + (X - M)$.

- Equilibrium national income is a level of national income which, if achieved, could be maintained.

- For equilibrium to be achieved, ... into the circular flow of income must exactly equal .... (in an open economy, $I + G + X = S + T + M$).

  o If actual national income exceeds the amount of national income at which there is full employment, the economy cannot produce any more output (since there is full employment) and so any further increases in national income will be inflationary, with prices rising (an ....).

  o If actual national income is less than full employment national income, there is a .... The economy could still produce more output with its unemployed resources and so national income in real terms could rise.

- The multiplier is a mathematical relationship between an .... in any item, C, I, G, X or M, and the .... in total national income Y, when Y gets back into equilibrium.

- Investment multiplier   =   Ratio of $\dfrac{\text{eventual change in national income}}{\text{initial change in investment spending}}$

- Government spending multiplier   =   Ratio of $\dfrac{\text{eventual change in national income}}{\text{initial change in government spending}}$

- Export multiplier   =   Ratio of $\dfrac{\text{eventual change in national income}}{\text{initial change in exports}}$

- If the output volume of consumption goods rises, firms must buy new equipment *in addition* to replacements, assuming a stable .... : .... ratio. The rate of increase in new investment will be faster than the rate of increase in consumption output (the .... effect).

- .... suggested that a combination of the multiplier and the accelerator causes the upswings and downswings of .... (with ceilings and floors being reached for various reasons, when the cycle turns from up to down or down to up).

TRY QUESTIONS 45-46

- *Possible pitfalls*

  Write down the mistakes you know you should avoid.

DID YOU KNOW? - NATIONAL INCOME ANALYSIS

- *Could you fill in the blanks? The answers are in bold. Use this page for revision purposes as you approach the exam.*

- **National income** is the sum of all the incomes obtained from the production of goods and services by a country's economy over a period of time, usually one year. It is the value of a flow of economic activity, and is *not* the value of a country's stock of wealth.

- The usual starting point for macroeconomic theory is a four sector economy (households + **firms** + **government** + **external trade**), with various income flows between these sectors.

  o National income can be measured in three ways. This is because economic activity can be seen as two related circular flows - a circular flow of **income** and **expenditure** and a related circular flow of **productive services (output)**.

  o Remember the basic equation: $Y = C + I + G + (X - M)$.

- Equilibrium national income is a level of national income which, if achieved, could be maintained.

- For equilibrium to be achieved, **injections** into the circular flow of income must exactly equal **withdrawals** (in an open economy, $I + G + X = S + T + M$).

  o If actual national income exceeds the amount of national income at which there is full employment, the economy cannot produce any more output (since there is full employment) and so any further increases in national income will be inflationary, with prices rising (an **inflationary gap**).

  o If actual national income is less than full employment national income, there is a **deflationary gap**. The economy could still produce more output with its unemployed resources and so national income in real terms could rise.

- The multiplier is a mathematical relationship between an **initial change** in any item, C, I, G, X or M, and the **eventual change** in total national income Y, when Y gets back into equilibrium.

- Investment multiplier   =   Ratio of $\dfrac{\text{eventual change in national income}}{\text{initial change in investment spending}}$

- Government spending multiplier   =   Ratio of $\dfrac{\text{eventual change in national income}}{\text{initial change in government spending}}$

- Export multiplier   =   Ratio of $\dfrac{\text{eventual change in national income}}{\text{initial change in exports}}$

- If the output volume of consumption goods rises, firms must buy new equipment *in addition* to replacements, assuming a stable **capital:output** ratio. The rate of increase in new investment will be faster than the rate of increase in consumption output (the **accelerator** effect).

- **Keynes** suggested that a combination of the multiplier and the accelerator causes the upswings and downswings of **trade cycles** (with ceilings and floors being reached for various reasons, when the cycle turns from up to down or down to up).

  TRY QUESTIONS 40-46

- *Possible pitfalls*

  o **Confusing 'savings' and 'investment'**
  o **Confusing productivity and output**
  o **Confusing growth in output and growth in output capacity**

---

40   TUTORIAL QUESTION: VOLUME OF PRIVATE INVESTMENT

According to J M Keynes, the volume of private investment depends on the rate of interest and the marginal efficiency of capital. Explain this proposition.

Approaching the question

1   First, define investment and summarise the factors determining it.

2   Then, explain the factors determining the rate of interest.

3   Next, explain the factors determining the marginal efficiency of capital.

4   Finally, explain the interaction of these two elements, emphasising the marginal efficiency of capital as the more important influence on changes in investment.

41   CIRCULAR FLOW OF INCOME (11/95)   *36 mins*

(a)   Explain briefly what is meant by the *circular flow of income*.   **6 Marks**

(b)   Describe the problems involved in using national income data to compare the living standards in different countries.   **14 Marks**

Total Marks = 20

42   METHODS (5/98)   *36 mins*

(a)   Explain the income, output and expenditure methods of measuring national income.   **6 Marks**

(b)   Describe some of the difficulties involved in their calculation.   **14 Marks**

Total Marks = 20

43   INJECTIONS AND WITHDRAWALS (11/97)   *36 mins*

(a)   Explain what is meant by 'injections' and 'withdrawals' in the circular flow of income model *and* show their role in determining the level of national income.

12 Marks

(b)   How might the business sector be affected if there were a rise in the savings rate in households?   **8 Marks**

Total Marks = 20

44   DATA RESPONSE QUESTION: CONSUMER EXPENDITURE (Specimen paper)
36 mins

Consider the following data and answer the following questions.

Consumer expenditure in the United Kingdom (£ billion in 1985 prices)

	1970	*1980*	*1990*
Consumer durable goods	9.4	15.5	27.8
Food	29.1	30.5	33.2
Drink and tobacco	19.7	24.2	23.2
Clothing and footwear	8.9	11.9	17.5
Energy products	14.4	17.3	20.5
Other goods	15.2	20.0	30.6
Rent, water and rates	20.7	25.4	29.3
Other services	40.6	52.4	90.9
Total expenditure	158.0	197.2	273.0

(Source: Economic Trends, HMSO)

Required

(a) Describe the main trends in consumer expenditure in the UK since 1970.   **5 Marks**

(b) Using economic concepts, provide possible explanations for these trends in consumption.   **10 Marks**

(c) Why would you expect the demand for consumer durable goods to fluctuate more than the demand for food?   **5 Marks**

Total Marks = 20

45   AGGREGATE MONETARY DEMAND (5/99)   *43 mins*

(a) Explain the concept of aggregate monetary demand and identify its four components.   **6 Marks**

(b) Explain what would happen to the level of aggregate monetary demand in the economy if there was:
(i)   an appreciation in the country's exchange rate;
(ii)   a fall in the propensity to save;
(iii)   a rise in business confidence.   **9 Marks**

(c) Identify three of the main objectives of government macroeconomic policy and show the effect on these of a rise in aggregate monetary demand.   **9 Marks**

Total Marks = 24

46   DATA RESPONSE QUESTION: TRADE CYCLE (11/96)   *36 mins*

The following data refer to the UK economy.

	Change in Gross Domestic Product from previous year	*Change in business investment (excluding dwellings) from previous year*	*Level of interest rates (London Inter-Bank Rate)*
1978	+ 3.5%	+ 10.1%	9%
1979	+ 2.8%	+ 3.4%	13%
1980	− 2.0%	− 3.9%	17%
1981	− 1.1%	− 4.8%	13%
1982	+ 1.7%	+ 8.4%	12%
1983	+ 3.7%	− 2.0%	10%
1984	+ 2.0%	+ 4.9%	10%
1985	+ 4.0%	+ 4.1%	12%
1986	+ 4.0%	+ 0.5%	10%
1987	+ 4.6%	+ 17.3%	9%
1988	+ 4.9%	+ 17.8%	9%
1989	+ 2.2%	+ 6.1%	14%
1990	+ 0.6%	− 3.1%	15%
1991	− 2.3%	− 9.5%	11%
1992	− 0.5%	− 5.1%	10%
1993	+ 2.0%	− 0.7%	6%
1994	+ 3.0%	+ 4.6%	5%

(Source: Economic Trends, HMSO)

Required

Using both your knowledge of economic theory and the data above:

(a) explain what is meant by the 'trade cycle' and show the recovery and recession phases of the trade cycle between 1978 and 1994;   **4 Marks**

(b) explain briefly what is meant by the accelerator principle and assess the extent to which the data show the presence of an accelerator effect;   **8 Marks**

(c) explain briefly how interest rates might affect the level of business investment and assess the extent to which the data support your explanation.   **8 Marks**

Total Marks = 20

DO YOU KNOW? - THE GOVERNMENT AND THE ECONOMY

- *Check that you can fill in the blanks in the statements below before you attempt any questions. If in doubt, you should go back to your BPP Study Text and revise first.*

- The aims of a government's economic policies might be:

  o   ....

  o   ....

  o   ....

- Key policy areas are .... policy (taxation, government spending and borrowing) and .... policy (policies on the money supply, interest rates and the availability of credit).

- The 'traditional' Keynesian approach to real economic growth, full employment and control over excessive (inflationary) rates of economic growth, was to ....

  o   Since AD = C + I + G + (X - M) this involves measures (especially fiscal policy, directly influencing C and G) to increase or restrict consumer spending, investment and government spending, or to influence the balance of payments.

  o   Problems with this approach include the difficulty of achieving full employment without inflation, and the difficulty of achieving real economic growth, rather than 'money' economic growth with excessive inflation.

TRY QUESTIONS 47-51

- In the 1950s, a connection between inflation and the level of unemployment was identified (the .... curve).

  o   Lower rates of inflation could only be achieved at the cost of rising unemployment. Lower rates of unemployment could only be achieved by accepting a higher rate of inflation.

  o   The .... curve could not, in its original form, explain rising inflation with rising unemployment.

- .... economists concentrate on low inflation as a policy objective, holding that in achieving price stability, the other elements of economic policy will naturally achieve a stable equilibrium.

- The aims of fiscal policy depend on the theoretical viewpoint adopted. .... would use tax and public spending as part of demand management, depending on the state of the economy. .... disfavour budget deficits which they believe may result in money supply increases and inflation.

- The emphasis of monetary policy is now usually on the control of inflation. In current policy-making, it is generally the price of money (interest rates) which is regulated rather than the supply of money.

- A government (eg the UK in the 1980s and early 1990s) might concentrate on a supply side approach to economic policy (favoured by monetarists). This concentrates on aggregate supply in the economy. When an economy is operating near its full employment level, and when increases in aggregate demand are inflationary, economic measures such as deregulation and the freeing of labour markets are proposed to shift the .... curve.

TRY QUESTIONS 52-58

- *Possible pitfalls*

  Write down the mistakes you know you should avoid.

DID YOU KNOW? - THE GOVERNMENT AND THE ECONOMY

- *Could you fill in the blanks? The answers are in bold. Use this page for revision purposes as you approach the exam.*

- The aims of a government's economic policies might be:
    - **steady economic growth, with stable prices to help ensure this;**
    - **full employment (no involuntary unemployment);**
    - **a fair distribution of economic wealth in society.**

- Key policy areas are **fiscal** policy (taxation, government spending and borrowing) and **monetary** policy (policies on the money supply, interest rates and the availability of credit).

- The 'traditional' Keynesian approach to real economic growth, full employment and control over excessive (inflationary) rates of economic growth, was to **manage aggregate demand (AD).**
    - Since AD = C + I + G + (X - M) this involves measures (especially fiscal policy, directly influencing C and G) to increase or restrict consumer spending, investment and government spending, or to influence the balance of payments.
    - Problems with this approach include the difficulty of achieving full employment without inflation, and the difficulty of achieving real economic growth, rather than 'money' economic growth with excessive inflation.

TRY QUESTIONS 47-51

- In the 1950s, a connection between inflation and the level of unemployment was identified (the **Phillips** curve).
    - Lower rates of inflation could only be achieved at the cost of rising unemployment. Lower rates of unemployment could only be achieved by accepting a higher rate of inflation.
    - The **Phillips** curve could not, in its original form, explain rising inflation with rising unemployment.

- **Monetarist** economists concentrate on low inflation as a policy objective, holding that in achieving price stability, the other elements of economic policy will naturally achieve a stable equilibrium.

- The aims of fiscal policy depend on the theoretical viewpoint adopted. **Keynesians** would use tax and public spending as part of demand management, depending on the state of the economy. **Monetarists** disfavour budget deficits which they believe may result in money supply increases and inflation.

- The emphasis of monetary policy is now usually on the control of inflation. In current policy-making, it is generally the price of money (interest rates) which is regulated rather than the supply of money.

- A government (eg the UK in the 1980s and early 1990s) might concentrate on a supply side approach to economic policy (favoured by monetarists). This concentrates on aggregate supply in the economy. When an economy is operating near its full employment level, and when increases in aggregate demand are inflationary, economic measures such as deregulation and the freeing of labour markets are proposed to shift the **aggregate supply** curve.

TRY QUESTIONS 52-58

- *Possible pitfalls*
    - **Confusing a government budget deficit with a trade deficit**
    - **Failing to distinguish between financing a budget deficit and correcting it**

47   TUTORIAL QUESTION: GOVERNMENT EXPENDITURE

Describe the methods a government may use to finance its expenditure.

What are the likely economic consequences of each method?

Approaching the question

1   To answer the first part of the question, mention the various types of taxation. Of course, borrowing is the other principal method.

2   Then, discuss the *effects* of taxation (consider fiscal policy effects, income distribution, incentives, savings and investment, wealth, indirect taxes) and of borrowing (especially with reference to the money supply).

48   MAIN OBJECTIVES (5/95, amended)   *43 mins*

(a) Describe briefly the main objectives of macroeconomic policy in a mixed economy.

6 Marks

(b) Explain how fiscal policy can be used to achieve these objectives.   **8 Marks**

(c) Explain what is meant by 'supply side' economic policies.   **10 Marks**

Total Marks = 24

49   PRODUCTION POSSIBILITY CURVE (5/97)   *36 mins*

(a) Explain briefly what is meant by the 'production possibility curve' *and* use it to explain the problems which arise from the scarcity of resources.   **8 Marks**

(b) Show how economic growth might affect the production possibility curve *and* describe the main sources of economic growth.   **12 Marks**

Total Marks = 20

50   DATA RESPONSE QUESTION: ECONOMIC TRENDS (11/98)   *36 mins*

The following financial data refer to the United Kingdom for the period 1992 to 1997.

	1992	*1993*	*1994*	*1995*	*1996*	*1997*
Interest rates						
Bank base rate (%)	8.5	7.0	5.5	6.8	5.8	6.0
Instant access account deposit rate (%)	6.3	4.9	3.8	4.2	2.8	2.3
90-day access account deposit rate (%)	8.8	6.2	4.5	4.9	3.9	3.9
Mortgage rate	11.0	9.4	7.7	8.4	7.0	7.4
Share prices						
FTSE 100 index	2521	2900	2919	2314	3711	4710
Inflation						
% rise in RPI (retail price index)	4.0	1.6	2.3	3.5	2.7	2.7

Required

Using both your knowledge of economic theory and the data above,

(a) describe and provide an explanation for differences in the various rates of interest.

5 Marks

(b) with respect to the bank base rate,

(i)   explain the difference between *nominal* and *real* rates of return   **2 Marks**

(ii)   calculate the real rate of interest for each year and comment on its value

3 Marks

(c) with respect to the FTSE 100 index,

    (i) explain what the FTSE 100 is;   **2 Marks**

    (ii) explain the factors which influence share prices;   **4 Marks**

    (iii) identify from the table and discuss two factors that may have contributed to the fall in share prices in 1996.   **4 Marks**

                    Total Marks = 20

51 PRIVATISATION (5/96)   *36 mins*

(a) Explain what is meant by 'privatisation' *and* discuss the economic arguments in favour of privatisation.   **12 Marks**

(b) Why do governments establish official bodies to regulate the privatised utilities such as gas and telephones?   **8 Marks**

                    Total Marks = 20

52 DATA RESPONSE QUESTION: UNEMPLOYMENT AND INFLATION (11/98)

36 mins

The following passage is based on a newspaper article, and discusses the unemployment situation in the UK in mid-1997.

> The number of people in unemployment fell sharply to a seven-year low last month but the fall failed to set off wage inflation, according to data released yesterday. The number of registered unemployed fell to 1.6 million, just 5,000 above its last low point in 1990. This is 5.7% of the workforce compared to 7.7% a year ago.

> The continued fall in unemployment clearly reflected the recovery from the recession. The rapid growth in consumer expenditure, partly fuelled by windfall gains from building societies as they converted to banks and issued free shares to their members, was likely to continue this process. However, the impact of the recent Budget, which contained significant tax increases to reduce government borrowing, and the effect on the export sector of the rise in the exchange rate for £ sterling, are likely to slow down the fall in unemployment in the medium term.

> Despite fears that the fall in unemployment might be fuelling inflation, there was no sign in yesterday's figures of a rise in earnings. The annual rate of increase for wages and earnings was 4.25% in June compared to 4.5% in May. 'There is evidence that the labour market is not strong and that inflationary pressures are easing' said Simon Briscoe, UK economist at Nikko Europe. 'The edge seems to have come off the economy's growth rate'. Mr Briscoe added that the fall in earnings growth and the continued strength of sterling could allows the Bank of England to leave interest rates at their current level.

Required

Using both your knowledge of economic theory and material contained in the passage:

(a) Identify and explain the main reasons for the recent fall in UK unemployment.

                    4 Marks

(b) Explain why the fall in unemployment might be slowed by:

    (i) recent budget measures;   **3 Marks**

    (ii) the strength of sterling.   **3 Marks**

(c) with the use of a diagram, describe the Phillips curve relationship between unemployment and inflation, AND use it to explain why the fall in unemployment might be expected to raise the rate of inflation. **7 Marks**

(d) identify and explain one of the factors that are operating to ease inflationary pressures in the UK economy. **3 Marks**

Total Marks = 20

53   PERSISTENT INFLATION (5/99)   *43 mins*

(a) Explain what is meant by the term inflation and show how the rate of inflation might be measured. **6 Marks**

(b) Describe the probable effects of persistent inflation in a country on:

    (i)   the distribution of income;

    (ii)   the trade balance;

    (iii)   the savings rate. **9 Marks**

(c) Identify and explain three economic problems that might arise if a government attempted to reduce the rate of inflation by raising the level of taxation. **9 Marks**

Total Marks = 24

54   UNEMPLOYMENT (11/96)   *36 mins*

(a) Distinguish between 'structural unemployment' and 'cyclical (demand deficient) unemployment'. **8 Marks**

(b) Explain how 'supply-side' policy might be used to reduce the level of unemployment. **12 Marks**

Total Marks = 20

55   FISCAL POLICY AND MONETARY POLICY (11/96)   *36 mins*

(a) Explain what is meant by 'fiscal (budgetary) policy' and 'monetary policy'. **8 Marks**

(b) Explain the means by which a government could conduct an expansionary monetary policy. **12 Marks**

Total Marks = 20

56   IDEAL TAX SYSTEM (11/98)   *36 mins*

(a) Describe the features of an ideal tax system, with special reference to the differences between direct and indirect taxes. **12 Marks**

(b) Explain the impact on a company producing a consumer good of:

    (i)   the imposition of an indirect tax on its product **4 Marks**

    (ii)   an increase in income tax on consumers. **4 Marks**

Total Marks = 20

57   DATA RESPONSE QUESTION: TAXATION (5/96)   *36 mins*

The following data refer to the principal sources of taxation revenue for the UK central government.

UK central government taxation revenue: main tax sources as percentage of total tax income

		1979 %	1993 %
1	Income taxes	34.1	30.0
2	Social Security taxes (National Insurance contributions)	19.2	20.0
3	Corporation tax	6.8	7.9
4	Value added tax	14.7	22.9
5	Excise duties	15.9	14.3
6	Other expenditure taxes*	7.7	3.7
7	Capital gains tax	0.9	0.6
8	Inheritance tax	0.7	0.6

*includes stamp duty and motor vehicle duties

(Source: National Income Accounts)

Required

Using both your knowledge of economic theory and material contained in the table:

(a) distinguish between direct and indirect taxes;   **4 Marks**

  and place *each* of the taxes shown above into one of these two categories;   **4 Marks**

(b) explain what is meant by a *progressive* tax, *and* what is meant by a *regressive* tax, giving an example of *each* from the table;   **4 Marks**

(c) identify the main changes which have occurred in the structure of UK taxation between 1979 and 1993;   **3 Marks**

(d) explain how these changes in the taxation system may have influenced incentives and the distribution of income.   **5 Marks**

Total Marks = 20

58   BUDGET BALANCE (5/98)   *36 mins*

(a) Explain what is meant by the 'government's budget balance'.   **4 Marks**

(b) Explain why the budget balance might vary over time.   **10 Marks**

(c) Describe how a government can finance a budget deficit.   **6 Marks**

Total Marks = 20

DO YOU KNOW? - THE INTERNATIONAL ENVIRONMENT

- *Check that you can fill in the blanks in the statements below before you attempt any questions. If in doubt, you should go back to your BPP Study Text and revise first..*

- The cost of producing goods in different countries can be compared in terms of their opportunity cost. One country has a .... over another in making a particular product if it has a lower opportunity cost of production, measured as production forgone of another product.

- .... describes government measures which prevent free trade. These measures will be aimed at:

  o protecting domestic industry against foreign competition (eg declining industries, infant industries);

  o possibly also protecting the country's inhabitants against unfair exploitation by foreign countries.

- The .... measure the ratio of export prices to import prices.

  o An improvement in the .... means that export prices have risen proportionately more than import prices. Given no change in export and import volumes, the balance of payments would improve.

  o A worsening of the .... means that import prices have risen proportionately more than export prices.

- Applying the equation $Y = C + I + G + (X - M)$, the .... is $(X - M)$. An improvement in the balance of payments adds to national income and a balance of payments deficit reduces national income.

  o Governments seeking to influence demand in their domestic economy must recognise the effect of their policy measures on exports and imports.

  o By boosting domestic demand (reflation) demand for imports goes up, and some domestic firms will divert output from exports to domestic markets. By reducing domestic demand (deflation) the opposite will happen.

  TRY QUESTIONS 59-64

- The .... is an institution that provides financial support, with conditions attached, to countries with serious external debt problems.

- Other international institutions you should be aware of include the .... (IBRD), the .... (BIS) and the .... (formerly GATT).

- Exchange rates can be allowed to vary up or down according to commercial supply and demand in the FX markets (.....................exchange rates).

- Alternatively, government might intervene (.....................), or participate in a fixed or semi-fixed exchange rate system (such as the ERM). Such a system implies that domestic economic policy (including monetary policy and therefore interest rates) must be subordinated to maintain a particular exchange rate or range of exchange rates.

- The effect of a currency depreciation on the balance of payments depends upon the elasticities of demand for .... and ....

  TRY QUESTIONS 65-68

- *Possible pitfalls*

  Write down the mistakes you know you should avoid.

DID YOU KNOW? - THE INTERNATIONAL ENVIRONMENT

- *Could you fill in the blanks? The answers are in bold. Use this page for revision purposes as you approach the exam.*

- The cost of producing goods in different countries can be compared in terms of their opportunity cost. One country has a **comparative advantage** over another in making a particular product if it has a lower opportunity cost of production, measured as production forgone of another product.

- **Protection** describes government measures which prevent free trade. These measures will be aimed at:

  o protecting domestic industry against foreign competition (eg declining industries, infant industries);

  o possibly also protecting the country's inhabitants against unfair exploitation by foreign countries.

- The **terms of trade** measure the ratio of export prices to import prices.

  o An improvement in the **terms of trade** means that export prices have risen proportionately more than import prices. Given no change in export and import volumes, the balance of payments would improve.

  o A worsening of the **terms of trade** means that import prices have risen proportionately more than export prices.

- Applying the equation $Y = C + I + G + (X - M)$, the **balance of payments on current account** is $(X - M)$. An improvement in the balance of payments adds to national income and a balance of payments deficit reduces national income.

  o Governments seeking to influence demand in their domestic economy must recognise the effect of their policy measures on exports and imports.

  o By boosting domestic demand (reflation) demand for imports goes up, and some domestic firms will divert output from exports to domestic markets. By reducing domestic demand (deflation) the opposite will happen.

TRY QUESTIONS 59-64

- The **IMF** is an institution that provides financial support, with conditions attached, to countries with serious external debt problems.

- Other international institutions you should be aware of include the **World Bank** (IBRD), the **Bank for International Settlements** (BIS) and the **World Trade Organisation** (formerly GATT).

- Exchange rates can be allowed to vary up or down according to commercial supply and demand in the FX markets (**free floating** exchange rates).

- Alternatively, government might intervene *(**managed floating**)*, or participate in a fixed or semi-fixed exchange rate system (such as the ERM). Such a system implies that domestic economic policy (including monetary policy and therefore interest rates) must be subordinated to maintain a particular exchange rate or range of exchange rates.

- The effect of a currency depreciation on the balance of payments depends upon the elasticities of demand for **imports** and **exports**.

TRY QUESTIONS 65-69

- *Possible pitfalls*

  o **Confusing a trade deficit with a government budget deficit**
  o **Confusing the balance of trade and the terms of trade**
  o **Failing to distinguish between financing a trade deficit and correcting it**

59   TUTORIAL QUESTION: TERMS OF TRADE

(a) Define 'the terms of trade'.

(b) Explain how changes in the terms of trade arise.

(c) Explain the effect which such changes may have on the economy.

Approaching the question

1   Once you have defined the terms of trade, you can go on to explain changes in terms of the definition, analysing the factors which determine the prices of imports and exports. Consider demand and supply, inflation and changes in the exchange rate.

2   The effects on the economy are to do with income, employment and the balance of payments. Emphasise the significance of demand elasticity.

60   TRADE BENEFITS (5/98)   *36 mins*

(a) Explain the economic benefits of trade to participating economies.   **12 Marks**

(b) Discuss the economic problems a country would experience if it ran a persistent deficit on its trade with the rest of the world.   **8 Marks**

                                                          Total Marks = 20

61   TRADE AND IMPORTS (11/96)   *36 mins*

(a) Using the comparative advantage model, explain the economic benefits of international trade.   **10 Marks**

(b) Describe the main methods by which governments might attempt to restrict international trade.   **5 Marks**

(c) Explain why, if trade is beneficial, governments often wish to limit the flow of imports into their economies.   **5 Marks**

                                                          Total Marks = 20

62   EXPLANATIONS (11/95, amended)   *43 mins*

(a) State the differences between free trade areas, customs unions and common markets.   **4 Marks**

(b) Explain what is meant by the *terms of trade* and describe *two* processes that would lead to a change in a country's terms of trade.   **12 Marks**

(c) Explain the effect on a country's balance of trade of a fall in its terms of trade.   **8 Marks**

                                                          Total Marks = 24

63   DEVALUATION POLICY (5/96)   *36 mins*

(a) Explain why a government might wish to reduce the exchange rate for its currency (devaluation) *and* discuss those factors that will determine the success of such a policy.   **12 Marks**

(b) Describe the possible effects on domestic companies of a significant devaluation of the currency.   **8 Marks**

                                                          Total Marks = 20

64   DATA RESPONSE QUESTION: UK TRADE (5/99)   *43 mins*

The following data refer to the pattern of UK trade in goods.

Structure of UK exports and imports

	Exports		Imports	
	1960	*1995*	*1960*	*1995*
Food and drink	5%	7%	33%	10%
Fuel and raw materials	8%	8%	33%	7%
Semi-manufactured goods and metals	36%	28%	22%	27%
Finished manufactured goods	48%	55%	11%	55%
Others	3%	2%	1%	1%

Destination of UK exports

	1960	*1995*
European Union	21%	58%
Other European countries	11%	4%
North America	16%	14%
Other OECD economies	13%	4%
Rest of the world	39%	20%

Based on: A Griffiths & S Wall Applied Economics 1997

Required

Using both your knowledge of economic theory and material contained in the tables,

(a) describe the main changes in the structure of UK exports and imports since 1960;

4 Marks

(b) explain briefly the comparative cost (comparative advantage) theory of trade;

6 Marks

(c) use the comparative cost theory to explain the changes in the structure of UK trade that you have identified;   **4 Marks**

(d) identify and describe two economic problems that a country might experience as the result of a rapid change in the structure of its international trade;   **4 Marks**

(e) identify the main changes in the destination of UK exports since 1960;   **2 Marks**

(f) identify and explain two possible reasons for the changes in the destination of UK exports.   **4 Marks**

Total Marks = 24

65   DEFICIT (11/97)   *36 mins*

(a) Explain what is meant by the term 'a balance of payments deficit'.   **5 Marks**

(b) Describe the main factors that might lead a country to experience a deficit on the current account of its balance of payments.   **10 Marks**

(c) Explain the difference between *financing* a balance of payments deficit and *correcting* that deficit.   **5 Marks**

Total Marks = 20

66   DATA RESPONSE QUESTION: EXCHANGE RATES (5/98)   *36 mins*

The following passage is based on a newspaper article published in February 1997, and discusses the effects of the rise in the sterling exchange rate in 1996.

'"UK companies are expressing alarm at the strength of sterling after seeing the rising exchange rate choke off their exports" the CBI (Confederation of British Industry) said yesterday as the pound sterling rose to DM 2.7070 in late trading.

The CBI said that demand for exports had levelled off for the first time since the autumn of 1993, with optimism and order books hit by the 9% appreciation of sterling in the final three months of 1996. According to the CBI survey, prices were regarded as more of a constraint on exports than at any time since October 1989. The picture which emerged was of weakening export orders balanced by the strength of domestic demand for UK-produced consumer goods.

The CBI said that the decision on whether the government should raise interest rates was "finely balanced". Any rise in interest rates to prevent the very rapidly recovery from recession leading to excessive inflation was likely to further strengthen sterling and have an adverse effect on exporters' order books.

However, the prospects of a rise in interest rates to slow inflation were lessened by the latest figures for the growth of the money supply. They showed that broad money growth fell from an annual rate of 10.8% in November to 9.6% in December. However, these were still well above the government's target for the growth of the money supply. In response, a Government source pointed out that the rise in sterling itself would act to reduce the rate of inflation through its effects on costs and on the level of aggregate demand.'

Requirements

Using both your knowledge of economic theory and material contained in the above passage:

(a) explain how exchange rates are determined in the foreign exchange market;

4 Marks

(b) explain why UK exporters might be worried by a rise in the exchange rate for sterling;   **4 Marks**

(c) show how a change in interest rates might influence the exchange rate for a currency;   **4 Marks**

(d) explain why the government might wish to see a rise in interest rates;   **4 Marks**

(e) explain why a rise in the exchange rate might act to reduce inflation.   **4 Marks**

Total Marks = 20

67   **DATA RESPONSE QUESTION: ECONOMIC RELATIONSHIPS (5/95)**   *36 mins*

The following data refer to the UK economy and are drawn from HMSO *Economic Trends*.

Consider the data and answer the following questions.

Year	Rate of growth of GDP	Public sector borrowing requirement	Balance of payments
	(1)	(2)	(3)
	%	£bn	£bn
1980	− 2.0	+ 11.8	+ 2.6
1981	− 1.1	+ 10.5	+ 6.7
1982	+ 1.7	+ 4.8	+ 4.6
1983	+ 3.7	+ 11.5	+ 3.5
1984	+ 2.0	+ 10.3	+ 1.4
1985	+ 4.0	+ 7.4	+ 2.2
1986	+ 4.0	+ 2.5	− 0.9
1987	+ 4.6	− 1.4	− 5.0

Year	Rate of growth of GDP (1)	Public sector borrowing requirement (2)	Balance of payments (3)
1988	+ 4.9	– 11.9	– 16.5
1989	+ 2.2	– 9.3	– 22.5
1990	+ 0.6	– 2.1	– 18.2
1991	– 2.3	+ 7.7	– 7.6
1992	– 0.5	+ 28.9	– 8.5

(1) Annual rate of growth of Gross Domestic Product (GDP)

(2) Public sector borrowing requirement (PSBR): + denotes net borrowing, – denotes repayment of previous debt.

(3) Balance of payments, current account: + denotes surplus, – denotes deficit.

Required

(a) Explain what is meant by the following terms and state briefly how they are measured.

(i)	Gross domestic product (GDP)	**4 Marks**
(ii)	Public sector borrowing requirement (PSBR)	**3 Marks**
(iii)	Current account of the balance of payments	**3 Marks**

(b) Identify and explain the possible relationship between the trend of the PSBR and the rate of growth of GDP. **5 Marks**

(c) Identify and explain the possible relationship between the trend of the current account of the balance of payments and the rate of growth of GDP. **5 Marks**

Total Marks = 20

68   FIXED OR FLOATING (11/98)   *36 mins*

(a) Explain the difference between a *fixed* exchange rate system and a *flexible* exchange rate. **10 Marks**

(b) Describe the appropriate policies for correcting a balance of payments current account deficit for each of these two exchange rate systems. **10 Marks**

Total Marks = 20

Multiple choice questions

69   SELECTION 1 (5/99)   *50 mins*

1   The opportunity cost of constructing a road is

   A   the money spent on the construction of the road.
   B   the value of goods and services that could otherwise have been produced with the resources used to build the road.
   C   the cost of the traffic congestion caused during the construction of the road.
   D   the value of goods that could have been produced with the labour employed in the construction of the road.

2   Which one of the following would cause the supply curve for a good to shift to the right (outwards from the origin)?

   A   A fall in the price of the good.
   B   An increase in the demand for the good.
   C   A fall in production costs of the good.
   D   The imposition of a minimum price.

3   When the price of a good is held above the equilibrium price, the result will be

   A   excess demand.
   B   a shortage of the good.
   C   a surplus of the good.
   D   an increase in demand.

4   If the price of a good fell by 10% and, as a result, total expenditure on the good fell by 10%, the demand for the good would be described as

   A   perfectly inelastic.
   B   perfectly elastic.
   C   unitary elastic.
   D   elastic.

5   Which one of the following would not lead directly to a shift in the demand curve for overseas holidays?

   A   An advertising campaign by holiday tour operators.
   B   A fall in the disposable incomes of consumers.
   C   A rise in the price of domestic holidays.
   D   A rise in the exchange rate for the domestic country's currency.

6   There is a rise in wage rates in an industry. Which one of the following will limit the amount of unemployment caused by the wage rise?

   A   The supply of substitute factors of production is inelastic.
   B   Labour costs form a high proportion of total costs.
   C   The demand for the industry's product is very price elastic.
   D   Labour and capital are easily substituted for each other.

7   Which of the following best describes the law of diminishing returns?

As more labour is added to a fixed amount of capital,

A   total output will fall.
B   increases in total output will become smaller for each additional unit of labour employed.
C   the marginal revenue from each additional unit of output produced will decline.
D   production costs will rise because higher wages will have to be paid to attract more labour.

8   Which one of the following is not a source of economies of scale?

A   The introduction of specialist capital equipment.
B   Bulk buying.
C   The employment of specialist managers.
D   Cost savings resulting from new production techniques.

9   Which of the following are characteristics of perfect competition?

(i)   Large numbers of producers.
(ii)   Differentiated goods.
(iii)   The absence of long-run excess profits.
(iv)   Freedom of entry to and exit from the industry.

A   (i), (ii) and (iii) only.
B   (i), (iii) and (iv) only.
C   (ii), (iii) and (iv) only.
D   All of them.

10   Which one of the following is not a feature of an industry operating under conditions of monopolistic competition?

A   There is product differentiation.
B   Producers operate at below full capacity output.
C   Firms maximise profits where marginal cost equals marginal revenue.
D   There is one dominant producer.

11   The public sector borrowing requirement (PSBR) is

A   the accumulated debts of the government.
B   the total amount borrowed by all members of the public.
C   the amount borrowed by the government and public authorities in a given period.
D   the amount borrowed to finance a balance of payments deficit.

12   Which one of the following is not a function of a central bank?

A   The conduct of fiscal policy.
B   Management of the national debt.
C   Holder of the foreign exchange reserves.
D   Lender of the last resort.

13   The current account of the balance of payments includes all the following items except which one?

A   The inflow of capital investment by multinational companies.
B   Exports of manufactured goods.
C   Interest payments on overseas debts.
D   Expenditure in the country by overseas visitors.

14 The main advantage of a system of flexible (floating) exchange rates is that it

A   provides certainty for international traders.
B   provides automatic correction of balance of payments deficits.
C   reduces international transactions costs.
D   provides policy discipline for governments.

28 Marks

70 **SELECTION 2 (11/98)**   *36 mins*

1   In a market economy, the allocation of resources between different productive activities is determined mainly by the

A   decisions of the government
B   wealth of entrepreneurs
C   pattern of consumer expenditure
D   supply of factors of production

2   If the demand for a good is *price elastic*, which one of the following is true?

When the price of the good

A   rises, the quantity demanded falls and total expenditure on the good increases.
B   rises, the quantity demanded falls and total expenditure on the good decreases.
C   falls, the quantity demanded rises and total expenditure on the good decreases.
D   falls, the quantity demanded rises and total expenditure on the good is unchanged.

3   Which of the following always rise when a manufacturing business increases its output?

(i)   fixed costs;
(ii)   marginal cost;
(iii) average variable cost;
(iv)   total costs.

A   (i) and (ii) only
B   (ii) and (iii) only
C   (iii) and (iv) only
D   (iv) only

4   The long-run average cost curve for a business will eventually rise because of

A   the law of diminishing returns
B   increasing competition in the industry
C   limits to the size of the market for the good
D   diseconomies of scale

5   The benefits to a company when it locates close to other companies in the same industry include all of the following *except* which one?

A   The benefits of bulk buying
B   The provision of specialist commercial services
C   The development of dedicated transport and marketing facilities
D   The supply of labour with relevant skills

6   Which one of the following statements about profit is correct?

   A   In the private sector, the profit motive encourages efficiency.
   B   Nationalised industries are always inefficient because they are not profit-motivated.
   C   Not-for-profit organisations do not have to worry about being efficient.
   D   In the private sector, companies cannot be profitable unless they are efficient.

7   In a perfectly competitive market, all producers charge the same price because

   A   they are all profit maximisers
   B   they have the same costs
   C   the product is homogeneous
   D   all firms are small

8   Which one of the following would be a sound economic reasons for a government to prevent a merger between two companies?

   A   Combined profits would increase
   B   Competition would decrease and prices rise
   C   The industry would become more concentrated
   D   The companies are operating in the same industry

9   The comparative cost model of international trade shows that trade arises because of differences between countries in

   A   the absolute costs of production
   B   patterns of consumer demand
   C   the opportunity costs of production
   D   the structure of production

10   A restriction imposed on the flow of imports into a country would be expected to lead to all of the following *except* which one?

   A   An improvement in the trade balance
   B   A reduction in unemployment
   C   Reduced competition for domestic producers
   D   A fall in the rate of inflation

20 Marks

71   **SELECTION 3 (5/98)**   *36 mins*

1   Which one of the following best describes the opportunity cost to society of building a new school?

   A   The increased taxation to pay for the school
   B   The money that was spent on building the school
   C   The other goods that could have been produced with the resources used to build the school
   D   The running cost of the school when it is opened

2   In a market economy the price system provides all of the following except which one?

   A   An estimation of the value placed on goods by consumers
   B   A distribution of income according to needs
   C   Incentives to producers
   D   A means of allocating resources between different uses ✓

3 According to the traditional theory of the firm, the equilibrium position for all firms will be where

A profits are maximised
B output is maximised
C revenue is maximised
D costs are minimised

4 The 'law of diminishing returns' can apply to a business only when

A all factors of production can be varied
B at least one factor of production is fixed
C all factors of production are fixed
D capital used in production is fixed

5 Which of the following statements about normal profit are correct?

(i)   It is the reward for risk taking
(ii)   It is the return to entrepreneurship
(iii) It is the cost of entrepreneurship
(iv)   It is earned only in the short run

A (i) and (ii) only
B (ii) and (iii) only
C (i), (ii) and (iii) only
D (i), (ii) and (iv) only

6 Which ONE of the following best describes the main purpose of the Monopolies and Mergers Commission (MMC)?

A To prevent the growth of large firms
B To investigate anti-competitive behaviour by firms
C To encourage mergers to enable firms to secure economies of scale
D To regulate the prices charged by privatised utilities

7 Which of the following would lead to a rise in the demand for money?

(i)   A rise in disposable income
(ii)   A fall in interest rates
(iii) An expectation of falling share prices
(iv)   A decrease in the money supply

A (i) and (ii) only
B (ii) and (iii) only
C (ii), (iii) and (iv) only
D (i), (ii) and (iii) only

8 Which one of the following would appear as a liability in a clearing bank's balance sheet?

A Advances to customers
B Money at call and short notice
C Customers' deposit accounts
D Discounted bills

9 Other things being equal, all of the following would lead to a rise in share prices except which one?

A A rise in interest rates
B A reduction in corporation tax
C A rise in company profits
D A decline in the number of new share issues

10   Which one of the following is not a valid economic reason for producing a good or service in the public sector?

    A   The good is a basic commodity consumed by everyone
    B   It is a public good
    C   There is a natural monopoly in the production of the good
    D   It is a merit good

20 Marks

72   **SELECTION 4 (11/97)**   *36 mins*

1   The demand curve for a good will shift to the right

    A   if there is an increase in the supply of the good
    B   if the price of the good falls
    C   if consumer incomes rise
    D   when the price of a substitute good falls

2   Which one of the following will tend to make the supply of labour to a particular occupation more elastic?

    A   Low skill requirements
    B   The need to pass professional examinations
    C   High wage rates
    D   A legal minimum wage

3   Which one of the following is not a function of profit in a market economy?

    A   A signal to producers
    B   A signal to consumers
    C   The return to entrepreneurship
    D   A reward for risk taking

4   Which one of the following comes closest to the model of a perfectly competitive industry?

    A   Oil refining
    B   Agriculture
    C   Motor vehicles
    D   Banking

5   Which of the following are common features of oligopolisitic industries?

    (i)   a small number of companies;
    (ii)   barriers to entry;
    (iii) product differentiation;
    (iv)   the absence of long-run excess profits.

    A   (i), (ii) and (iii) only
    B   (ii), (iii) and (iv) only
    C   (i), (ii) and (iv) only
    D   (i), (iii) and (iv) only

6   Arguments for allocating resources through the market mechanism rather than through government direction include three of the following.

Which one is the exception?

    A   It provides a more efficient means of communicating consumer wants to producers
    B   It ensures a fairer distribution of income
    C   It gives more incentive to producers to reduce costs
    D   It encourages companies to respond to consumer demand

7   Which one of the following will tend to increase competition within an industry?

   A   Economies of scale
   B   Barriers to entry
   C   Low fixed costs
   D   Limited consumer knowledge

8   Which one of the following is likely to result from an increase in the size of the public sector borrowing requirement?

   A   A decrease in the rate of inflation
   B   A reduction in the level of taxation
   C   A rise in the price of shares
   D   A rise in the rate of interest

9   The theory of comparative advantage suggests that countries should

   A   diversify their production as much as possible
   B   engage in trade if the opportunity costs of production differ between countries
   C   engage in trade only if each country has an absolute advantage in at least one good or service
   D   aim to make their economies self-sufficient

10 Which one of the following is not a benefit from countries forming a monetary union and adopting a single currency?

   A   International transaction costs are reduced
   B   Exchange rate uncertainly is removed
   C   It economies on foreign exchange reserves
   D   It allows each country to adopt an independent monetary policy

20 Marks

73   **SELECTION 5 (5/97)**   *36 mins*

   1   Which *one* of the following would be a variable cost to a firm?

      A   Mortgage payments on the factory
      B   The cost of raw materials
      C   Depreciation of machines owing to age
      D   Interest on debentures

   2   The supply curve of labour will be more elastic:

      A   the more training is required for the job
      B   the greater is the immobility of labour between occupations
      C   for a single firm than for the industry as a whole
      D   the higher is the wage

   3   Which of the following statements about a policy of privatising a public sector industry are *true*?

      (i)   It will permit economies of scale.
      (ii)   It is a means of widening share ownership.
      (iii) The industry would become more responsive to the profit motive.
      (iv)   It is a source of funds for the government.

      A   (i) and (ii) only
      B   (i), (ii) and (iii) only
      C   (ii) and (iii) only
      D   (ii), (iii) and (iv) only

4   Which *one* of the following would *not* act as a barrier to the entry of new firms into an industry?

A   Perfect consumer knowledge
B   Economies of scale
C   High fixed costs of production
D   Brand loyalty

5   In the theory of the demand for money, the transactions demand for money is determined by the:

A   level of consumers' incomes
B   expected changes in interest rates
C   expected changes in bond prices
D   level of notes and coins in circulation

6   Which of the following are functions of a central bank?

(i)   Issuing notes and coins
(ii)   Supervision of the banking system
(iii)   Conducting fiscal policy on behalf of the government
(iv)   Holding foreign exchange reserves

A   (i), (ii) and (iii) only
B   (i), (ii) and (iv) only
C   (i), (iii) and (iv) only
D   (ii), (iii) and (iv) only

7   Venture capital is best described as:

A   investment funds provided for established companies
B   short-term investment in Eurocurrency markets
C   capital funds that are highly mobile between financial centres
D   equity finance in high-risk enterprises

8   Which *one* of the following would cause a fall in the level of aggregate demand in an economy?

A   A decrease in the level of imports
B   A fall in the propensity to save
C   A decrease in government expenditure
D   A decrease in the level of income tax

9   Which *one* of the following is *not* an economic advantage of international trade?

A   It encourages international specialisation
B   Consumer choice is widened
C   It enables industries to secure economies of large-scale production
D   Trade surpluses can be used to finance the budget deficit

10 Which of the following policies for correcting a balance of payments deficit is an expenditure-reducing policy?

A   Cutting the level of public expenditure
B   Devaluation of the currency
C   The imposition of an import tax
D   The use of import quotas

20 Marks

74   SELECTION 6 (11/96)   *36 mins*

1   The 'central economic problem' means:

   A   the output of goods and services is limited by scarce resources
   B   market prices do not always equal costs of production
   C   all businesses must make a profit
   D   consumers cannot maximise their utility because of limited information

2   Decreasing returns to scale can only occur:

   A   in the short run
   B   in the long run
   C   if there is one fixed factor of production
   D   if companies have monopoly power

3   When only a small proportion of a consumer's income is spent on a good:

   A   the demand for the good will be highly price elastic
   B   the good is described as 'inferior'
   C   a rise in the price of the good will strongly encourage a search for substitutes
   D   the demand for the good will be price inelastic

4   The conditions necessary for a successful policy of price discrimination by a company include which of the following?

   (i)   There are at least two separate markets
   (ii)   Marginal costs are different in each market
   (iii) The price elasticities of demand are different in each market
   (iv)   The price elasticities of demand are the same in each market

   A   (i) and (ii) only
   B   (i) and (iii) only
   C   (i), (ii) and (iii) only
   D   (ii) and (iv) only

5   A multi-national company is best described as one which:

   A   engages extensively in international trade
   B   sells its output in more than one country
   C   produces goods or services in more than one country
   D   is owned by shareholders in more than one country

6   A yield curve shows how:

   A   the rate of return on financial assets varies with their maturity dates
   B   the productivity of capital goods falls with increasing age of those goods
   C   company profits rise or fall over time
   D   the total amount of tax collected rises as tax rates are raised

7   Which *one* of the following will cause the demand curve for a good to move to the right (outwards from the origin)?

   A   A decrease in the costs of producing the good
   B   A fall in the price of the good
   C   An increase in the price of a complementary good
   D   An increase in the price of a close substitute good

8   Marginal cost is best defined as:

   A   the difference between total fixed costs and total variable costs
   B   costs which are too small to influence prices
   C   the change in total costs when output rises by one unit
   D   fixed costs per unit of output

9   Which of the following is most likely to cause a country's balance of payments to move towards a deficit?

A   A devaluation of that country's currency
B   An expansionary fiscal policy
C   A contractionary fiscal policy
D   A rise in the rate of domestic saving

10 Which *one* of the following is a characteristic of floating (flexible) exchange rates?

A   They provide automatic correction for balance of payments deficits and surpluses

B   They reduce uncertainty for businesses

C   Transactions costs involved in exchanging currencies are eliminated

D   They limit the ability of governments to adopt expansionary policies

20 Marks

75 **SELECTION 7 (5/96)**   *36 mins*

1   The term 'mixed economy' implies all of the following conditions except which *one*?

A   The allocation of resources is mainly through the price system
B   Producers have an incentive to advertise their products
C   There is some government planning of the use of resources
D   All industries have a mix of small and large companies

2   If the demand for a good is price inelastic, which *one* of the following statements is correct?

A   If the price of the good rises, the total revenue earned by the producer increases

B   If the price of the good rises, the total revenue earned by the producer falls

C   If the price of the good falls, the total revenue earned by the producer increases

D   If the price of the good falls, the total revenue earned by the producer is unaffected

3   The purpose of a cartel is to:

A   rationalise production
B   reduce consumer uncertainty
C   standardise product quality
D   ensure that all producers charge the same price

4   Economies of scale:

A   can be gained only by monopoly firms
B   are possible only if there is a sufficient demand for the product
C   do not necessarily reduce unit costs of production
D   depend on the efficiency of management

5   Which of the following are characteristics of monopolistic competition?

(i)   Freedom of entry into the industry
(ii)   Homogeneous (ie uniform) products
(iii) Advertising
(iv)   A downward sloping demand curve

A   (i) and (ii) only
B   (i) and (iv) only
C   (i), (iii) and (iv) only
D   (ii) and (iv) only

6   A shift to the right in the supply curve of a good, the demand remaining unchanged, will reduce its price to a greater degree:

A   the more elastic the demand curve
B   the less elastic the demand curve
C   the nearer the elasticity of demand to unity
D   the more elastic the supply curve

7   Which *one* of the following statements is *incorrect*?

A   Wages are determined mainly by the forces of supply and demand in imperfect markets

B   The supply of labour does not consist of homogeneous (ie uniform) units

C   An increase in wages will always result in a rise in unemployment

D   The marginal product of labour theory attempts to explain the demand for labour

8   Structural unemployment is best defined as that caused by:

A   the long-term decline of particular industries
B   the trade cycle
C   an insufficient level of aggregate demand
D   seasonal variations in demand for particular goods and services

9   Which *one* of the following would appear as a DEBIT item on the current account of the balance of payments?

A   Payment of interest on debts owed to overseas commercial banks
B   Expenditure by tourists visiting the country
C   Overseas capital investment by domestic companies
D   Repayment of debts to overseas central banks

10 A favourable movement in the terms of trade for a country means that:

A   the balance of trade has improved
B   the volume of exports has risen relative to the volume of imports
C   the prices of exports have risen relative to the prices of imports
D   the revenue from exports has risen relative to the revenue from imports

20 Marks

76   SELECTION 8   *50 mins*

1   Which one of the following statements is *not* true?

   A   The basic economic problem is the same in planned and free market economies

   B   The basic economic problem is one of choice between alternatives

   C   Factors of production are limited in supply

   D   Choice is necessary because of limited consumer wants

2   When a government wishes to increase its expenditure on education but can do so only at the expense of expenditure elsewhere, this is said to be an example of:

   A   diminishing marginal utility
   B   opportunity cost
   C   scale of preferences
   D   equi-marginal returns

3   Vertical integration means:

   A   a merger between two competing firms in the same industry

   B   the take-over by Firm X of the suppliers to Firm Y

   C   the establishment of a cartel to maintain price levels

   D   the combination of a firm with its suppliers or customers in the chain of production

4   Which of the following statements is true under conditions of monopolistic competition?

   A   Each firm fixes its price irrespective of other firms.
   B   There is no freedom of entry into the industry in the long run.
   C   Buyers and sellers have perfect information.
   D   Firms tend to rely heavily on product differentiation.

5   The real rate of interest is:

   A   the rate at which the central bank lends to financial institutions
   B   bank base rate
   C   the difference between the money rate of interest and the rate of inflation
   D   the annualised percentage rate of interest

6   The law of diminishing marginal utility states that:

   A   as more of a good is consumed, total satisfaction diminishes

   B   as more units of a good are consumed, the amount of satisfaction obtained from each additional unit will fall

   C   as more units of a good are produced, the price will fall

   D   increased use of variable factors reduces their marginal productivity

7   Which one of the following statements about the elasticity of supply is *not* true?

   A   It tends to vary with time
   B   It is a measure of the responsiveness of supply to changes in price
   C   It is a measure of changes in supply due to greater efficiency
   D   It tends to be higher for manufactured goods than for primary products

8 GNP (Gross National Product) at factor cost may be best defined as:

   A the total of goods and services produced within an economy over a given period of time

   B the total expenditure of consumers on domestically produced goods and services

   C all incomes received by residents in a country in return for factor services provided domestically and abroad

   D the value of total output produced domestically plus net property income from abroad, minus capital consumption

9 Which one of the following can be used by governments to finance a public sector borrowing requirement?

   A A rise in direct taxation
   B The sale of public assets
   C An increase in interest rates
   D An issue of government savings certificates

10 Which one of the following will result if a firm is taxed by an amount equal to the external costs that its productive activities impose on society?

   A Resource allocation will be improved since prices more closely reflect costs and benefits

   B There will be a misallocation of resources because the price mechanism has been interfered with

   C The increase in costs will lead the firm to raise output in order to maintain profits

   D The firm will maintain output and profits by passing the costs of the tax on to its customers

11 Which of the following are common features of oligopolistic markets?

   (i) advertising
   (ii) barriers to entry
   (iii) interdependence of decision making
   (iv) price stability

   A (i) and (ii) only
   B (i), (ii) and (iii) only
   C (i), (ii) and (iv) only
   D All of them

12 A progressive tax is one where the tax payment:

   A rises as income increases
   B falls as income increases
   C is a constant proportion of income
   D rises at a faster rate than income increases

13 Which one of the following *cannot* be used to finance a deficit on the current account of a country's balance of payments?

   A Running down foreign exchange reserves
   B Increased taxation
   C Borrowing from foreign central banks
   D Attracting inflows of short-term capital

14 The imposition of which one of the following would *not* act as a barrier to international trade?

A A value added tax
B Tariffs
C Import quotas
D Exchange controls

28 Marks

Answer bank

1   TUTORIAL QUESTION: NEW PRODUCT

> **Pass marks.** As mentioned in the notes accompanying the question, an alternative way of answering this question to that suggested below, which relies on marginal utility analysis, is one using indifference curves if you are aware of this form of analysis. The new product may change the indifference curve for each commodity relative to all other commodities, since the satisfaction derived from a given amount of all other commodities changes depending upon the marginal rate of substitution of the different commodities.

Consumers demand products because they expect to derive **utility** from them. The approach of **marginal utility analysis** enables us to examine the effect of the introduction of a new product on the demand for other products.

As used by economists, the term 'utility' refers not to a property of a good or service, but to the derivation of satisfaction from the use of such a good or service. Thus, for example, bread has the same 'properties' whether in a period of glut or famine. However, bread's utility is to the consumer: the consumer's utility will vary according to his state of body and mind.

For each consumer the relationship between **utility** and **price** will determine the **equilibrium** of the consumer. From this it is possible to derive the consumer's demand curve for individual products.

Central to this approach to consumer equilibrium and the derivation of the **demand curve** is the concept of marginal utility and the hypothesis of **diminishing marginal utility**. Marginal utility is the extra utility derived from the consumption of one more unit of a good, the consumption of all other goods remaining unchanged. The hypothesis of diminishing marginal utility states that as the quantity of a good consumed by an individual increases, the marginal utility of a good will eventually decrease. Consider, for example, the utility derived by a thirsty consumer from successive glasses of milk. The first glass will yield a great deal of utility, ie the marginal utility of the first glass is very high. A second glass may be welcome, but is unlikely to yield as much utility as the first, and a third glass of milk is likely to yield even less utility. Once his thirst is quenched, the consumer may have no further desire for liquid refreshment and any more milk would yield disutility. The hypothesis of diminishing marginal utility appears to be a valid generalisation about consumer behaviour: the more a consumer has of a commodity, the less utility he is likely to derive from the consumption of an additional unit.

The introduction of a new product will result in the consumer assessing the product in terms of its utility to him. If the ratio of marginal utility to price for the first unit consumed of the new product exceeds the same ratio for existing products (assuming consumer equilibrium), the consumer will decide to buy the product. He will adjust the pattern of all of his purchases until the ratios of price to marginal utility are again equal for all products.

The decision to consume a quantity of the new product is of course likely to affect the quantity of consumption of close **substitutes** most markedly. For example, with the introduction of the compact disc, the consumption of vinyl records would be expected to fall considerably, as indeed it has over recent years. Suppose that the price of a compact disc is twice the price of a vinyl record: in that case, a consumer with the facilities to use each is only going to buy a compact disc instead of a record if the marginal utility of the compact disc (with its superior sound reproduction, user convenience and so on) is more than twice that of a vinyl record. The pattern of consumption will be adjusted until the ratios of price to marginal utility equate for each product.

However, as already suggested, the introduction of the new product affects the pattern of purchases of products in general. The consumer's **income** - and therefore the amount he has to spend on products in general - is not affected by the introduction of the new product, and so he must 'redistribute' his spending over products in general if he is to purchase a quantity of the new product. He will do this until, again, the ratios of price to marginal utility are the same for all products. Another way of viewing the situation is to observe that every product is, to some extent, a 'substitute' for all other products.

2   TUTORIAL QUESTION: ELASTICITY OF SUPPLY

Supply is the quantity of goods which existing or potential suppliers would be prepared to supply to the market at a particular price. The upward-sloping **supply curve** illustrates the general fact that suppliers will be prepared to supply greater quantities of output as price increases.

The **elasticity of supply** is a measure of the responsiveness of supply to a change in price. This responsiveness is quantified as the percentage change in the quantity supplied divided by the percentage change in price. A good for which supply increases by 10% as the result of a 5% increase in price has an elasticity of 2.

The two **limiting values of elasticity** are infinity and zero. The elasticity of supply may be close to zero for very rare goods or services. It will not be possible to increase the quantity supplied as the price increases. Examples here would be the services of a top rock star, or a unique work of art. The supply curve will be vertical in cases where the supply elasticity is zero.

Perfect elasticity describes a situation where the elasticity of supply is infinite, and the supply curve is horizontal. Supply is said to be **elastic** when the percentage change in the amount which producers want to supply exceeds the percentage change in price. Otherwise, supply is **inelastic**.

Elasticity of supply will be determined in large part by:

(a)   the time period over which its measurement is made;
(b)   the opportunity cost of using the factors of production necessary;
(c)   fixed costs and variable costs of production.

The effects of **time** on supply and to the response of supply to changes in price can be considered for analytical purposes in terms of three lengths of time period. Firstly, the market period reflects a short time period within which output cannot be altered. Supply of the commodity is limited by existing stocks of the good, and is therefore inelastic.

The **'short-run' period** is long enough for output to be increased or decreased in order to alter supply of the commodity. However, fixed equipment such as plant and machinery cannot be altered in the short run. Although suppliers will be able to reduce output fairly quickly, suppliers will be able to produce larger quantities only if they are not already operating at full capacity. The degree of inelasticity in the market and short run periods will depend upon how much stock or how much spare capacity exists.

In the **'long-run' period**, capital investment is possible. New factories and machines can be built, and old ones closed down. New firms can enter the industry. Over this length of period, supply elasticity will be relatively more elastic.

Costs can be analysed into fixed and variable elements, and it will be the opportunity costs of using the factors of production required in particular combinations which will determine the amount of a product which a firm will make available.

It is not surprising that an important determinant of the elasticity of supply is the **change in costs** as output is varied, since the basis of the supply curve lies in the costs of production. If the firm operates in perfect competition then the firm's marginal cost curve (from the point it intersects the average variable cost curve) is the firm's supply curve, as this indicates what quantities the firm will supply at different market prices. Clearly the costs of factors of production will affect the elasticity of supply. If demand for the firm's product increases, the supplier must attract more factors of production in order to increase output. If the cost of attracting new amounts of the factors is high then the costs per unit of output will rise rapidly as output expands. The stimulus to expand production from any given price rise would therefore quickly be choked off by increasing costs and supply would tend to be rather inelastic.

Conversely, if costs per unit of output rise only slowly as production increases, for any given increase in the price of the product there will be a larger increase in the amount supplied before the increase in costs halts the expansion in output. Supply in this case would therefore tend to be rather elastic.

Supply in the market period cannot be varied beyond the stocks that are available. Production costs have already been incurred, and an unanticipated difference in price will result in windfall gains or losses when judged against opportunity costs.

In the short run, increases in supply must come from greater output from **existing capacity**. This will involve additional variable costs, which must be met from sales revenue for supply to be worthwhile. Obtaining extra output may be more costly than existing output if plant is more efficient at the existing level of output.

In the long run, **fixed costs** as well as **variable costs** may change. Fixed costs may rise as capital investment occurs. The new capital investment necessary to increase supply in the long run may lead to economies of scale being gained, which will reduce unit costs. This may permit a large increase in supply over the long run period. However, it should be recognised that capital investment over this time scale - typically, several years - may be influenced by various factors other than the price mechanism. Demographic or other market changes foreseen by entrepreneurs, and corporate strategic objectives, are as likely to influence the investment decision as changes in current price levels.

3   **DATA RESPONSE QUESTION: EUROTUNNEL**

> **Pass marks.** You may well be aware of the issues covered in the extract in the question but this is not necessary to produce a good solution. What is necessary is that you *apply* your knowledge of economic theory to the details of the case.
>
> **Examiner's comment**. This question was, on the whole, answered quite well. The better scripts contained clear explanations of price and cross elasticity of demand and good attempts to apply them to the particular issues of Eurotunnel pricing. Weaker answers tended to provide textbook explanations of demand elasticity, often with extensive examples, but failed to apply these concepts to the issues raised in the extract.

(a)   **Price elasticity of demand** (PED) measures, in respect of a product or service in a particular market, the extent of responsiveness of quantity demanded to changes in its price.

A commonly used means of measuring PED is as follows.

$$PED = \frac{\text{Percentage change in quantity demanded}}{\text{Percentage change in price}} = \frac{(\Delta Q / Q) \times 100}{(\Delta P / P) \times 100}$$

Demand is **elastic** (PED > 1) when a cut in price results in a bigger percentage expansion in demand. A seller who cuts the price of his goods under these conditions would find his revenue increasing.

Demand is **inelastic** (PED < 1) when a cut in price leads to a smaller percentage expansion in demand. Under these conditions, total revenue would fall.

PED will be negative for all 'normal' demand curves. Hence it is usual to omit the use of + and – signs.

Price elasticity can, of course, apply also to price rises. What has been stated so far merely operates in reverse. Therefore, if price is increased and revenue falls, demand is elastic.

In summary:

Price		*Revenue*		*Demand*
Decrease	$\longrightarrow$	Rises	}	Elastic
Increase	$\longrightarrow$	Falls		
Decrease	$\longrightarrow$	Falls	}	Inelastic
Increase	$\longrightarrow$	Rises		

The key factor determining PED is **substitution**. Thus, food as a whole has a highly inelastic demand, as there is no real substitute for it. However, between different foods much substitution is possible.

Whether a good is a 'necessity' has relevance up to a point. For the basic essentials of living, demand tends to be inelastic (often very much so). Even if price rises noticeably, we will still strive to buy them (though perhaps in smaller quantities or lower in quality).

Those items which represent only a minor part of income are likely to have inelastic demand. A large percentage increase in the price of such products would probably make little difference to demand, whereas the reverse is true of major budgetary items.

Some goods are bought as a matter of habit, eg cigarettes. Price changes may need to be substantial to make any difference to demand, and so demand will be relatively **inelastic**.

The **durability or potential life of a product** will also be a determining factor. If the price of durable products rises we can, if necessary, defer their replacement, whereas expendable products must be replaced. Demand for durable products will therefore tend to be price elastic.

Time will also be important. Elasticity of demand will tend to be greater in the long run: buying habits can then more easily adjust in response to price changes.

(b) (i)   In the market for transport across the English Channel, a **substitute** for the tunnel services is the alternative ferry services. The existence of substitutes will make consumers more sensitive to changes in price of a good, since they have an alternative to switch to if prices are set too high. Therefore, where there are substitutes, the **price elasticity of demand** will be higher.

In the article extract, Dr Szymanski argues that Eurotunnel could double profitability by lowering its prices and that it could feasibly halve its prices when the tunnel is running at full capacity. This implies that the price elasticity of demand is more than 1 and that total revenue can be increased by lowering prices: the revenue lost through lowering the prices for all customers is more than compensated for by the additional revenue gained from extra traffic. If it is true that halving prices will increase Eurotunnel's revenue, it must be that this action will more than double the volume of customers.

If Eurotunnel sets its prices too high, more customers will choose the substitute services offered by ferry companies and much of Eurotunnel's capacity will remain unused.

In its **pricing policy**, Eurotunnel will consider the **current capacity** of its services. When it first opened, the capacity of the tunnel was relatively low. Setting prices relatively high at first avoids the risk of demand exceeding capacity, which could result in customers being disappointed by delays. At the same time, this policy tests the market, seeing how much is demanded at the initial price set. As capacity increases, Eurotunnel can reduce its prices in stages to allow more capacity to be taken up. Again, this will 'test' the market at different prices, providing information on the demand curve faced by the firm.

(ii) The **cross elasticity of demand** refers to the responsiveness of demand for one good to changes in the price of another good. Given no change in the price of good A:

Cross elasticity of demand $= \dfrac{\text{\% change in quantity of good A demanded}}{\text{\% change in the price of good B}}$

If the two goods are substitutes, cross elasticity will be greater than 0 and a fall in the price of one will reduce the amount demanded of the other. If the goods are complements, cross elasticity will be negative and a fall in the price of one will raise demand for the other.

Cross elasticity thus involves a comparison between two products. Cross elasticity is significant where the two goods are close substitutes for each other, so that a rise in the price of B is likely to result in an increase in the demand for A. The cross elasticity of demand between two complementary products can also be significant because a rise in the price of B would result in some fall in demand for A because of the fall in demand for B.

Since tunnel and ferry services are very close substitutes for one another, the cross elasticity of demand between them will be significantly positive. If Eurotunnel raises its prices, for example, more people and more freight carriers will switch to ferries and the volume of ferry services demanded will increase.

The article suggests that either Eurotunnel or the ferry companies could face eventual curtailment of services, depending upon the pricing policies which Eurotunnel adopts. If Eurotunnel's prices are too high, it will be unable to attract enough custom away from the ferries and may face bankruptcy as a result. If its prices are set low enough, ferry companies will attempt to compete by lowering their prices. However, it will then become difficult for these companies to generate enough traffic to cover their overheads and their services may consequently be 'killed off'.

(iii) The addition of Eurotunnel as a competitor to the ferries widens the choice of services available to the cross-channel car traveller and freight carrier. There are some differences between the various services available, for example with respect to the journey time and the susceptibility to cancellation in bad weather.

In the **short run**, Eurotunnel's strategy is to set prices close to those of the ferries. There is then no cost saving for consumers. The possible consumer benefits are those relating to increased choice and increased capacity. Increased cross channel transport capacity makes it less likely that customers will have to queue for services, and more likely that they will be able to travel when they want.

In the **longer term**, it is likely that price competition will ensue. Prices will move closer to the firms' marginal costs and both ferry and tunnel users will benefit from paying lower prices. This will cause more cross-channel trips to be made. If the prices fall to levels at which ferry companies can no longer make a profit, these companies may exit from the market. If this process happens on a wide scale, consumers will face a reduction of choice compared with the short-run situation. If Eurotunnel then becomes the dominant firm in the market, it will be a monopolist and might raise its prices again. Consumer choice will then be limited and consumers would have to pay more. The tunnel company, as the monopolist producer, could be protected by high start-up costs which would form an entry barrier against re-entry of ferry firms into the market.

4 DATA RESPONSE QUESTION: ELASTICITIES

> **Pass marks**. For the first four parts, much of the marks were in the data. Part (e) required slightly more elaboration with an understanding of pricing policy and product range strategy.
>
> **Examiner's comment.** This was the more popular of the two Section B questions and most candidates gave good answers. Most candidates grasped the basic concepts but some were unable to link causes of elasticity of demand with relevance and usefulness.

(a) **Price elasticity of demand** is a measure of how sensitive consumers are to changes in price and is measured by the formula:

$$\frac{\% \text{ change in quantity demanded}}{\% \text{ change in price}}$$

For a **normal good**, we would expect quantity demanded to rise if price fell and to fall if price rose, and so the PED will have a negative value. If the PED is greater than 1, demand is said to be elastic. If it is less than 1, demand is inelastic.

(b) If the amount of quantity demanded rises more than the price falls, then demand is **elastic**. The data show that services, entertainment, travel abroad and catering fall into this category.

If quantity demanded changes less than the price change, then demand is **inelastic**. Fuel and light, food, alcohol, durable goods, dairy products and bread and cereals are all categories with inelastic demand.

Two factors which affect elasticity of demand are the type of good and the proportion of income spent on it. An essential good with few close substitutes, such as fuel and light, will be price inelastic. Entertainment is less essential and so will exhibit price elasticity.

A good where a low proportion of income is spent (eg dairy produce) will have a low (inelastic) elasticity of demand. A good which represents a high proportion of income spent (eg travel abroad) will have a high (elastic) elasticity of demand.

(c) **Income elasticity of demand** (IED) measures how sensitive consumers are to changes in income and is measured by the formula:

$$\frac{\% \text{ change in quantity demanded}}{\% \text{ change in income}}$$

For a normal good, we would expect quantity demanded to rise as income rises, which would indicate a positive income elasticity of demand. If the rise in demand is greater than the rise in income, demand is said to be **income elastic**. If the rise in demand is less than the rise in income, demand is **income inelastic**.

(d) **Inferior goods** are goods that have a negative income elasticity of demand, which include coal, and bread and cereals in the data given. Necessities will have low income elasticities while luxury goods will have higher elasticities.

Higher-priced products, such as consumer durables, will tend to have a higher IED as more consumers will be able to afford them as incomes rise.

(e) Price elasticity is important to **businesses** since if they know what the price elasticity of demand of their product is, they can work out their revenue maximising output. For many goods and services, demand is elastic and revenue might be increased by cutting price, as the increase in demand will be proportionately higher than the cut in price and total revenue will be increased. If demand is inelastic, a firm should consider raising its prices: the consequent drop in demand will be proportionately smaller than the rise in price, and revenue should rise.

Total revenue will be maximised where the PED is 1. Thus, knowledge of PED will help a company in its **pricing strategy**. Knowledge of the IED of products is useful for a company's **output strategy**. As living standards improve, businesses need to produce goods with higher income elasticity of demand. This can be particularly important for those individuals working in marketing with a company that has a range of products. For example, motor manufacturers will target their luxury cars towards a certain income group and small cars will be targeted towards a lower income group. A firm which produces only goods with a low IED, or even inferior goods, may fail to take advantage of consumer affluence.

5 PRICE SYSTEM

> **Pass marks.** Better answers need to show not only an awareness that markets may not function efficiently but also an understanding of why this may be so.
>
> *Other points.* Part (b) of the question ranges widely. An efficient allocation of resources requires that all costs, both social and 'private' are taken into account and rationally assessed. Market imperfections arise from inadequate information, inability to use that information effectively, difficulties in adjusting to changed market conditions and excessive concentration of seller or buyer power.
>
> **Examiner's comment.** Weaker answers were often limited to a description of the supply and demand model without any attempt to show how this influenced resource allocation. There were many digressions into irrelevant issues such as the determination of price elasticity. In part (b), some candidates could reproduce the monopoly diagram but failed to draw the relevant conclusions from it.

(a) The **price system** in a **market economy** is essentially a decentralised system, with decisions being taken by individual consumers, workers and firms. These decisions collectively have the effect of allocating resources in the economy, determining what is produced, how things will be produced and to whom what is produced will be distributed.

The system functions through the processes of:

(i) **signalling**: price is an indicator of relative value;

(ii) **allocating**: resource decisions are made in anticipation of or in response to price changes;

(iii)   **rewarding** the seller through profit obtained or loss avoided and the buyer through satisfaction derived.

In a free market economy, the decisions and choices about resource allocation are left to the forces of supply and demand, of which the price system is a part. What is produced and what consumers will buy are kept in balance by the price that producers want for their product and the price that consumers are willing to pay. Each price is an expression of relative value, enabling the purchaser and seller each to know the opportunity cost of any transaction they might be entering into.

The working of the price mechanism is such that a rise in demand creates a potential shortage so that price rises. If however demand falls, this indicates an excess of supply over demand and price falls. Any rise in price induces suppliers to place more goods on the market. At the same time, the rise in price will tend to deter people from buying the product so that demand will fall back. At some point - the '**equilibrium point**' - a balance will be established, and the initial shortage will be eliminated.

The **allocation of resources** can be explained as follows. Consumers express their preferences through purchases in the goods market. The producers of goods use their income from sales to purchase resources in the factor market. When consumers' preferences change, the demand for some goods rises, and the prices of these goods are likely to rise, so increasing the profits of the producers. The increased profits - the reward element - will encourage existing producers to increase output and additional suppliers may enter the market. If, instead, demand had fallen, the scenario would be reversed. Firms will cut production and some firms will have to close down. Productive resources will then become available to be used by other firms in the production of other goods. Resources are thus allocated according to the expressed wishes of consumers.

(b)   For markets to allocate resources efficiently requires all factors affecting opportunity cost to be taken into account: **social** as well as **private costs**; **longer term** as well as immediate consequences. However, the market system may operate imperfectly.

The working of the **free market** is based on the assumption of full information and full knowledge on the part of both producers and buyers of products and their possibilities, including alternatives. This is the pre-requisite of fully rational decision-making. In reality, this is not the case: producers are often buying in factor markets with inadequate knowledge while consumers are likely to be at an even greater disadvantage.

The free market theory also assumes, potentially, a condition of complete responsiveness and adjustment in the various markets. **Signalling through the price system** is assumed to bring prompt readjustment of resources according to changing consumer preference. This is far from the real world in which many resources (labour, machines etc) are specific and not necessarily mobile. Resources may not easily be switched from one industrial application to another. The free market system is also based on the assumption of an absence of intervention by the State or otherwise. For political and social reasons this often is not the case; so the market process becomes distorted.

A further assumption is that production will remain relatively small in scale such that any one firm by itself cannot determine market price. There will remain a reasonable balance between producers and consumers. Yet the logical outcome of much competition, reinforced by the search for scale economies and the application of technology, is that supply becomes concentrated in fewer hands, as the more profitable firms survive. As monopolisation develops, the balance between producers and consumers is changed. **Monopsony** - the exertion of buying power by a single organisation - also distorts the market. Monopolists can charge 'excessive' prices and use their supernormal profits to subsidise other products and thus compete unfairly in other markets. This can result in resource misallocation.

The basic price system does not take account of **externalities**: the free market fails to take account of social costs and benefits. Hence a satisfactory allocation of resources in wider social terms is not achieved. Externalities occur when the actions of producers or consumers affect not only themselves but also third parties, and these are not taken account of through the normal workings of the price mechanism. Thus, the siting of a factory which emits noxious fumes in a restricted area is clearly to the disadvantage of the health and welfare of the residents. For the most part, such social costs are mostly ignored. As a consequence, the prices of the products of many firms are lower than they would be if social costs were also taken into account.

The disparity is sometimes the other way round. Some organisations confer benefit on society beyond what is incorporated into the pricing of their products, eg basic research which in due course has much wider application and from which the firm itself may only partially benefit.

6   NORMAL PROFIT

> **Pass marks**. Profit as incentive and the reward of the entrepreneur is your starting point, but you must cover its signalling function also. Good, clear, simple diagrams are essential for part (b).
>
> **Examiner's comment**. Some candidates tried to deal with part (b) in terms of changes in *demand*. Its often worth pausing for a moment and asking yourself if you have hold of the right end of the stick.

(a) Profit is the reward for entrepreneurship and as such, part of the cost of a firm's activities. Normal profit is the level of profit that is just large enough to prevent the entrepreneur from leaving the current activity and entering another market. Normal profit is thus one of the opportunity costs of production. If revenue exceeds the total of those opportunity costs, the surplus is abnormal profit.

Profit has several functions in a market economy. First, as the reward for entrepreneurship, it encourages risk-taking economic activity such as the introduction of new products and techniques. This, in turn, contributes to economic growth. Second, it sends signals into the wider economy. When demand exceeds supply, prices and profits will rise. Entrepreneurs will be attracted and more resources will be introduced into the market. Conversely, reducing demand will see entrepreneurs leave a market to seek better profits elsewhere. Profit thus influences resource allocation within a market economy. Finally, profit enables the accumulation of surpluses for re-investment and therefore contributes to economic growth.

(b) (i)

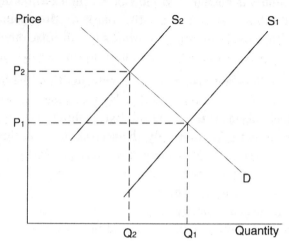

A rise in profits in another part of the economy would tell entrepreneurs that the opportunity cost of remaining in their present market had gone up. If they could not cover this increased opportunity cost, they would begin to move their resources into the more profitable market. This would cause a reduction in the amount supplied at any price, shown in the diagram as a leftward shift in the position of the supply curve from S_1 to S_2. Quantity supplied would be reduced to Q_2 and the equilibrium price would rise to P_2.

(ii)

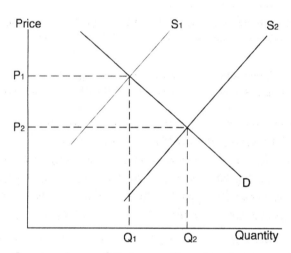

Conversely, a fall in profits elsewhere would have the opposite effect. Entrepreneurs would be attracted by the higher profits and move their resources into the market. There would be an increase in the quantity supplied at any price, shown in the diagram as a rightward shift of the supply curve from S_1 to S_2. The equilibrium price would fall from P_1 to P_2 and the quantity supplied would increase to Q_2.

The implication of these processes is that we should expect a single level of normal profit to prevail in all markets where the conditions of perfect competition (particularly cost-free entry and exit) apply.

(c) Traditional theory of the firm assumes that, whatever the market form, firms will aim to maximise profit. This is because firms are assumed to be managed by entrepreneurial owners. Where this is not the case we may expect different motivations to apply. Public sector businesses may have a number of non-profit objectives such as provision of service, environmental protection and the maintenance of employment. Charities are not businesses in the strict sense, but they are part of the economy: by definition their objectives differ from those of the private sector.

There is a separation of ownership from control in larger businesses run by professional managers. The owners may continue to desire maximum profits but the motivations of the managers may be different. One model suggests that managers will aim to maximise revenue, since their financial rewards are typically linked to turnover, and growth brings prestige and career development. Another model suggests that managers will *satisfice* rather than maximise, that is, they will address several objectives including profits and growth, but will seek levels of performance that are satisfactory rather than maximum. This allows the needs of other stakeholders to be recognised.

7   TUTORIAL QUESTION: COMPETITION AND ECONOMIES OF SCALE

Economies of scale will cause **average total costs of production**, spread over the units produced, to fall as the size of the plant increases. **Diseconomies of scale** will tend to lead to average total costs being increased as plant size increases beyond a certain level. It is believed that economies of scale predominate as output rises from relatively low levels, leading to a downward-sloping curve of average total costs. As the plant size increases, certain diseconomies of scale begin to take effect, and this may lead the average total cost curve to rise at higher levels of output. An enterprise may grow as a result of growth through internal expansion, through take-over, or through mergers.

Economies of scale include those which result from the **division of labour** - from the ability to create **specialisation** in particular areas. There may be economies resulting from the technical advantages of larger scale production. A larger scale of production may enable economies to be gained in management costs, and there may also be financial economies: central services can be spread over a number of units without incurring additional costs in proportion to the number of units.

Economies can arise from external factors such as the growth of an industry overall which may enable facilities to be established which the firms in the industry may take advantage of.

It is believed that diseconomies of scale may result from an excess of bureaucracy and an increasing inability to co-ordinate activities effectively within the business. It is also thought that incentives may become eroded by the growth in size of organisations. Employees feel more remote from the organisation, and a diminishing of competition may inhibit management's willingness or ability to perform to full effectiveness.

The **minimum efficient scale** in an industry is the lowest level of output at which long-run average costs are minimised. This is illustrated in Figure 1, in which it can be seen that long-run average total costs (LRAC) fall up to a particular level of output, Q_1.

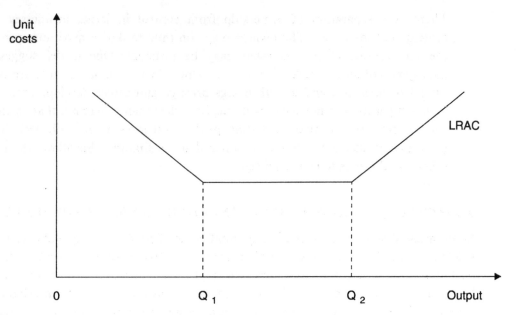

Figure 1

From this level up to Q_2, constant returns to scale are obtained and over that band of output, LRAC is flat. (In reality, it is to be expected that the curve will not completely flatten off at one particular point.) In the middle band of output, between Q_1 and Q_2, constant returns to scale are earned. In other words, efficiency cannot be improved by adjusting the scale of output within this range, and firms may coexist within the industry with plants of different sizes but similar unit costs.

It can be appreciated that if the band at which constant returns to scale are gained is relatively narrow, or if there is no flattening off to the curve at all, but rather a 'sharper' minimum point as in Figure 2, there will be a single minimum efficient scale of operations at this minimum point. In an industry which has these conditions, producers are likely to operate with plants of similar sizes.

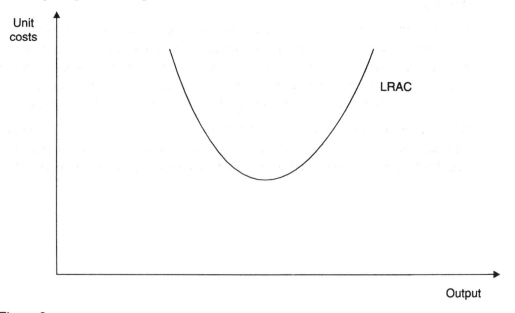

Figure 2

In many industries, it may be that there are few if any genuine diseconomies of scale. In such a case, the LRAC curve will flatten off, but will not rise significantly, as shown in Figure 3.

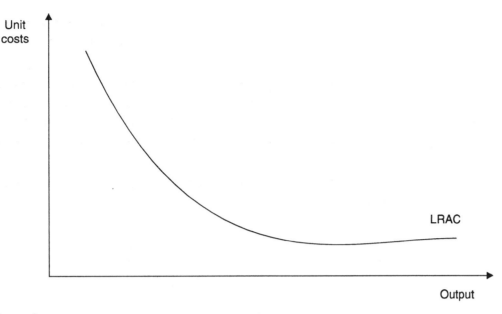

Figure 3

In such cases, the very large scale plants will be the most efficient. Competition may be reduced as production becomes concentrated among a few very large producers. Small firms will not be able to match the larger firms in efficiency and will therefore not survive in the industry. A situation of '**natural monopoly**' may be enjoyed by a single producer if economies of scale can be gained indefinitely within the range of output in the whole industry. In such a case, there will be no competition in the industry.

The **structure of an industry** is determined by various factors, including historical factors, regulatory and legislative restrictions, and the geographical spread of the business engaged in. As we have seen above, another significant determinant of the structure of an industry, apart from the competitiveness of the industry in which it operates, is the extent of economies and diseconomies of scale in the industry.

8   DATA RESPONSE QUESTION: REVENUE AND COSTS

> **Pass marks**. Remember that the profit-maximising quantity produced is always where MC = MR.
>
> **Examiner's comment.** This was by far the most popular of the two data response questions and was, on the whole, well answered with a good number of candidates gaining very high marks indeed. However, a minority of scripts suggested a poor grasp of basic concepts of revenue, costs and elasticity.

(a) (i)   The **marginal cost** and **marginal revenue** at different levels of demand are as follows.

Quantity sold	Price £	Total revenue £	Marginal revenue £	Total cost £	Marginal cost £
1	34	34	34	12	12
2	30	60	26	20	8
3	27	81	21	34	14
4	25	100	19	53	19
5	23	115	15	75	22
6	21	126	11	102	27
7	19	133	7	131	29

The marginal cost is the increase in total cost brought about by producing the last unit of output of a good. Thus the marginal cost of the second item in the question is £8, that is the difference between the total cost of producing the items and the total cost of just producing the first item, ie £20 – £12.

(ii) The marginal revenue is the **amount added to total revenue** by the sale of the last unit of good produced. To get the total revenue, we multiply the quantity sold by the price prevailing at that quantity. The marginal revenue added by the second one sold is thus £26, the difference between £60 total revenue for a quantity of two units and £34 total revenue for a quantity of one unit.

(b) The level of **profit** at each level of output, that is total revenue less total cost, is shown below.

Quantity sold	Total revenue £	Total cost £	Level of profit £
1	34	12	22
2	60	20	40
3	81	34	47
4	100	53	47
5	115	75	40
6	126	102	24
7	133	131	2

The profit-maximising level of output is the point at which marginal revenue equals marginal cost, that is at the point at which a quantity of 4 is produced, when marginal cost is £19 and marginal revenue is also £19.

(c) The **price elasticity of demand** (PED) is calculated as:

$$\frac{\% \text{ change in quantity demanded}}{\% \text{ change in price}}$$

The new price is £23.

$23/25 \times 100 = 92\%$ of £25.

Therefore, the percentage change is –8%. The price has dropped by 8%.

At the same time the quantity sold has increased from 4 to 5, a percentage increase of 5/4 = 25%.

$$\text{PED} = \frac{\% \text{ change in quantity demanded}}{\% \text{ change in price}} = \frac{25}{-8} = -3.125$$

The PED is greater than 1 and therefore the demand for the good in question is said to be **price elastic** - in this case, highly elastic.

(d) The following factors which might explain the relatively high *value* of the elasticity of demand for the good.

(i) **Substitutes**. A high value may indicate there is a number of substitutes with which this good must compete. It could be one brand of tea trying to compete with a number of other brands. If we put up the price of our tea by say 1%, assuming others keep the price of their tea unchanged, we might expect to see around 3% of our consumers **switch away** from our brand to the other brands.

(ii) **Time**. Over a relatively long period, all goods have a high price elasticity of demand, in theory at least. For example, if gas prices go up substantially more than electricity prices, in the long run consumers will switch to electricity. In the short run, no change can be made because of the high cost of the obsolescence of fixed appliances like gas cookers.

(iii) **Proportion of income.** The good might be a **mortgage,** the monthly interest payments on which could take up a large proportion of a consumer's monthly income. A rise in the monthly price of a mortgage, here the interest rate, would cause many to respond to increases in mortgage rates and either to seek a lower-priced mortgage from another provider, or to buy less new mortgage finance.

(e) As more new firms come into the industry, new close substitutes could emerge. As we saw above, more substitutes could increase the value of the price elasticity of demand, making the demand curve **flatter**.

As well as this, more competition could give each firm a smaller share of the market and drive prices down, changing the position of the profit maximisation level of production for each firm. This point would be at a lower level of production than before, because of a leftward shift in the demand curve for the individual firm. Not only will the firm receive lower prices, but it could also suffer a drop in volume as a result of greater competition.

9   FALLING COSTS

Pass marks. In part (a), the central point is economies of scale, but a distinction needs to be made between those arising with each function of the firm (eg production, marketing) and those attributable to the firm as a whole.

The consequence of marked economies of scale (part (b)) is high minimum levels of efficient operation and resulting barriers to entry. The greater concentration of supply may mean reduced competition, or a move towards new price competition.

Prizewinners' Point. There may also be major structural consequences: whole new (sub-) industries may arise to act as feeder firms (eg parts, specialised components) to the 'main' (original) producers who now specialise in design and assembly of completed products.

Examiner's comment. Many candidates failed to identify economies of scale as the focus of part (a) and few could see the relevance of scale economies to the structure of an industry.

(a) A business may experience **falling long-run average costs** due to **economies of scale** - the 'long run' signifying a period long enough for all of a firm's costs to become variable. The economies of scale arise from an increase in resource inputs resulting in a proportionately greater increase in output. The **long-run average cost curve** (LRAC) therefore falls with increases in output. Economies of scale may be **internal,** with average costs falling as a result of the individual firm (or any sector of the firm) growing in size, or **external** when average costs fall with the growth of the industry as a whole.

The various forms of **internal economies of scale** include the following.

(i) **Technical economies.** Larger machines (as in printing) may provide vastly greater outputs with little or no increase in the labour which operates and controls them. The larger plant may provide greater scope for specialisation of processes and therefore of labour. The division of labour is facilitated and productivity can be improved. Computerised control of operations and the use of sophisticated, integrated equipment are likely to raise the minimum size at which production effectively can be carried out. Overall the result, at a sufficient level of working, can be a marked fall in unit costs.

(ii) **Purchasing economies.** Larger firms can buy in bulk, thus deriving discounts. They can also buy more effectively, ensuring reliable delivery and higher quality. The larger firms may find it economic to employ specialists in purchasing.

(iii) **Marketing economies**. These may arise in market research, marketing planning, distribution, advertising and promotion.

(iv) **Financial economies**. The larger firms may be able to raise funds more effectively and at lower rates than smaller firms.

(v) **Research and development economies**. The small firm may not satisfactorily be able to run its own R & D capability. The large firm can benefit from ongoing product and process development.

(vi) **Managerial economies**. The larger firm may be able to employer more specialised management personnel, eg in financial management, at relatively low cost.

The average plant size has not grown that much over the past 40 years, though the concentration of capital in sophisticated, integrated resources within these plants has increased noticeably. The growth of the size of firms in the medium to large firm sector of the economy has been more significant. Long-run average costs at firm level embrace a number of functions, some of those functions providing more scale economies than others. The unit cost of product development will fall with growth in the size of the firm. Marketing and finance both have great potential for scale economies with growth of the firm.

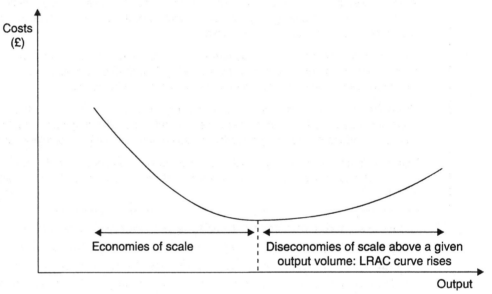

Figure 1

Cost structures may vary considerably between firms. In Figure 1, total average costs fall up to a point, beyond which they rise as diseconomies set in. Inefficiencies arise with the increasing size of operation.

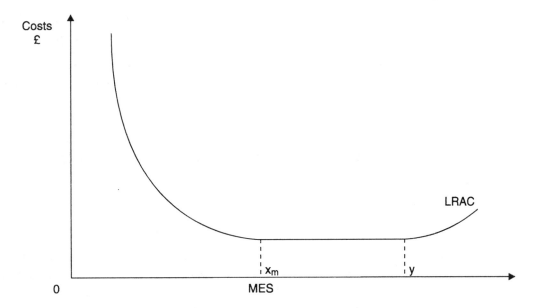

Figure 2

In Figure 2, MES signifies the **minimum efficient scale of activity**. Beyond that to point 'y' average costs are constant. Beyond 'y' they rise as diseconomies apply. Between x and y, fixed costs (as in finance and marketing) continue to fall by these - approximately - are offset by a rise in variable costs, eg unit costs of control and operation begin to rise as the firm grows in size.

(b)   In Figure 1 the **lowest point on the LRAC curve** represents the **optimal** point of operation. In Figure 2, x_m represents the first point at which minimum cost is achieved, though this level of costs continues to point y. If the point at which minimum cost is achieved is large relative to the size of the industry, only a few firms will be able to survive. Firms with a high proportion of 'unavoidable' fixed costs will be especially vulnerable. The tendency will be towards a greater concentration of supply, as firms merge, close down, or abandon their particular industry for other, more advantageous industries. By an expansion in the average size of operation, fixed costs can be more widely spread and profitable operation can continue. In some cases, for example steel, volume motor vehicle assembly or cement, there may be very few firms remaining in the industry.

In some instances, firms will try to combine activities straddling two or more industries (or 'product groups') which have resource commonality, to achieve a better spread of overheads. As a result, more firms may be able to survive within given industries than otherwise would be the case.

The variation in optimum level of working between the different functions of the firm has important **structural consequences**. Much diversification and/or takeover activity of firms is driven by the need to achieve a high level of working in those functions, such as higher management, finance, marketing, research and product development, where fixed costs are relatively high and tend to increase in real terms as time goes on.

Industrial structures may encompass **joint venture** and **resource-sharing arrangements** between firms, eg between motor vehicle manufacturers. Such arrangements may enable individual firms to concentrate their efforts where their strengths are greatest and to achieve a more acceptable spread of costs. They may also facilitate their survival in their main industry.

With fewer firms in any given industry, competition is likely to lessen. The increased MES, with high costs of setting up and high ongoing fixed costs will constitute a barrier to the entry of new, perhaps smaller, firms. The fewer the firms existing within an industry, the easier it is for unofficial price-fixing to be practised.

The consequence is likely to be a change in the **nature of competition**. With industries that are **oligopolistic** or **monopolistic**, the tendency may be towards less competition directly on price and more non-price forms of competition, for example product modification and consumer competitions. There is likely to be a move of resources into marketing and advertising which from the consumer viewpoint partly offsets the benefits resulting from lower unit operating costs.

10 TUTORIAL QUESTION: DIVISION OF LABOUR

(a) **Advantages** of **specialisation** and the **division of labour** are as follows.

(i) A worker who spends his time performing one relatively **simple task** becomes extremely skilful at that particular operation. This is summed up in the phrase 'practice makes perfect', which is the common sense view of the notion that constant repetition leads to great dexterity.

(ii) There is the **saving of time** in the **training** of workers. As each process is broken down into relatively simple tasks then a worker has only to learn how to use one set of tools in order to undertake one operation. A man or woman can therefore be trained very quickly for the performance of a single operation.

(iii) Time is saved through **not having to switch** from one operation to another. As the worker concentrates on performing one task, the necessity of moving from one work station to another is eliminated and there is no longer a need to put down one set of tools and pick up another.

(iv) Each person may be employed in the job for which he or she is **best suited**. Specialisation means that many different occupations are created, each one of which calls for some particular aptitude. By specialising at what they do best the combined production of the workforce will be greater than it otherwise would be. Even if one person is more efficient in all tasks than another person the theory of comparative advantage shows that specialisation can still be advantageous.

(v) The division of labour makes possible a much **greater use of specialised machinery**. When a complex process has been broken down into a series of separate simple tasks, it is possible to devise machinery to carry out each individual operation. It would, for example, be very difficult to construct a machine that would carry out the whole process of making a table. Once this process has been reduced to a series of separate operations, however, it becomes possible to use such specialised machines as electric saws and power-driven lathes. These specialised tools are economic because they are in constant use, and output from them is much greater.

(vi) The process of increased specialisation has in fact produced **many new types of craftspeople**, for example the designers and inventors of new machines, and many new occupations which require a high degree of skill and applied knowledge. This is particularly the case with **computers** which have created a demand for software writers, programmers, systems analysts and so on.

(vii) The use of machines has reduced the **drudgery** of much heavy manual toil associated with hand methods of production. Consider the physical effort required to dig a tunnel or lay a pipeline if heavy earth moving and lifting equipment were not available.

(b) **Disadvantages** of specialisation and the division of labour are as follows.

(i) With the extension of specialisation has come a great increase in the use of machinery which has meant that production processes have become more **automated**. Some of the basic skills of the worker are thus no longer required as these may be performed by more sophisticated machines. For instance the machine will control the design, the quality and the quantity of the product, not the machine operator. This trend has increasingly meant that the **degree of craftsmanship** required of the average industrial worker has declined significantly.

(ii) Associated with the loss of craftsmanship is a **reduction in job satisfaction** and increase in monotony and boredom on the job. A highly specialised production process composed of a cycle of simple movements which is repeated every few minutes is all that is required of a large number of operations. Such work provides no opportunity for individuals to exercise initiative, judgement, manual skills, or responsibility. The worker instead is faced with a daily grind of monotony and boredom. The frustration associated with highly routine work may spill over into poor industrial relations between workers and management, and may lead to an increased incidence of strikes.

(iii) The highly skilled and specialist worker may incur a greater **risk of becoming unemployed**. A specialised worker does not have the wide industrial training which would tend to make him adaptable to changes in the techniques of production. A specialised function can become obsolete when a new machine is invented; for example the firemen required on steam locomotives were no longer required following the introduction of diesel engines.

More generally, because the demand for labour is derived from the demand for goods and services, where these are no longer required then the demand for labour will fall. As many industries are located in specific geographical areas, the fall in demand for particular types of labour can lead to severe structural unemployment which hits particular regions very hard. There will thus be a high level of social costs associated with the increased level of unemployment, and individuals will have to retrain in order to regain employment. This may be particularly difficult for some individuals, especially older workers who may be reluctant to acquire new skills, and hence many only have a remote possibility of ever returning to work.

(iv) **Different sectors of the economy** will come to depend on one another to a more significant extent, the greater is the overall level of sophistication in the economy. Modern industries consist of a large number of firms each specialising in the production of only one, or a relatively few, components, which are brought together in large assembly plants. Probably the best example of this is the car industry where several hundreds of different components are manufactured by specialist firms and are then brought together on an assembly line. Although this is an efficient, low cost method of production, it is vulnerable to a breakdown in any one of the large number of links in the chain. Should the headlight manufacturer experience production difficulties and be unable to supply the requisite number of headlight components, for example, this may cause massive hold-ups throughout the industry. Such interdependence also means that strike activity in one sector can have widespread repercussions across significant areas of the economy leading to a large number of lay-offs.

11 DEMAND FOR LABOUR

> **Pass marks.** Note that the demand for labour is a derived demand, and then you can use the marginal productivity theory to explain this, using an appropriate diagram.
>
> **Examiner's comment.** Many candidates were unsure of the marginal productivity theory of wage determination although they could remember some of the relevant terminology. Some confused the law of diminishing returns with the law of diminishing marginal utility and some confused the demand curve for labour with the supply curve for labour.

(a) The **demand for labour** is a **derived demand,** meaning that labour is a factor of production whose demand is derived from the demand for the final good which the labour contributes to producing. The demand for labour can be explained using marginal productivity theory.

This theory employs two concepts.

(i) The **marginal physical product** (MPP) of labour represents the additional units of output obtained from employing one additional unit of labour. Given the law of diminishing returns, the MPP of labour falls as more and more labour is used.

(ii) The **marginal revenue product** (MRP) of labour is the marginal revenue gained from the MPP of labour. In other words, MRP is the extra revenue which firms in the industry would gain from the extra output provided by each additional unit of labour. Like the MPP, the MRP of labour will decline as the quantity of labour employed increases.

For a firm in conditions of perfect competition, the price of the product is determined by the market and will not change as the output of the firm changes. The MRP of labour will equate with the MPP multiplied by the price of the product.

A firm in conditions of imperfect competition faces a downward sloping demand curve for its product. Price will fall as output increases, and the MRP of labour (= MPP × price) will be lower than the MPP.

A firm which maximises profits will employ additional labour up to the point at which the final additional worker no longer adds more revenue than costs. The demand curve for labour will be given by the MRP curve.

The equilibrium condition will be that the marginal cost of labour equals the MRP of labour.

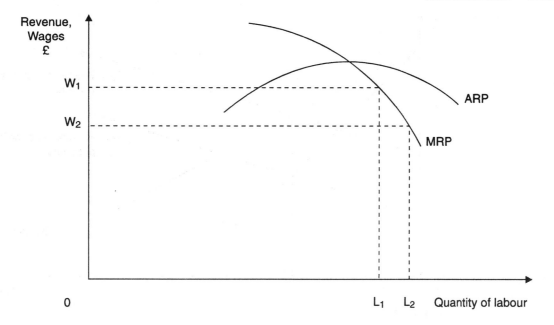

Figure 1

The MRP curve is illustrated in Figure 1. Under assumptions of perfectly competitive markets, the wage rate will be constant and will be equal to the marginal cost of labour. At a wage rate of W_1, L_1 units of labour are demanded. If the wage rate falls to W_2, then the demand for labour increases to L_2.

An increase in the productivity of labour will lead the MRP curve to shift to the right reflecting the resultant improved value of the marginal revenue product. In turn, productivity will depend upon various factors, such as the level of specialisation and the acquired skills of individual workers.

(b) The **elasticity of demand** for a factor of production such as labour is the sensitivity of demand with respect to changes in price (ie wages).

$$\text{Elasticity of demand} = \frac{\% \text{ change in quantity of labour demanded}}{\% \text{ change in wage rate}}$$

The determinants of demand elasticity for a factor of production can be identified using Figure 2, which shows the level of output and price which will be set by a profit-maximising firm. If we begin with an initial position shown by P_1, Q_1 then an increase in the price of any factor of production will raise the cost curve from C_1 to C_2, reduce the level of output and reduce the demand for factors of production. The size of this reduction depends upon a number of factors.

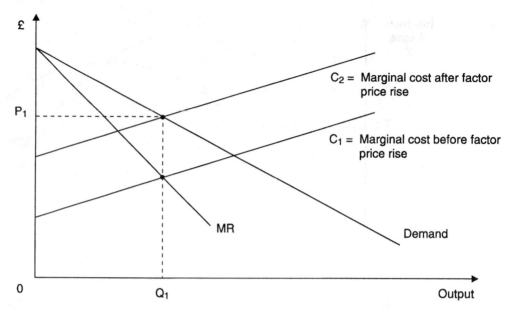

Figure 2

First, it depends upon the **elasticity of demand** for the firm's final product. The steeper is the demand curve in Figure 2, the smaller will be the reduction in output and the reduction in the demand for factors. Conversely, as demand is more elastic, and the demand curve flatter, so will the demand for factors be more elastic. In a very competitive market demand will be highly elastic, implying that the demand for the labour of both factory managers and assembly workers will be more elastic than it would be in less competitive industries.

Second, the elasticity of demand for a factor depends upon the **proportion of total costs** which is accounted for by that factor. In terms of the diagram, if the wages of assembly workers rise, and those wages account for 70% of total costs, then the cost curve will rise substantially, output will be reduced substantially, and the elasticity of demand for assembly workers will be relatively high. For the factory manager, on the other hand, his wages are unlikely to make up a substantial proportion of total costs and as a result demand for his services will be less elastic.

An increase in the cost of a factor of production will **reduce the demand** for it as a consequence of reducing the firm's level of output. However, it will also be reduced as the firm attempts to substitute other factors. A third major determinant of the elasticity of demand for a factor, then, is the ease and cheapness with which substitutes may be found. In the case of unskilled workers it will be relatively easy to find substitutes. In the case of a skilled manager who represents considerable 'know-how' of the firm's operations, substitutes will be more difficult to find. As a result, the elasticity of demand for a factory manager's services will be lower than that for assembly workers.

A fourth factor is the **price elasticity of supply for alternative factors of production**. If the supply of capital is inelastic, it may prove too costly to substitute labour with capital even if it is technically feasible to do so. It may be cheaper to employ more labour than to switch to capital, causing the demand for labour to be relatively inelastic.

12   LABOUR MOBILITY

> **Pass marks.** You need to distinguish between occupational and geographical mobility and to give a sound analysis of the determinants of each.
>
> *Other points.* Don't be side-tracked into discussing the role of trade unions and the factors determining their bargaining power or the problems of policing a minimum wage. These issues are of limited relevance here.

(a)   In the 'ideal' case of a perfect market, **factors of production** will move to whichever use of the factor provides the highest reward. If the labour market were perfect, labour would move in response to better wage rates obtainable in other regions or in other jobs. Labour mobility refers to the movement of labour from one industry or job to another, and from one geographical region to another. A move from one firm to another may be a 'lateral' move to do similar work for another firm, or it may be a change to a different kind of work. This latter form of mobility is referred to as **occupational mobility of labour.**

In the real labour market, a number of factors serve to restrict the mobility of labour. Barriers to entry into jobs in particular industries serve as obstacles to the lateral and occupational mobility of various kinds of labour. Such barriers will result, for example, from a 'closed shop' agreement between employees and trades unions which restricts particular jobs to members of those trades unions. Even if a person has the necessary skills and aptitudes for the job, a trades union might refuse to admit that person as a member. The union may wish to use the agreement to restrict the supply of labour available in order to keep wages higher than they would otherwise be.

Professional associations such as those for accountants and solicitors generally restrict occupational mobility by controlling entry to the work done in their profession by means of professional examination. A period of training on low pay may be required, and this may deter those who cannot easily afford to live on low pay for such a period. Rather than the supply of labour being determined in the market place in response to the demand conditions generated by consumers of professional services, the supply is controlled by the professional associations acting as 'gatekeepers' to the profession. Barriers to entry such as these may be supported by legislation or regulations which entitle professional bodies to control entry into roles such as those of company auditor or court advocate.

Geographical immobility of labour may be aggravated by the structure of the housing market or of government housing provision. Non-monetary considerations, such as a desire to be close to friends and relatives or a reluctance to move children from one school to another, may discourage people from moving to areas where higher paid jobs are available. Younger people are often less reluctant to move to where a job is available. However, even if people are willing in principle to move to a different area, a shortage of suitable housing may make this more difficult and more costly. Local authority housing provisions will vary from one area to another. An owner-occupier who wishes to move faces the problem that houses are relatively illiquid assets which may take some time to sell, particularly at times when the housing market is depressed. The cost of moving itself will need to be taken into account by someone considering whether it is worthwhile to move to another area to take a higher paid job.

(b)   The effect of a government imposing a **minimum wage** may be considered with reference to the diagram below.

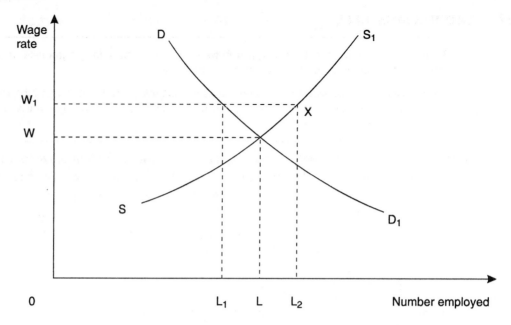

Curve DD₁ and SS₁ represent the free market **demand and supply curves** for a particular type of **labour**. The free market wage will be OW and OL people will be employed. If the minimum wage is set below OW it will have no effect as at a wage below OW there will be excess labour demand which would lift wages back up to their equilibrium level of OW. If though the government enforces a minimum wage of OW₁, this means that the part of the labour supply curve from S to X has no relevance; this is because although some workers will be willing to work for less than OW₁, they will not be allowed to do so. The supply of labour to the industry is now represented by the line W₁XS₁ and the equilibrium position is where the demand curve crosses this line. At this point OL₁ workers will be employed. The result of the introduction of the minimum wage is to reduce employment by LL₁ workers. The lucky workers who remain in employment will be better off than before as they now receive a higher wage rate. Those workers who lose their jobs will however be worse off.

At the minimum wage of W₁ there is an **excess labour supply** of (L₂ − L₁). Since firms cannot be forced to employ workers they do not want, employment will be at L₁ and the quantity of workers (L₂ − L₁) will be involuntarily unemployed. Workers are involuntarily unemployed if they are prepared to work at the going wage but cannot find jobs. Thus for low skill, low wage occupations a minimum wage in excess of the free market equilibrium wage will raise the wage for those lucky enough to find jobs but will reduce the total amount of employment relative to the free market equilibrium level of employment. Minimum wage agreements may thus explain involuntary unemployment among low-skilled workers.

Where the higher wage costs are passed on to consumers in the forms of higher prices the imposition of a statutory minimum wage may trigger an **inflationary spiral**. Hence the opponents of minimum wage legislation argue against it because it tends to cause both inflation and unemployment.

The extent to which minimum wage legislation causes a **fall in employment** will to a large extent depend on the nature of the demand for labour in the industries where the minimum wage lies above the equilibrium wage rate. The **elasticity of demand for labour** depends on a number of features.

(i)   The elasticity of demand for labour is directly related to the elasticity of demand for the product. If labour is producing a commodity which has a very inelastic demand, an increase in wages caused by the introduction of a minimum wage will have a relatively small effect on the demand for labour.

(ii) The elasticity of demand for a given type of labour varies according to the proportion of total costs accounted for by labour costs. Where wages account for only a small proportion of total costs, the demand for labour will tend to be inelastic.

(iii) The demand for labour will be more elastic the easier it is to substitute other factors for it. An increase in wage rates, ceteris paribus, will increase the cost of labour relative to the costs of the other factors. Where possible, therefore, firms will tend to substitute other factors for the now relatively dearer labour.

The supporters of minimum wage legislation argue that raising wage rates above the comparative equilibrium will ultimately lead to an increase in the productivity of labour. Firms faced with higher wage rates might stimulate efforts to improve the productivity of labour. If this occurs the demand for labour will increase - which would be shown by a rightward shift of the demand curve in the diagram above. If this happens there might well be no net reduction in the numbers employed.

13 LABOUR PRODUCTIVITY

Pass marks. It is important to cover all angles of the question if you are to gain as many marks as possible. For example, in (b), you should cover the aspect of corporate taxation as well as personal taxation.

Examiner's comment. Few candidates had any real understanding of the term 'labour productivity'. In response to part (b), many candidates appeared to regard the question as quite separate from part (a). Even those candidates who correctly identified the issues were rarely able to produce good answers. These answers were often lacking in economic theory and depended too heavily on popular opinion and prejudice.

(a) **Labour productivity** is indicated by the average product of labour and can be defined as the output per worker over a given period of time. According to the use of the measure, labour productivity may be measured at the level of the firm, for sectors of the economy or for an overall economy. Indices tracking gross domestic product per worker for a given year can be used for the economy as a whole. A number of factors influence the productivity of labour, as follows.

(i) The productivity of labour is influenced by its **quality**, which will depend on the amount of **education and training** which it has received. Education and training is a form of investment in human capital which can raise productivity, not only by equipping workers with direct vocational skills but also by encouraging people to become more innovative, more flexible and more capable of taking on work responsibilities.

(ii) The degree of **combination of other factors of production** with labour also influences labour productivity. Physical capital in the form of modern technology can dramatically increase the amount and quality of output which a worker can produce. Such new technology may require additional training in some cases; in other cases a worker with a lower level of skill may take on the same task.

(iii) The pattern of **remuneration** of employees and the perceived effect of the tax burden operating on them are further possible determinants of labour productivity. Profit-related pay and employee share option schemes represent two types of remuneration which are designed to make employees feel more motivated to ensure the success of the firm in which they work. Increased motivation will accordingly increase output per worker. It is also sometimes argued that the structure of taxation has an effect on the incentive of workers.

(iv) **Other macroeconomic factors** can also influence labour productivity. A steadily growing economy is likely to produce conditions more conducive to high labour productivity than an economy with a more erratic economic cycle in which periodic recessionary conditions may inhibit a firm from maximising output effectively.

High levels of labour productivity will only be achieved in firms or organisations in which the factors of production are organised to maximise efficiency, so avoiding wasted effort. The economies of scale which larger firms can often achieve will enhance the productivity of labour. Specialisation will be most readily achieved in larger productive units; where it occurs, workers are likely to be more productive when engaged in specialised work. It is management's task to ensure that work arrangements encourage the maximum possible efficiency for the firm, and thus to minimise 'X-inefficiency'.

(b) It is sometimes claimed that high levels of taxation of personal incomes erode work incentives. A rise in levels of personal taxation will lead *ceteris paribus* to a fall in personal disposable income.

(i) In theory, the resultant **income effect** will lead the individual to work harder so as to regain the income lost through additional taxation.

(ii) By the **substitution effect,** the person will tend to work less hard because the opportunity cost in terms of disposable income forgone of choosing more leisure instead is now reduced.

If the substitution effect outweighs the income effect, a government could increase labour productivity by cutting taxes on personal incomes. There is however inconclusive evidence on whether this can be achieved in practice.

Other aspects of taxation policy may also influence labour productivity. Corporation tax changes, for example changes in capital allowances, may enhance incentives for firms to invest in new capital equipment. Tax concessions may also be applied to encourage firms to implement training schemes or to provide personal tax relief for individuals in respect of expenditure on their own education and training.

Policies such as those mentioned above which seek to influence the pace of development of physical and human capital (ie labour) need to be seen as long-term policies which are likely to take some time to work.

14 DATA RESPONSE QUESTION: SIZE OF FIRMS

> **Examiner's comment**. This was not a popular question. There were a few good answers but the majority did little more than reproduce the data given. Common errors were inadequate discussion of trends in the data given, and failure to identify the economic concepts involved, for example diseconomies of scale, and to apply them to the particular issues involved.

(a) The data given relates to the number of enterprises within five different size bands which are defined according to the number of employees working for the manufacturing enterprise. For the two years 1978 and 1989, data is provided on the numbers of enterprise in each band and also the percentage of the manufacturing labour force which is employed by enterprises in each band.

Manufacturing enterprises generally remain in existence for a number of years, and the process of growth and amalgamation of enterprises occurs over the medium to longer term. Because of this, it is not necessary to question whether 1978 and 1989 are representative years to choose: the trends which are observed in the size distribution of firms are likely to be medium to longer term trends.

There was a large **increase in the overall total number** of manufacturing enterprises in the UK between 1978 and 1989: during the 11-year period, a net figure of over 60,000 manufacturing businesses were formed, increasing the total number from 90,000 to over 150,000. Although a few new enterprises will have been created by the splitting up or demerger of existing larger businesses, the vast majority of this net increase must be due to formation of new enterprises.

The size band within which most new enterprises would be expected to fall is the smallest - up to 99 employees, and this is evident from the increase in the total number of enterprises in this band from 84,000 in 1978 to 143,000 in 1989.

The numbers of enterprises in the next two size bands (100 to 499 employees and 500 to 999 employees) also each increased by over 50% over the 11 years to 1989. Some of the enterprises added to these bands will be newly formed businesses, but there will also be smaller businesses which have expanded over the period and larger businesses which have contracted in number of employees. Such contraction may reflect the **shedding of workers** where efficiency is improving as well as where operations are being scaled down.

The two largest size bands (1,000 to 4,999 employees and 5,000 plus employees) both declined in total number, but the fall is much more marked for the largest band, which accounted for only 41 enterprises in 1989 compared with 179 in 1978. The data on the percentage of the manufacturing labour force employed reflects the marked **shift from larger enterprises to smaller ones**. While almost 40% of this labour force was employed in the band of largest businesses in 1978, this dropped to 8.7% by 1989. By 1989, 58.6% of the manufacturing workforce was employed in enterprises of up to 500 employees, compared with 35.6% in 1978.

(b)   The two main trends underlying the changes in the size distribution of firms over the period in question are the general **decline in manufacturing industry** as a sector of the UK economy and the **creation of small firms** which has taken place with government encouragement.

During the early stages of economic development, it is common for the secondary sector of the economy, which includes manufacturing, construction, energy and water, to grow. In economies like that of the UK which are at a **later stage of industrial development**, it is not unusual for this sector to be in decline. Much of the decline in manufacturing employment between 1978 and 1989 has affected larger enterprises such as those in shipbuilding and heavy engineering, contributing to the substantial fall in the number of manufacturing enterprises employing over 5,000 people.

The Conservative governments in power from 1979 to 1997 aimed to create conditions for growth in output and employment by stimulating the **supply side** of the economy, with special attention being paid to the small firms sector. There were three main facets of this policy.

(i)   Firstly, there were measures to improve the **availability of equity (share) capital and loan capital** to those wishing to set up a business or expand an existing one.

(1)   The Business Start-up Scheme was set up in 1981 with the aim of encouraging investors to buy shares in new unquoted companies. This was succeeded in 1983 by the Business Expansion Scheme, which had similar aims and offered full income tax relief on investments of up to £40,000 per year as well as capital gains tax relief for investments held for at least five years. This scheme was in turn replaced by the **Enterprise Investment Scheme**, in 1993.

(2) The **Loan Guarantee Scheme** was introduced in 1981 and is still in operation following periodic modifications. The scheme is intended to allow borrowing by individuals with insufficient collateral or where the risk of lending goes beyond the banks' usual lending criteria.

(3) The Unlisted Securities Market was established by the London Stock Exchange to enable small and medium sized more easily to obtain venture capital on the stock market. The rules of the USM were less stringent than those which must be complied with to obtain a full listing on the main market. The USM was replaced in 1995 by a new **Alternative Investment Market** whose rules are also less stringent than the main market.

(4) **Changes in the law** made it possible for owners of small businesses to sell shares to outside investors with an agreement that the company would buy back the shares after a certain period of time. This helped small firms wanting to raise capital without parting with the equity permanently.

(ii) Secondly, **tax allowances and grants** were made more favourable to small businesses. A reduced rate of corporation tax was introduced for companies with profits below a certain limit. The Enterprise Allowance Scheme has offered an allowance for up to 66 weeks to help unemployed people set up their own businesses. By 1992, more than 500,000 people had benefited from the scheme. The **Enterprise Initiative** has provided Regional Enterprise Grants for investment and innovation projects. The Small Firms Merit Award for research and technology has offered phased financial support for new technology projects.

(iii) Thirdly, a number of measures were taken to **reduce government regulation and administrative interference**, and to create a climate in which advice and training is more readily available to small firms. For example, some small firms have been exempted from employment law requirements, schemes have been introduced to simplify VAT accounting for smaller businesses, and Local Enterprise Agencies and Training and Enterprise Councils have been established to help and advise smaller firms.

(c) The heavy engineering and other large scale manufacturing sectors which, as mentioned earlier, have experienced decline in recent years, are sectors in which **economies of scale** are great. These sectors have often provided the conditions in which a monopolist producer can prosper. With the decline of such industries, the tendency has been towards smaller firms. In many cases, the formation of many smaller firms has led to increased competition between enterprises. One of the aims of supply side economic policies is to lower barriers to entry by new firms. If it is easier to set up new enterprises, existing firms face an increased possibility of competitors entering the market and should therefore be encouraged to keep costs down and not to over-price products.

The existence of many smaller firms widens choice for consumers in general and increases the number of firms competing in many markets. However, where markets are highly segmented or specialised, it may still be possible for a producer to take advantage of monopoly conditions.

15 PROFIT

> **Pass marks**. The concept of 'normal profit' is fundamental to answering part (b). Supernormal profits act as the magnet attracting newcomers to an industry but equilibrium will be achieved only with all surviving firms earning normal profits.
>
> **Examiner's comment**. Weak answers often gave no more than a simple accounting notion of profits without explaining the wider role of profit in a free enterprise economy. Some candidates clearly had little knowledge of the perfect competition model and responded to part (b) with general discussions of the competitive process.

(a) **Profit**, in economic terms, is regarded as the reward to the factor of production 'enterprise', ie the return for undertaking the risk of investing in business activity as well as for overall organising of the remaining factors.

The expectation of profit provides incentive to take non-insurable risks, whether that be by individuals or organisations. Much is done by means of market research, marketing and advertising, careful planning and control to minimise business risk but consumer tastes can change quite unpredictably while developments in technology can be rapid and costly. The possibility of profit commensurate with the risk is needed if the production/supply of goods and services is to be undertaken.

Hence, profit is not merely a consequence of successful change: the expectation of profit can itself help to bring about successful change. It is a necessary spur to innovation, be that as new products or through business and industrial processes. Profit has been described as 'the reward for a risk successfully taken', implying that much innovation ends in costly failure. It is therefore essential to ensure that the innovation which maximises consumer and public welfare is adequately rewarded. An appropriate reward system will foster the dynamic elements within an economy and improve international competitiveness.

Profit also acts as a signal for the movement of resources, directing them to where society wishes them to go. When demand for product X exceeds its supply, its price will rise and profits also. Resources will then be attracted to the supply of the product. The demand for other products may be falling, hence their profitability will fall also. In due course, resources will move out of the supply of those declining products. Resource allocation which maximises consumer welfare is thus achieved through market processes.

Profit (or rather profitability, or rate of return) in a competitive economy becomes an approximate measure of efficiency. In order to maintain or improve their position in 'league tables', companies need to ensure the effective organising and application of resources towards meeting or developing customer demand. This therefore results in overall benefit to consumers.

Profits are also a source of funds for investment. Profits may be distributed as dividends to shareholders, this money then being potentially available for reinvestment in business through the capital market. Alternatively, they may be retained within companies and thus be directly available for investment. Profits are indeed essential for sustained growth in a free enterprise economy.

(b) A **perfectly competitive industry** is comprised of a large number of firms:

    (i)   producing homogenous products;

    (ii)   all of which are 'price acceptors' (none by itself being powerful enough to determine price);

    (iii) with each firm being involved in that industry alone (no cross-subsidisation).

It is also assumed that there is complete freedom of entry to and exit from the industry.

It is unrealistic to assume that all the member firms will operate under exactly the **same supply conditions**. Some **diversity** of conditions is likely to arise from different distances from customers, variations in labour resources, differences in management as well as differences of 'maturity' as organisations. Thus, there may be some difference in average cost levels between the firms, although not necessarily a marked difference.

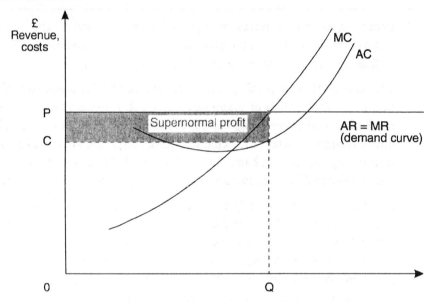

Figure 1

Normal profit is the minimum profit necessary to keep a firm in the industry. **Supernormal profit** is anything in excess of that. In the short term, some at least of the firms may be making supernormal profit, with average cost AC below average revenue (= price).

In Figure 1, supernormal profit is represented by the shaded area ($= (P - C) \times Q$).

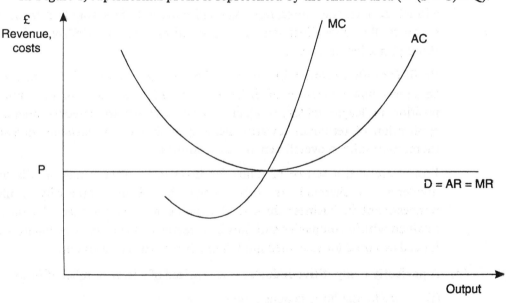

Figure 2

In the longer run, the supernormal profit attracts new firms into the industry and the 'excess' profit is competed away (see Figure 2) until the remaining firms earn only normal profit.

With the diversity of supply conditions between the firms, as selling price falls the more marginal firms will be forced out of the industry. Equilibrium in the longer term will be with all firms making a 'normal profit' and operating at lowest average cost, where MC = AC.

The number of firms could be calculated thus:

$$\text{Number of firms} = \frac{\text{Aggregate market demand}}{\text{Optimal operating size (per firm) (= point of lowest ATC)}}$$

Therefore, if total market demand were to expand/(contract), the number of firms would accordingly increase/(diminish).

As is usual in the theory of the firm, the above analysis has included normal profit in **average total cost**. Normal profit is an expression of **opportunity cost**: the amount of profit needed to keep a firm within a particular industry will be set by the profit which could be earned by leaving that industry and transferring the firm's resources into another industry. Within an industry there is likely to be some difference in practice between member firms in their power or willingness to transfer resources to another industry. Hence normal profit can vary between the firms. If so, a perfectly competitive industry at full equilibrium can accommodate firms with different levels of total operating costs. This would suggest that in practice perfectly competitive industries may, at times, be slower to adjust to a fall in aggregate demand than the theory indicates.

16   REGIONAL SPECIALISATION

Pass marks. The relative importance of factors influencing location vary greatly between firms (part (a)). Nearness to resources remains a key factor for some industries though overall has declined in importance as the selling market has exerted a greater pull. Part (b) of the question is concerned with external economies of scale, such as benefiting from shared facilities. Part (c) is about external diseconomies such as a rise in rates of pay for particular skills. It is also about the danger of over-dependence on one industry.

Examiner's comment. The best answers used economic theory clearly to answer the question. In part (a) these candidates emphasised the importance of total costs in the location decision and gave examples of how costs might vary from one site to another. The best answers also identified external economies of scale as the relevant concept for part (b) and could give appropriate examples. However part (c) was rarely well answered.

(a)   The factors influencing **business location** are various. Among the main factors will be the considerations of total costs, resource availability, selling markets, government policy, and, increasingly, the personal preference of management.

Historically, **resource availability** was a major influence upon the locating and development of industries. This is less so nowadays. Raw materials and natural resources now generally constitute a diminished proportion of the cost of finished goods. Also, if completed products are relatively bulky, then movement costs will tend to pull centres of production closer to the selling market. As the average real value of products relative to weight and bulk rises, manufacturers and distributors are more free to incur greater movement costs and so the firm has much greater scope in choosing its location.

However, there continue to be absolute requirements regarding natural resources and other inputs. For example, the aluminium industry, a vast user of electric power, is mostly located in those countries with much cheaper electric power. Power stations tend to be located near to where vast amounts of water are available for cooling processes. The availability of particular human skills can be a key factor in the location decisions of some firms. The availability of pools of less skilled labour has also been an important factor, though this is less so where most areas of a country have pools of unemployed semi-skilled or unskilled labour. Increased mechanisation can also be an alternative for some firms, so further diminishing the importance of this point.

The pull of the **selling market** has, in general, become of growing importance over the years. Goods which are fragile and expensive to transport are often better produced near to the market where they are to be sold. Thus, London has many consumer goods industries in close vicinity. Also, service industries (eg professional services, catering) mostly have to locate near to their delivery points. The ability to supply the market reliably and speedily means that transport and communications will be vital considerations. Proximity to main transport routes can be a major advantage in the distribution of products as well as in providing a service to business or members of the public.

Government policy and its implementation can be a great influence on location decisions. Planning permission may be refused on grounds of congestion or for other environmental reasons. Some industrial activities might be regarded as unsuitable for location close to centres of population. On the other hand, government policy might be aimed at encouraging firms to locate in certain areas in order to stimulate economic activity and provide employment opportunities. Grants, tax relief or rent-free accommodation might be made available.

Location decisions can also be taken on grounds of the **personal preferences of management**. Some areas might be favoured because of their climate, pleasantness, amenities or favourable residential accommodation. This has been regarded as partly accounting for the development of the 'sunrise' industries on both sides of the M4 motorway. The assertion of personal preference on location is, however, likely only where the firm is footloose as to location. Only rarely does one factor alone determine location: more usually it is a combination of factors.

(b) The potential for **external economies of scale** is often a reason why competing firms locate near to each other. They might benefit from operating in the same area, where specialist ancillary services are available, eg financial services, various agents or specialist advisers; or where the firms can benefit from common transport or distribution facilities. The practice of firms concentrating their activities and sub-contracting work may result in the feeder firms setting themselves up within fairly easy reach of the purchasing company.

Training facilities for developing particular skills may be established in an area and this may tend further to attract into the area firms requiring those skills. Recruitment of labour is thus facilitated. If firms within an industry or firms associated with it are located close to one another, transport costs can be minimised and communication between the firms might be helped.

(c) External diseconomies may result from the **concentration of industry** within a given area. As the number of firms within an area increase, congestion could result. This could lead to a fall in efficiency. With the increased size of an industry, unit costs could begin to rise among the member firms. The rise in demand for resources to be used within the industry could result in a rise in input prices, eg a rise in wage rates for particular skills.

Concentration of a particular industry **within an area or region** can also mean that the area becomes over-dependent upon that industry. Success in the development of that industry might have crowded out other alternative industries. Changes in technology or in consumer demand could undermine or change drastically the future of that industry. The result could be a major downturn in the fortunes of the area. Any resulting redundancy among the workforce or a forced reduction in the working week would reduce spending power. The situation will then be worsened by the multiplier effect, so adding to the adverse economic effects. Reduced spending would cause increased unemployment and therefore further retrenchment in spending. The absence of a diversity of economic activity and skills would make the process of readjustment the more difficult.

17 TUTORIAL QUESTION: PERFECT MARKET

The word **market** originally designated a place where certain things were bought and sold, for example, Billingsgate market (the former London fish market). The modern usage of the word is in terms of a medium through which buyers and sellers negotiate the exchange of a well defined commodity. The word 'market' refers to the totality of buyers and sellers (both actual and potential) of a particular good or service. Hence it is possible to discuss the market for cabbages, the housing market, and the equity market. It is not necessary for markets to have a physical existence. For example, the foreign exchange market does not constitute a physical place but is a system of communications between those who wish to buy and those who wish to sell foreign currencies.

A market is thus an **exchange mechanism** that brings together sellers and buyers of a product, a financial security or a factor of production. Economists define a market as a group of products which consumers view as being substitutes for one another. A free market economy is one in which the allocation of resources is determined by production, sales and purchase decisions taken by firms and households. At the opposite extreme is a centrally controlled economy, in which all the decisions about the allocation of resources are taken by the central authorities.

The theory of markets distinguishes between markets according to their various **structural characteristics**. A perfect market is one that contains the following characteristics.

(a) All units of the commodity are exactly the same, ie there are **homogenous products**, with one unit of the good being exactly like another. If this is the case, then buyers will be completely indifferent as to which seller they purchase the commodity from.

(b) There are a **large number of sellers** and a **large number of buyers** in the market. Each seller and each buyer constitutes so small a part of the whole market that the behaviour of the individual buyer or seller will have no significant influence on the market price. For example, an individual seller may significantly change the volume of the commodity that he brings to the market. Although this represents considerable change in his quantity of output, the total market supply will change by only a very small amount and hence will have no perceptible impact on market price.

(c) There is assumed to be **perfect knowledge on the part of sellers and buyers**. Sellers are fully aware of the activities of buyers and other sellers. Buyers are fully informed as to the strength of demand from other buyers and of the intentions of sellers. Should a particular seller raise his price above the prevailing market price, for example, buyers will immediately recognise that other sellers are supplying exactly the same good at a lower price and hence the demand for the seller's product would fall to zero.

(d) There are **no barriers to entry or exit** from the market. If abnormal profit is being earned in the market this will encourage entrepreneurs to move into the market, thus increasing supply and causing price to fall until only normal profit is earned. The reverse process will occur if firms are making losses in the perfect market.

All of these conditions mean that the focus of competition in a perfect market is **price competition**. In a perfect market there will be one, and only one, market price, and this price will be beyond the influence of any one buyer or seller. Many buyers and sellers ensures that individual buyers and sellers have no market power. The assumption of perfect knowledge ensures that buyers will not pay different prices, while homogeneity of product ensures that preferences will not arise which might be converted into price differences. Finally, the assumption of free entry to and exit from the market ensures that factors of production will move to eliminate any price differentials which might tend to arise.

Imperfections occur where the underlying assumptions associated with perfect markets do not apply. The clearest example of this is the market situation of monopoly. This is a type of market structure characterised by a single supplier. This means that the market demand curve is the monopolist firms' demand curve. Given that the market demand curve is downward sloping this provides the monopolist with some discretion over the setting of price. The **monopolist** could for instance set a high price and accept a low volume of sales, or conversely, produce a high volume of output and accept a lower price for his product.

The monopolist is in part able to do this because of a **lack of substitute products**, ie there are no close substitutes for the monopolist's product. In other types of markets imperfections may occur because of differentiated products, that is, the products offered by competing firms are differentiated from each other in one or more respects. These differences may be of a physical nature, involving functional features, or may be purely 'imaginary' in the sense that artificial differences are created through advertising and sales promotion. The less well informed buyers are of the qualities of competing brands, the more susceptible they are likely to be to persuasive advertising.

The purpose of such differentiating activity is to secure an initial demand for the firm's products and to cultivate brand loyalties to ensure that sales are increased. **Product differentiation** is significant in that it widens the dimensions of competitive actions, with firms competing against each other in quality, advertising, product features and so on, rather than on price alone. Although product differentiation is an aspect of market imperfection, this does not imply that heterogeneity of products is bad. Genuine differences among products imply greater diversity and therefore greater choice for consumers.

A third characteristic of monopoly is that of **barriers to entry** which make it impossible for new firms to enter the market. These obstacles may arise in a number of ways. For example, lower cost advantages of established firms from the possession of substantial market shares and the benefits of economies of large scale production; strong consumer preferences for the products of established firms resulting from product differentiation, as discussed above; large capital outlays required by new entrants to set up production; the control of raw materials, technology and distribution channels by established firms either through direct ownership or through patents and exclusive dealing contracts.

Barriers to entry are significant in that by blocking entry to markets by new firms they enable established firms to earn **abnormal** (ie above normal) **profits** and prevent the allocation of factor resources in line with patterns of consumer demand.

18   BARRIERS TO ENTRY

> **Pass marks**. We can explain barriers to entry by using real life examples. Most markets today are oligopolistic – airlines, diamonds, soap powder, soft drinks, football clubs. Consider some of these industries and work out where and why these barriers exist.

(a) A **barrier to entry** is an obstacle which prevents firms from entering a market. Barriers to entry may stop new firms starting up, or they may prevent existing firms from diversifying into new markets. Existing firms in the market therefore have an advantage.

One reason why barriers to entry exist is because of prohibitive **entry costs**. Each country only has a small number of airlines because the industry is capital intensive. Regulation by governments is also a barrier to entry where it determines which companies are allowed into certain markets.

Related to cost is the amount of money spent on **research and development** and in some cases companies will have technologically superior products to their competitors. **Patent rights** may prevent new firms from entering the same market.

The soft drinks industry is a special type of oligopolistic market, a duopoly, where two firms (Coke and Pepsi) dominate the market. There is no magic formula for making fizzy drinks but the industry is still difficult for outside firms to penetrate because Coke and Pepsi spend large sums each year on **advertising** building up and maintaining their brand images. Heavy advertising expenditure makes entry costs for new firms high.

Predatory pricing, although illegal in some countries, is another way in which firms are prevented from entering a market. This is where pricing is set below costs to stop a new firm from entering or forcing an existing one out of business. A cartel of firms which fixes price and/or output levels can make it difficult for new firms to enter.

Finally, a firm may exercise control over its markets through **vertical integration** in ways that deny new firms access to raw materials or sales outlets.

(b) Barriers to entry will reduce the number of firms which can enter an industry. Established firms will become dominant and there will be a concentration of larger firms in the industry. This will tend to weaken the competitive conditions in the industry. Where effective barriers to entry exist, the market structure will tend to be either oligopolistic or a monopoly.

A monopolist may be defined as someone who can earn excess or **supernormal profits** in the long run without attracting competition. Assuming that the firm is seeking to **maximise profits**, a monopolist will produce where marginal costs equal marginal revenues. In such a structure, prices will tend to be higher and output would be restricted. The **oligopolist** is also able to earn **supernormal profits** in the short run and the long run.

Under fully competitive conditions, the prospect of profits acts as a signal to firms on which markets to enter. The entry of new firms raises supply, thus lowering prices until only normal profits are earned. Barriers to entry prevent this process from operating, and the existing firms in the industry reap the rewards through supernormal profits. In the absence of regulation, firms may take advantage of part of these profits to strengthen entry barriers further.

19 PUBLIC INTEREST

Examiner's comments. The best answers contained an accurate diagram of equilibrium for the monopoly firm, showing both cost and revenue curves and indicating price, output and profits. These answers provided clear explanations of the price and output outcomes using the concepts of profit maximisation and entry barriers. In response to part (b), the best scripts could show the disadvantages of monopolies in terms of their high prices and restricted output, as well as their potential benefits, especially in relation to economies of scale and investment in research and development.

(a) A firm will **maximise its profits** when the price and output combination is such that the **marginal revenue** of an additional unit of output is equal to the **marginal cost** of producing it.

A market dominated by a single firm is called a **monopoly**. The monopolist can choose to set price at different levels and, as a **price-maker**, faces a downward sloping demand (average revenue) curve.

Because there are **barriers to the entry of new firms** to the industry, in a monopoly supernormal profits are not 'competed away' by other firms. The long-run equilibrium price and output of a monopoly firm is illustrated in the diagram below.

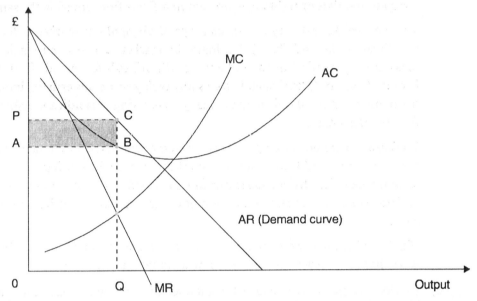

The **profit maximising position** for the firm is where MC = MR. This occurs at output Q in the diagram above, where the price paid by consumers is P. In this equilibrium position, the monopolist is achieving supernormal profits represented by the area of the rectangle PABC, which is the output quantity multiplied by the difference between average revenue (price) and total average costs (AC).

If demand for the firm's product is relatively inelastic, then the demand curve is more steeply downward sloping and the position of the monopolist is further removed from that of perfect competition: the monopolist is then more able to earn supernormal profits than if demand is more elastic.

The monopolist illustrated by the diagram is not producing at the lowest point of its average cost curve. This indicates a misallocation of resources since the firm is not operating as efficiently as it could be. Additionally, the earning of supernormal profits by the monopolist could be viewed as a maldistribution of income compared with perfect competition, with which all firms earn normal profits only.

(b) Monopoly conditions can clearly operate against the consumer's interest and against public policy, and can therefore be bad for an economy. For example, the profit maximising output of a monopolist is likely to be at a price and output level which leads to supernormal profits being earned. At the same time, such an output level can never coincide with the level at which average costs are minimised, so that monopolies are inherently inefficient. A monopolist is also free to carry out restrictive practices, such as price discrimination and the exploitation of **barriers to entry**.

Without government measures to control these problems the activities of a monopolist can operate against the public interest. Nevertheless, governments (including the present Conservative government of the UK in recent years) have sometimes encouraged the development of private monopolies relatively free from such controls. There are a number of possible reasons for this.

(i) The **minimum efficient plant size** may be such that the market is large enough only to accommodate a single firm. For example, it would clearly be a waste of resources for there to be two separate national systems for the distribution of electricity or gas to consumers.

(ii) **Competition from foreign firms** (sometimes benefiting from government subsidies) may threaten the existence of domestic producers. It may be that the only way to protect them is to confer on them the advantages of monopoly status.

(iii) Governments may believe that private enterprise is **more efficient** than public enterprise. In the case of the so-called natural monopolies a government might prefer to place the industry in the hands of a private organisation rather than a public one.

In practice, however, **supernormal profits** can be beneficial to an economy since they permit firms to invest for the longer term in both fixed capital (eg new equipment) and in other ways (eg expenditure on research and development). In some sectors, a monopoly may be necessary for profits to be achieved.

For example, in the pharmaceutical industry, the development of new drugs requires a high level of current profits to support current expenditure. There must also be an expectation that the development will, if successful, earn high profits in the future to recover its development costs and also the costs of those projects which fail (of which there will inevitably be some). Although the pharmaceutical industry is not an entire monopoly, some monopoly powers are available through patent legislation and the simple expedient of being first into the market with a new drug.

A monopoly may be able to exploit **economies of scale** by increasing its size and output to a scale which could never be achieved in a competitive market because of the entry of new firms into the market. This could result in lower prices to the consumer even though the monopolist still earns good profits. On the other hand, the lack of competition means that the monopolist does not necessarily have to be efficient to earn a satisfactory profit. Competitive markets do, in general, produce more efficient producers.

These two features (economies of scale and inefficiency) can, of course, exist simultaneously, making it very difficult to judge the overall impact of the monopoly.

There are certain sectors which operate on an **international basis** (eg aerospace) and an apparent monopoly in the home market does not have any impact in practice. Indeed, there may be other reasons (such as **national security**) why certain sectors need to be particularly strong and the creation of a monopoly may achieve this.

20   **OLIGOPOLY MARKETS**

> **Pass marks.** The examiner is always very keen on the ideas of uncertainty and
> interdependence when considering oligopoly and emphasised them in his comments on
> the May 1999 examination. The reference to 'an appropriate model' indicates that one
> such as the kinked demand curve model should be described. We can make a distinction
> between collusive and competitive oligopoly. The former, where not outlawed, is more
> likely where products are homogeneous and there is common interest between the firms.
> The latter is likely to be characterised by product differentiation, non-price competition, and
> variability of market conduct. Barriers to entry and interdependence will be common to all
> oligopolies. The interdependence (greater where the products are homogeneous) in turn
> constrains market behaviour.

(a)   The actions of firms in an oligopolised industry are dominated by **interdependence**
of possible actions/reactions of competitors. Because individual firms must consider
the effects of their actions on rival producers, there is **uncertainty** because they
cannot be certain how rivals will react. Each of the oligopolists is faced by a
downward sloping demand curve, commonly portrayed in the form of a kinked
demand curve.

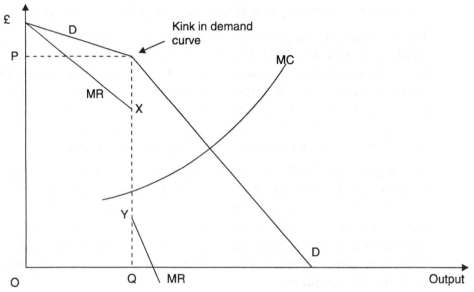

It is assumed that the market is relatively mature, in the sense that the firms are
well established in the market, and that the present market position is the outcome
of much interaction between them. Price is now at point P because any attempt in
the past to raise the price would have been followed by rivals. Owing to the
elasticity of demand above that point, any price raiser, through loss of sales, would
soon have been forced back to price P. The relevant consideration is therefore
possible price cuts below P. Throughout that lower part of the demand curve,
demand is inelastic.

On the assumption that elasticity of demand in the aggregate market (the combined
output of oligopolists X_1, X_2 and X_3) is fairly low, then a price cut by X_1 would soon
be followed by equivalent price cuts by X_2 and X_3, as each strives to maintain its
market share. All would be worse off as total revenue would fall. Indeed, there could
be the added disadvantage for all (though not necessarily in equal proportions) of
the advertising and promotional costs which might be necessary to make any price
cut effective, apart from any decline in buyer confidence in the product.

The kink in the demand curve is due to the nature of the marginal revenue curve,
MR. At price P, the MR curve falls vertically because at higher prices the curve

corresponds to the elastic section of the demand curve, and at prices below P it reflects the inelastic section of demand.

The greater the **cross elasticities of demand** between the products of X_1, X_2 and X_3, ie the more they are substitutes for one another, the more the model on pricing response will hold and the sooner, initially, will the sales of X_2 and X_3 drop as customers switch to buying from X_1. At the same time, the higher the level of 'committed costs' of X_2 and X_3, the greater their need to maintain revenue through market share. However, the more effectively X_2 and X_3 have differentiated their products and the greater the loyalty of their customers, the slower will be the switch of sales to X_1. As time goes by, though, the basic similarity of the products will be increasingly recognised and demand will switch to X_1.

Awareness of this **switching process** leads oligopolists to avoid intra-industry price warfare where possible and to compete on points other than price eg by product. Nevertheless, price cutting does take place. If X_1 were to cut prices to exploit a growth in total demand for the industry product, the others would follow in order to hold market share as well as to exploit possible economies of scale. Alternatively price cutting could take place in the later stages of a product's life cycle, as demand declines, or in the later stages of a recession. Stocks might be liable to deterioration, or the firms might be facing cash flow problems.

(b)   Oligopolistic industries are characterised by **heavy advertising expenditure** in part because advertising forms a very effective barrier to entry. If we consider the soft drinks industry, this is a special type of oligopoly, a duopoly where the market is dominated by two key players, Coca-Cola and Pepsi. Both companies spend heavily in advertising in order to keep up the brand image and consumers built up a certain amount of loyalty to their brands which makes it difficult for new firms such as Virgin to penetrate this market. Firms in oligopolistic markets often enjoy large profits which can be invested in further advertising, which can make it very difficult for new firms to come into the market.

Heavy advertising is also an example of **non-price competition**. Although the products of different firms may be very similar, the firms seek to differentiate their own product by building up a strong brand through advertising, or by emphasising small distinctive features of their products.

Advertising may increase the size of the overall market without affecting the revenues of individual firms adversely. This can help firms to reduce the uncertainty of what will happen if prices are raised. If brand loyalty can be established, the demand curve for rises in price will become less elastic.

21   MONOPOLISTIC COMPETITION

The concept of **monopolistic competition** is based on the following assumptions.

(a)   There is a **large number of quite small firms** with each firm acting independently of others in the industry.

(b)   There is **free entry and exit** from the industry in the long run.

Free entry means that when abnormal profits are being earned by established firms in the industry, this will attract other firms to the industry who face no barriers to entry. Conversely, where established firms are making a loss they face no barriers to leaving the industry.

Under monopolistic competition each firm faces a **downward-sloping demand curve**. This means that each firm can influence its market share to some extent by changing its price relative to its competitors. Every firm has a downward sloping demand curve because the goods produced by each firm are not perfect substitutes for the goods produced by other firms in the industry. Firms compete with each other by selling goods which are similar but not perfectly homogeneous: **product differentiation** is a feature of monopolistic competition. This differentiation may come about by branding and the build up of brand loyalty; for small restaurants and corner shops it may arise because of their particular location. Product differentiation will allow a firm to charge a slightly higher price than other producers in the industry without losing all of its customers. Similarly it may charge a slightly lower price than other firms but would not gain all of their customers because it is not providing exactly the same kind of good. However, the availability of close substitutes will mean that each firm's demand curve will be fairly elastic.

The market situation for a firm under monopolistic competition is illustrated in Figure 1. In the short run, output is determined at the profit maximising level, that is, where marginal cost equals marginal revenue. Given the marginal cost curve MC, and the marginal revenue curve MR, the firm will produce output level Q_0.

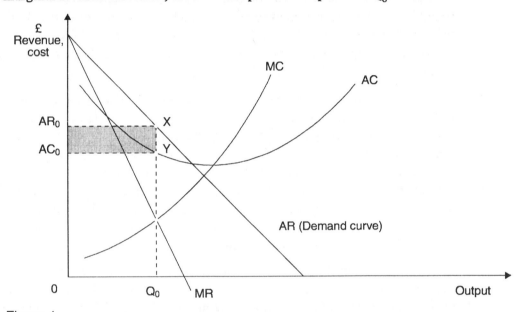

Figure 1

Figure 1 shows that if the firm produces OQ_0, the price charged will be AR_0 and the firm will have average costs of AC_0. The firm will be making short-run profits equal to the shaded area $Q_0 \times (AR_0 - AC_0)$.

The firm is thus earning **abnormal profits** equal to the rectangular area $AR_0 \, XY \, AC_0$, in Figure 1. These abnormal profits will attract new firms to the industry. The effect of the entry of a number of new firms will be to reduce the market share of each firm in the industry, which will cause the demand curve of each firm to shift to the left. New firms will continue to enter the market, causing the demand curve of each firm to shift to the left, until abnormal profit has been eliminated for each firm. This results when each firm's demand curve has shifted so far to the left that average revenue (or price) equals average costs, so that firms are just breaking even and earning only normal profit.

The **long-run equilibrium** is shown in Figure 2. In the long run the firm's demand curve will be tangential to the average cost curve at the output level where profit is maximised. Again the firm will equate MC and MR to obtain the profit maximising level of output shown by Q_1 in Figure 2. Although the firm is maximising profit, there are no abnormal profits being earned because average revenue (AR_1) equals average cost (AC) at output level Q_1. There is therefore no incentive for new firms to enter the industry and hence Figure 2 shows a position of long-run equilibrium.

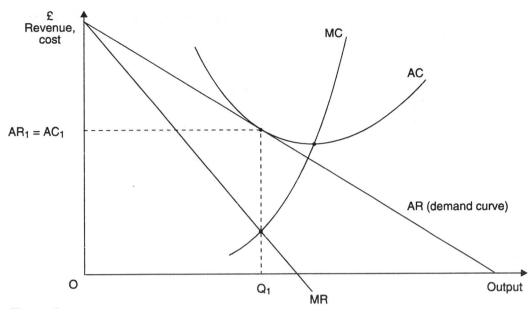

Figure 2

Figure 2 shows that in long-run equilibrium the firm will not be producing at minimum average cost, but produces with excess capacity. The firm could reduce average costs by increasing output beyond Q_1; however, average revenue would fall faster than average cost so this would not be profitable for the firm. Also the firm retains some monopoly power because of the special features of the products it supplies, and so the firm sells at a price which is greater than the marginal cost.

22   DATA RESPONSE QUESTION: BREWING INDUSTRY

> **Pass marks**. Identify the barriers to entry in the passage to illustrate part (a). The standard diagram is essential for part (c).
>
> *Prize winner's points.* Strategy in a non-collusive oligopoly is complicated by the interdependence of the firms involved; they cannot act without considering their rivals' reactions. At the same time, those reactions are never certain.

(a) Barriers to entry affect firms wishing to enter a market and compete with the existing suppliers. They may make entry impossible, as when a legal monopoly exists, or impose onerous costs, as when heavy capital expenditure is required to build up operations to the minimum efficient scale. The large brewers protect themselves against effective competition in two ways: they control the majority of pubs and bars and they spend heavily on advertising their products. Control of distribution makes it difficult for competitors to supply their products to the consumers; extensive promotion must be matched at great expense if competitors are to attract the widespread attention of the consumers.

(b) Oligopoly is a market form in which a small number of large firms control supply. Each has significant market power in that it can increase its sales by reducing its price. A price reduction will normally be matched by competitors, resulting in unchanged market shares but reduced total revenue in the market. However, a firm which increases its price will probably not be imitated by its competitors who will thus gain market share and revenue at its expense. As a result, price competition is unusual in an oligopoly and competitive efforts are concentrated on achieving product differentiation. Methods include high spending on promotion and brand development, providing high quality service and technical developments in the products themselves. The firms involved are interdependent in that their actions are always likely to affect those of their competitors, but those reactions are uncertain and difficult to forecast.

(c)

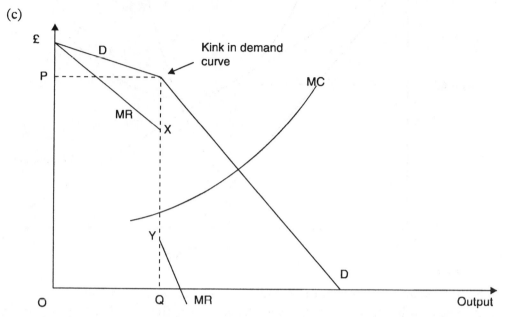

The oligopolist believes that if he increases his prices, his competitors would not do the same and he would lose trade to them. This implies elastic demand at prices greater than the prevailing market price. Conversely, the oligopolist expects that competitors will match a price reduction, thus preserving their market shares. This would have the same effect as inelastic demand at prices lower than the prevailing market price. The overall effect is that the oligopolist perceives a kinked demand curve as shown in the diagram.

Since the demand curve is also the average revenue curve, the kink implies a discontinuous marginal revenue curve, effectively vertical at output Q and prevailing price P. Profits are maximised at the output at which marginal revenue and marginal cost are equal; the vertical section of the marginal revenue curve implies that output is likely to be maintained at Q and price at P, even if significant changes in marginal cost occur.

Instead of competing on price, it is common for oligopolists to defend and build market share by extensive promotion, as is mentioned in the final paragraph of the passage.

(d) Forward vertical integration occurs when a firm amalgamates with a customer and backwards vertical integration when it amalgamates with a supplier. Thus, if a brewer bought farms growing malting barley, it would be integrating backwards. If it bought a chain of pubs it would be integrating forwards. Horizontal integration takes place when a firm amalgamates with a competitor, as when Bass took over Carlsberg-Tetley.

Any of these forms of growth may be undertaken as a strategic move. Vertical integration can safeguard sources of supply and chains of distribution. Horizontal integration will increase market share and the ability to influence market price. It enables the firm to increase productivity and avoid over-capacity in the industry by closing less efficient plant. Increases in efficiency will bring absolute cost advantages which will form a barrier to entry into the market against other firms.

Both vertical and horizontal integration can bring cost benefits. Economies of scale may be achieved, particularly in management, purchasing, distribution, training and stock-holding. Dimensional economies may be particularly relevant in the brewing industry, where it may be possible to use fewer, but larger fermentation vessels.

23   DATA RESPONSE QUESTION: OPEC

> **Pass marks**. A key skill required here is to draw clear *diagrams*. Be clear about the difference between shifts in the curves, the slopes of the curves and movements up and down the curves.
>
> **Examiner's comments**. Those who combined both appropriate analysis and correct diagrams to explain what had happened in the market for oil were rewarded with very high marks. Most answers only achieved low marks, partly because of numerous errors and partly because of a tendency to consider supply and demand in the abstract rather than in relation to the particular issue of oil prices.

(a)   The OPEC's cut-back in supply is illustrated in Figure 1 by an upward and leftward shift of the supply curve S_1. Consequently the **equilibrium** moves from E_1 to E_2. This caused prices to rise (P_1 to P_2) and output (Y_1 to Y_2) to fall.

The price of oil is determined by the **interaction of supply and demand** for oil within the oil market. There is a limited number of suppliers, and so the market for oil is not perfect. However, price change will be influenced by changes in supply and demand.

The extent of the price changes will depend upon the respective elasticities of supply and demand for oil. As the passage points out, OPEC were able to 'put up the price of oil from \$3 to \$12 per barrel' almost immediately. The price rise was large because supply and demand are relatively inelastic.

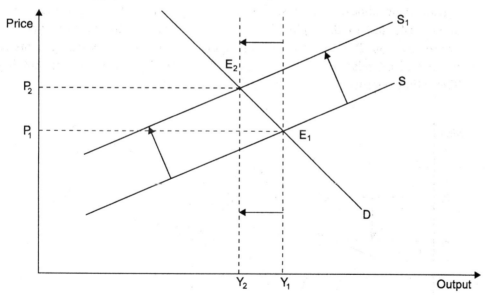

Figure 1

(b)   In the **long-run,** the elasticity of **demand** for oil becomes more responsive. In other words the demand curve gets **flatter**.

We might also expect to see a **shift in the demand curve,** from D_1 to D_2 in Figure 2, brought about by the following two factors:

(i)   **aggregate demand** for oil in the consuming countries fell as **substitutes** for oil, like natural gas, were put in place.

(ii)   **unemployment** brought about by a deflationary fall in national income would also reduce the demand for oil. In turn this could bid down wages to bring the demand for oil down even further.

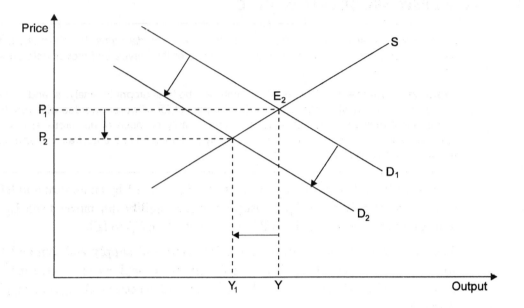

Figure 2

(c)   The higher price of oil made it more profitable for non-OPEC members to produce oil, so that oil **exploration and technology** developed further and oil output increased. Also, some OPEC members breached their own agreements to stay within their allocated quotas. These factors caused the supply curve to **shift** downwards and to the right, as shown in Figure 3. This brought prices down eventually from P_1 to P_2 as shown in Figure 3. This will apply where firms restore the use of oil relative to other sources of energy. In Japan this did not happen. There they restructured their industrial base to one using less oil.

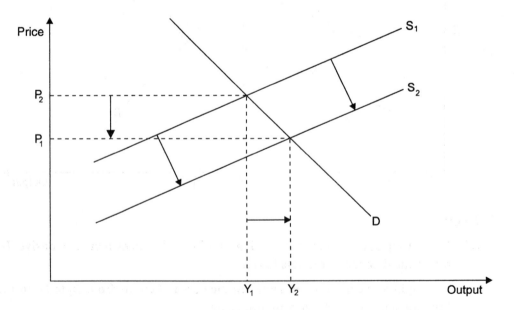

Figure 3

(d)   **Income elasticity of demand** measures the **responsiveness** of the demand for a good, oil in this case, to changes in **real income**.

$$\text{Income elasticity of demand} = \frac{\% \text{ change in quantity demanded}}{\% \text{ change in real income}}$$

As explained in the passage, income growth in the main industrial economies was slowing down under the impact of serious recessions. This fall in real national income growth **in the long term** inevitably caused a fall in the quantity of oil demanded.

In response the OPEC countries, anxious to keep up their **total oil revenues,** responded by bringing down oil prices towards the equilibrium point at which they were before the oil shock of 1973.

The income elasticity of demand for oil is likely to be low because consumers in developed countries see it as a basic product which they are already buying in sufficient quantities for their needs. Any additional disposable income is likely to be spent on non-oil related products, including services. Lower income growth combined with low income elasticity of demand for oil will tend to dampen the long-run demand for oil. Along with the expanded supply of oil, these factors will result in downward pressure on the long-run oil price.

24   DATA RESPONSE QUESTION: COMPACT DISCS

Pass marks. This question requires you to apply the theory of price discrimination. It is not enough to produce a general answer based only on the information in the article.

Other points. The question was a very topical one at the time it was set. In June 1994, the MMC found after an 11-month inquiry that although the dominance of firms like EMI, Polygram and the retailer W H Smith did constitute monopoly, they did not operate against the public interest nor make excessive profits.

Examiner's comment. Those candidates who understood the concept of price discrimination also tackled part (b) quite well, but many resorted to irrelevant descriptions of the development of CDs. You should show clearly that it was geographical distance and the copyright laws that permitted market segmentation - the essence of price discrimination.

In part (c), too many candidates merely asserted that cost differences or the ability to buy tapes was a sufficient reason for non-intervention by the MMC. Others recommended price controls rather than the removal of the sources of price discrimination especially the copyright laws.

(a)   The term **price discrimination** refers to a situation in which a firm sells the 'same' product at different prices in different markets.

Three conditions are necessary for price discrimination to be effective.

(i)   Firstly, the seller must be able to **control the supply of the product,** a condition which will apply under monopoly conditions. The monopoly seller has control over the quantity of the product offered to a particular buyer.

(ii)   The seller must be able to **prevent the resale of the good** by one buyer to another. This means that the markets must, be clearly separated so that those paying lower prices cannot resell to those paying higher prices. The ability to prevent resale tends to be associated with the character of the product, or the ability to classify buyers into readily identifiable groups. Services are less easily resold than goods while transportation costs, tariff barriers or import quotas may separate classes of buyers geographically and thus make price discrimination possible.

(iii)   There must be **significant differences in the willingness to pay** among the different classes of buyers. In effect this means that the elasticity of demand must be different in at least two of the separate markets so that total profits may be increased by charging different prices.

(b)   The average prices of CDs in Europe is around 40% higher than CD prices in North America, which appears to indicate **significant price discrimination**. The prices of different CD titles also vary widely in each of these markets. However, there is only limited substitution between different titles and therefore these price differences do not represent price discrimination.

It will be found that there are significant differences in price for the same CD titles in Europe compared with North America, and there are two reasons why record companies are able to practise this price discrimination.

(i)   **Copyright law** makes it easier for record companies to segment the market by prohibiting retailers from buying CDs at lower wholesale prices in other countries for re-sale at home.

(ii)   **Physical separation** between the European and North American markets reduces the extent to which European consumers can easily buy CDs in the lower-priced North American market.

(c)   The **Monopolies and Mergers Commission** (MMC) can carry out an investigation into an industry if the case is referred to it by the Director General of Fair Trading or by the President of the Board of Trade, a government minister.

An MMC investigation can be called for to see whether a monopoly situation exists in an industry, or if the industry is pursuing practices which are against the public interest. The UK CD industry cannot be said to be a monopoly, although by the nature of the product a 'mini-monopoly' could be said to exist for each title, reinforced by copyright law. There is also lack of evidence of a price-fixing cartel. Reference to the MMC would need to be on the grounds that the large price difference between European and North American CD prices is against the public interest.

Some would argue that the price discrimination which exists is **in the best interests of consumers,** since it allows a wider range of music to be marketed than would otherwise be the case. However, this argument will only be borne out if it can be shown that the price differential allows a wider range of music to be available in Europe than in North America.

To reduce or eliminate price discrimination, the MMC would need to address the issue of why the price discrimination is taking place.

Obviously, it is not possible to reduce the **physical distance** between the European and North American markets. However, it might be possible for the MMC to press for changes in copyright law so that it is possible for retailers to source CDs from wholesalers in either market. This might intensify price competition in European markets and lead to a lower price differential between Europe and North America.

25   TUTORIAL QUESTION: TOO LITTLE MONEY

Monetarist economists stress the significance of the **role of money** in the workings of the economy. They base their arguments on the quantity theory of money which, in its classical form, was developed by Irving Fisher in 1911.

The **quantity theory of money** takes the following identity as its starting point:

$$MV \equiv PT$$

where   M   is the money supply
          V   is the velocity of circulation
          P   is the price level of goods and services
          T   is the number of transactions

In other words, monetarists assume a relationship between the money supply on the one hand and the level of prices and/or the **number of transactions** (economic activity) on the other.

The **amount of money** in an economy could fall because there is a tight control over credit creation through the banking system. Alternatively, it could fall because there is a level of saving and a reduced level of consumption. One could assume that a significant part of this saving is dormant in financial institutions and not being lent on for investment purposes. The tightness of the credit control methods could make this so. These dormant funds are not then forming part of the *effective* money supply, even though they very much form part of potential money supply.

The effect of the reduced level of national income flow would be under-utilised production capacity. Given the cost structure of many firms, this might result in a rising of unit costs as fixed costs become higher per unit of output. This, in turn, could make domestic producers' costs and prices compare unfavourably with overseas competitors. The result of this would be an increased propensity to import and a further reduced national income flow. The country might then experience the phenomenon of the 'vicious circle', as the cut-backs in production bring about the closure of marginal enterprises and so reduce further the flow of national income. In practice, in a modern society there would be likely to be some 'compensating' social security payments (and perhaps subsidies to firms) to offset partially these deflationary effects.

It is possible that although there is tight **government control** of the money supply, people's expectations of inflation lead them to make compensating wage demands, so that the rate of increase in average prices will be in excess of any increase in the money supply. If the government is effective in its limiting of the growth of the money supply, but wages rise at a faster rate, then the higher wages will mean less real income and less real output. This will exacerbate the recessionary situation. There is thus a need for the government both to communicate its intentions as to reducing the money supply and to make any 'demand management' decisions consistent with doing so.

Although an **uncontrolled increase in money supply** is undesirable, there is a need for an optimal increase in money supply to facilitate healthily based economic growth. This can help to develop growing demand, falling unit costs and falling real product prices (though this depends upon productivity performance and factor-reward demands not outstripping factor 'contribution').

26   INTEREST RATES

> **Pass marks.** It is often useful to categorise different theoretical perspectives, where relevant, into the two main camps of economic analysis, the Keynesians and the monetarists. This will clarify the different arguments you are putting forward. Part (a) of this question provides a good example of this. Regarding (b), (i) it is perhaps worth pointing out that despite the implication in the question, investment is believed by some economists to be autonomous. That is, business people invest or otherwise depending on how confident they are about economic prospects. Do learn to draw economics diagrams like the two shown in the answer.
>
> **Examiner's comments.** There were some very good answers where candidates clearly coped well with all three parts of the question. The weaker answers often included poor responses to part (a).

(a)   One theory to explain how the **general level of interest rates** is determined in a market economy is the **loanable funds theory**. This is illustrated in Figure 1.

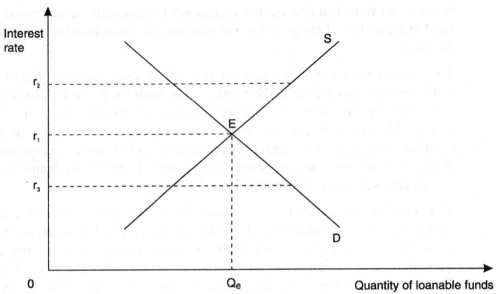

Figure 1 Loanable funds theory of interest rates

The loanable funds theory is a **monetarist theory,** in which money is treated like any other commodity. Demand comes from potential investors; supply comes from potential savers. The **demand curve** slopes downwards from top left to bottom right. The supply curve slopes upwards from bottom left to top right. The point at which they cross is the equilibrium E. This settles the rate of interest, the price of money.

At the higher rate of r_2 in Figure 1, there will be excess sums supplied and at the lower rate of r_3 there will be excess sums demanded.

The demand for money comes from potential investors, while the supply of money comes from potential savers. Changes in demand and supply conditions may shift the D and S curves and thus change the equilibrium point E.

To the **supplier** or **lender,** the interest rate is the reward for saving. As interest rates rise, so does the opportunity cost of current consumption. To the 'demander' or borrower, the interest rate is the price paid to consume or invest today rather than having to wait until some time in the future.

The second theory about how the general level of interest rates is determined is the Keynesian liquidity preference theory.

Liquidity preference (LP) theory not only concentrates on *why* people hold money rather than invest it in bonds, it also deals with the **demand and supply of money** rather than loanable funds. Adding together the three main types of demand for money creates the LP curve: these are the **transaction, precautionary and speculative demands.**

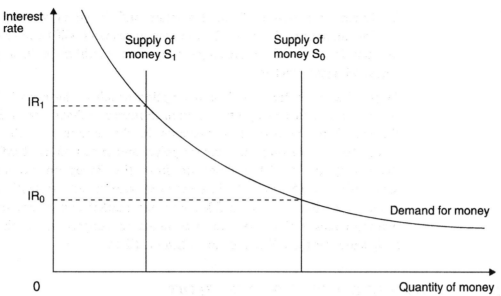

Figure 2 Liquidity preference theory

Money is a liquid asset according to Keynes. The opportunity cost of holding money is the rate of interest forgone. When interest rates are high, the opportunity cost is high and *vice versa*.

The **liquidity preference function**, another name for the downward sloping money demand curve (see Figure 2), is inversely related to the rate of interest and purports to represent people's preferences for money liquidity.

Another feature of the LP theory is the shape of the **money supply curve**, which is vertical and thus completely inelastic.

As the amount of money is reduced from S_0 to S_1 in Figure 2, the interest rate rises from IR_0 to IR_1.

(b) (i)   A **change in the rate of interest** affects the **level of business investment** in a number of ways.

   If an interest rate change is perceived to be only a short-term change, or if it was expected by businesses, the level of investment will not be affected. An unexpected change in longer term interest rates will alter the rate of return on a project and this will cause businesses to put some projects off if longer term interest rates go up, or to begin new projects if the rate comes down.

   There is also the **capital/output ratio** to bear in mind. This affects the level of business investment. As interest rates fall, so does the cost of capital. Assuming the cost of labour stays the same, the tendency will then be to *substitute*, at the margin, capital for labour.

   As interest rates go up, firms will also dis-invest by reducing stock levels, or reinvest in higher stock levels if interest rates come down.

   When interest rates go up, **borrowing by firms** from the banks comes down until equilibrium is restored, and *vice versa* when interest rates come down.

(ii) The **exchange rate** of a country's currency is the price of that currency in terms of other currencies, and is determined by the supply and demand for that currency in foreign exchange markets.

   If **interest rates** on financial assets denominated in one currency, say sterling, rise, then *ceteris paribus* depositors will wish to invest more funds in those assets because these assets are now relatively more attractive, compared to assets denominated in other currencies. There will be inflows of mostly short-term 'hot' money into sterling assets, and thus there will be an increase in demand for sterling from depositors and investors wishing to hold sterling-denominated assets. The increase in demand will be reflected in an increase in the sterling exchange rate, until equilibrium in supply and demand is again reached.

In practice, the **ceteris paribus** assumption which we have made here will rarely hold, in that many other factors influence exchange rates, including the confidence of market participants in the economy of the country, speculation concerning government policy and expectations of inflation. In the run-up to the UK's departure from the **European exchange rate mechanism (ERM)** in 1992, interest rates were raised substantially by the government, but lack of confidence in the market and severe speculative pressures meant that the rate rises failed to support the exchange rate sufficiently for the UK to remain within the ERM.

27   TUTORIAL QUESTION: BUSINESS CREDIT

Credit enables firms and individuals to purchase goods and services without paying for them immediately. Credit may be defined as **any form of deferred payment for goods and services**.

Credit is available to businesses in a variety of forms. As a general rule, the length of credit should not exceed the life of the asset which it finances. The various forms of credit differ in the time scale over which they are provided. Credit may be categorised as taking the forms of trade credit, bank credit or consumer credit.

For the purposes of short-term credit, almost all businesses make use of **trade credit**, which is the credit provided by suppliers of raw materials, components and other goods and services in the normal course of trade. Trade credit is typically granted for 30, 60 or 90 days before invoices must be paid. Trade credit permits a producer to defer payment until after materials or services purchased have been used in production, and thus reduces the level of working capital which would otherwise be necessary for the business to operate. If the business supplies on trade credit to other businesses, it will effectively be providing short-term finance through trade credit to its customers on the one hand, and receiving short-term finance from suppliers on the other hand. Many retail businesses can gain a significant cash flow advantage from the fact that they receive payment from customers in cash at the time of sale, but do not need to pay their suppliers promptly.

Bank overdrafts offer an alternative form of short-term credit. Bank overdrafts will be more flexible than trade credit in terms of amount, within the limits which a bank will permit for the business, but interest must be paid. Bank overdrafts should not be treated as a permanent or long-term form of credit. In general, short-term credit should enable a firm to retain sufficient liquidity, and a firm should keep its current ratio (the ratio of current assets to current liabilities) at a sufficiently high level.

A further form of short-term credit which is important to a business is the credit which a retailer is able to provide to customers through informal credit arrangements, customer credit accounts, credit cards and charge cards. These forms of **consumer credit** can provide a way for a business to increase sales. In many retail markets, a major retailer could lose sales significantly if it did not provide the various forms of credit which its competitors provide.

Medium-term and long-term credit is available to businesses to finance fixed assets with a comparable or longer life. For example, **medium-term credit** might be used to finance the purchase of cars or items of plant and machinery. Bank loans, hire purchase and leasing finance offer alternative means of financing such purchases. A firm may borrow from a bank in a foreign currency as well as in the domestic currency: such 'eurocurrency' loans could be used as part of an arrangement whose objective is to hedge the risks of exchange rate movements.

A business may make use of sources of **long-term credit** as an alternative method of finance to equity shares. Larger companies can issue debentures or loan stock may be quoted on the Stock Exchange. Such loans will normally be secured with a fixed or floating charge over the company's assets. The largest firms can raise capital on worldwide markets in the form of eurobond issues, or for short and medium-term borrowing through commercial paper or medium term notes respectively. If a company is able to generate returns on the capital which exceed the cost of capital, it will be able to secure the benefits of higher dividends for its shareholders. However, if the costs of capital exceed returns made, shareholders in a firm with a high 'gearing' or debt/equity ratio may suffer heavily. Mortgages offer a form of long-term finance which is secured on land and buildings.

Levels of credit are of great **economic importance** because of their implications for the money supply and in turn for the level of demand in the economy. Higher levels of credit are likely to result in higher levels of bank deposits and hence to an increase in the money stock. Credit provides for the consumption of goods and services now in anticipation of future income. Increasing levels of credit can increase consumer demand and create inflationary pressures which a government may seek to control, for example by increasing rates of interest or by direct credit controls.

28   DATA RESPONSE QUESTION: CORPORATE SECTOR

Pass marks. In part (a), use of the term 'appropriation account' together with the phrase 'uses to which income may be put' may appear confusing, given the contractual commitment to pay interest charges. However, the question obviously requires an answer in somewhat broader terms that would be provided in financial accounting.

Other points. In part (c), financial intermediation does not refer to the relatively limited agency role of, for example, linking lender and borrower through advisory and support services. The financial intermediary itself supplies funds as a principal to a deficit party.

Examiner's comment. Common errors included:

- failure to relate answers to the data given in the table

- misunderstanding of the notion of financial intermediation; many claimed it was related to a government role of helping the economy out of recession

- failure to show the relevance of financial intermediation, even when correctly explained, to the data given

(a)   UK companies are contractually obliged to pay interest charges on borrowed funds and by statute are committed to pay corporation tax on profits. Subject to this proviso, **companies** may use their **income** in the following main ways.

(i)   As payment of interest on borrowed funds, as mentioned above.

(ii)   In payment of corporation tax on profits, as mentioned above.

(iii)   For resource or organisational improvement. This might include the closing down (including redundancy costs) of part of the firm, or a major training programme.

(iv)   To finance capital investment. This may be:

(1)   for payment on projects already planned or entered into:

- replacing existing assets,
- purchase of additional assets;

(2) for capital expenditure thought likely over, say, the next year.

(v) In payment of dividends to shareholders.

In practice, companies need to strike a balance between (iv) and (v), with an eye on retaining the support of shareholders with voting rights. 'Interim' dividends will usually already have been paid anyway, during the course of the year.

(b) One accepted definition of an **economic recession** is two quarters in succession with an actual fall in national income/output. With output falling, company profits will fall. The companies most affected will be those with high levels of unavoidable fixed costs.

The data in the extract indicates a recession as follows.

(i) A fall in gross trading profits ('undistributed income'), ie between 1989 and 1991 by 6¼% in unadjusted terms - more in inflation-adjusted terms.

(ii) A fall in expenditure on capital investment, ie between 1989 and 1992 by 20% in unadjusted terms; more in inflation-adjusted terms.

(iii) An actual decline in stock levels. In 1989 there was a rise of £9bn in stock levels; in 1991 there was a fall of £5bn.

In 1989, the company sector had a financial deficit of £30bn: its expansionary posture (capital investment and stock increases amounting to £71bn) required the support of other sectors of the economy. By 1993, this was changed to a surplus of £1bn, clear evidence of the overall effects of the recession.

(c) It is possible for a **direct contractual relationship** to exist between supplier(s) and user(s) of funds, ie between surplus units and deficit units. However, in respect of a major part of funds movement, a third party effectively is interposed between the suppliers and users of funds (**financial intermediation**). Savers of funds might for example take up units in a unit trust which in turn buys new shares in an industrial company which needs to finance a deficit resulting from its programme of investment.

The process of financial intermediation provides three benefits.

(i) **Maturity transformation**. Individual providers of funds may not wish to commit their funds for a lengthy or indefinite period of time whereas the users of funds may require them for long periods. Through financial intermediation the needs of both parties can be satisfied: the fund provider can, for example, dispose of company shares on the secondary market while the industrial user continues to have use of the funds.

(ii) **Aggregation**. Financial intermediation is the means of collecting together a large number of relatively small amounts to pass on in aggregated large amounts to industrial/commercial users.

(iii) **Risk transformation**. Direct funds provision by an individual can be very risky. However, the financial intermediary can pool risk, ie minimising the impact of any loss by setting loses off against a greater number of profitable loans/investments. Further, the financial intermediary can apply his expertise and experience in judging investment proposals in order to lessen the extent of risk undertaken.

Companies, in general, are both **users** and **providers** of funds. The use of funds is indicated in the data through the existence in the four years 1989 to 1992 of a cumulative financial deficit in the industrial/commercial company sector amounting to £72bn. This deficit was met either by direct provision of funds by outsiders (loans, purchase of company shares) or by funds obtained from financial intermediaries, for example investment trusts and unit trusts.

Some companies are in a position to have funds surplus to their operational needs and these funds can be placed either temporarily or on a longer term basis with other institutions/industrial companies. Thus, under 'capital account' the item 'other' includes funds spent on acquiring or having a partial share ownership in other companies as well as funds placed temporarily in the money market. This, in turn, provides income to the investing companies by way of dividends or interest, reflected in the item 'other income'. Funds placed temporarily with a bank would be an example of financial intermediation: the funds so placed enable the bank to lend to other parties.

29 FINANCIAL INTERMEDIATION

> **Pass marks**. Note that the term 'financial intermediation' covers institutions other than the banks. The main advantages to individuals apply also to the business sector, but the advantages to the business sector do not usually accrue to individuals. The main advantages lie in the services offered by the various intermediaries to different types of business institution.
>
> **Examiner's comments**. Too many candidates regarded this as a general question about the functions and services of banks, rather than about the particular process of financial intermediation. Thus part (b) tended to be poorly answered since the answers were often much too general. Those candidates who understood the concept and stuck to the question were able to secure high marks.

(a) **Financial intermediaries** (FIs) are the organisations which channel funds from institutions and individuals who have a **financial surplus (lenders)** to institutions and individuals which are in **financial deficit (borrowers)**. By intermediating between lenders and borrowers, the FIs earn profits from the difference in the rate of interest paid to depositors and the rate of interest charged to borrowers.

FIs operate in both **money markets** and **capital markets**. The main financial intermediaries in the UK economy are:

(i) the banks

(ii) the building societies

(iii) other institutions, including insurance companies, pension funds, unit trust companies and investment trust companies

The different FIs operate in various ways. **Banks** are largely involved with lending in the money markets, where loans are repayable within one year, and may have funds on deposit from individuals and businesses. Banks also provide business loans, and mortgage loans to individuals, the latter traditionally being the main activity of the **building societies**. As well as intermediating between savers and borrowers in the housing market, in recent years the building societies have also become important providers of banking services. **Insurance companies** and **pension funds** generally operate over a long time scale as they are dealing with long-term investments, and are likely to be heavily involved in capital markets.

(b) The most obvious advantage of financial intermediation to both individuals and businesses is in providing ways of **linking lenders of money with potential borrowers**. A lender does not need to find an individual borrower, but can deposit his money with a bank, building society, investment trust company or other financial intermediary. Most of the funds deposited with FIs come from the personal sector, and FIs may use these funds to provide finance within the personal sector or to businesses.

This role in linking lenders and borrowers has the important consequence that the intermediary is able to 'package' or **aggregate** the amounts lent by savers into the amounts which borrowers require. For example, numerous individuals' building society accounts containing deposits of relatively small sums may be used to finance the smaller number of relatively large sums which mortgage borrowers require.

The intermediation process leads to **risk reduction** by the pooling of the risks of lending money to borrowers among the various lenders who deposit money with the intermediary. Risk reduction is also effected by unit trust companies through the spreading of investments across a variety of stocks and shares in a way which enables a small investor to take advantage of the effects of portfolio diversification which are normally only easily available to the larger investor. Many FIs operate globally, allowing risks to be spread very widely.

The role of the financial intermediary provides what is called **maturity transformation**. That is, the intermediary bridges the gap between the desire of many lenders for liquidity and the need of most borrowers for loans over longer periods. The intermediary does this by providing investors with financial instruments which are sufficiently liquid for investors' needs and by providing funds to borrowers on a long-term basis.

The existence of FIs which offer a wide range of products to potential lenders may serve to encourage **savings** and **business investment**. This may enhance the prospects of economic growth in the economy in general, and will assist the general functioning of economic activity. If the intermediaries do not perform this role effectively, the economy may suffer. For example, commercial banks in the UK have been criticised for their unwillingness to provide long-term investment funds to the business sector in recent years.

Furthermore, FIs oil the wheels of the economy by allowing individuals to obtain **consumer finance**, which is an important driver of consumer demand. As well as enabling individuals to make larger purchases more easily, this boosts demand in the business sector for such goods. If we consider the housing sector, it can be appreciated that the sector could not exist in its current form in the UK without the FIs. There is a high level of owner-occupation, which is only possible because of the ready availability of mortgage finance. Other business sectors, such as the car industry, are heavily dependent on the existence of consumer finance in making sales to individuals. Thus, both personal and business sectors gain from the existence of FIs.

(c)   The **Financial Times Ordinary Share Index** is designed to reflect short-term equity price movements and the 'mood' of the market. It is based on the unweighted geometric mean of the prices of 30 leading UK shares. This number has been found to give a good balance between the need to achieve reasonable stability (which might be lost if a smaller number were used) and the need for the index to be reasonably sensitive to market changes. The inclusion of many second line shares would tend to deaden the impact of sudden changes in market sentiment since many of them are dealt in relatively infrequently.

Although changes in the index reflect movements in prices generally, it is not a particularly good measure of price movements within the market as a whole because:

(i)   the index is based on only 30 shares;

(ii)   its main constituents are 'industrial' companies. Banks, insurance companies and property companies are not fully represented;

(iii)   the index is unweighted and so takes no account of the relative size of the different companies.

The **Financial Times Actuaries All-Share Index** is a weighted arithmetic index of the share prices of approximately 850 companies and includes a representative number from each sector. The weightings used are the market capitalisation of each company, so that a change in the price of shares in a large company will have a greater effect on the index than a similar change for a small company. The selected companies are classified according to the sectors to which they belong. A separate index is calculated for each sector, together with an estimated average earnings yield, dividend yield and P/E ratio.

Because of its representative nature and its method of construction, the All-Share Index provides a useful yardstick against which the performance of particular portfolios can be measured. The individual sector indices provide a useful guide for assessing different sectors with a view to increasing or decreasing the extent to which each sector is represented within a single portfolio.

30   FINANCE NEEDS

> **Pass marks.** You can use knowledge of accounting to help answer this question. The key point in (b) is to distinguish between internal and external funding.

(a)   We can define **short-term finance** as finance that is repayable within one year or less, to accord with usual accounting conventions. Business need short-term finance in order to deal with the cash flow needs arising from timing differences between receipts and payments. It is considered to be good practice for firms to avoid using short-term finance to finance the purchase of assets for long-term use, such as plant and machinery or other 'fixed' assets of the business. Short-term assets of the business comprise its **working capital** and include cash, debtors and stocks, including work-in-progress, and short-term financing may be used to finance accumulation of working capital. Short-term finance may typically take the form of overdraft finance, or trade credit gained from suppliers.

Long-term finance could be used to finance freehold and leasehold premises, as well as other fixed assets. The fixed assets of the business provide it with the basis on which it can generate output over a sustained period of time.

(b)   **Sources of long-term finance** can be divided between internal funds, such as depreciation and retained profit, and external funding such as share issues or long term loans.

The main internal source of long-term finance arises from retained profit from previous years. Not all profit is paid out in dividends; some can usually be kept for future investment. Depreciation is purely an adjustment to taxable profit, and underestimates the amount of cash coming in from generated profit.

For publicly quoted companies, one way to raise long-term finance is to **issue shares**. The shares can be bought and sold daily on the London Stock Exchange and, although share prices fluctuate on a daily basis, the company has already received its injection of capital.

There are various types of long-term loans available to a company, eg **debentures** or forms of **loan stock**. One advantage to the company borrowing is that dividends need not be paid and only interest is repaid, while the full amount must be repaid at the end of the loan period.

Debentures will generally be **secured** by legal charge on some of the company's assets. In the event of liquidation, the debenture holder (ie the lender) takes priority in the list of creditors. Loan stock, or corporate bonds, are not always secured on company assets. The lender will be relying on the credit rating of the company, and may charge a higher rate of interest to compensate for the higher level of risk.

A further form of long-term finance is mortgages, in which case the lender has a legal charge over freehold or long leasehold property. Others include long-term bank loans, and franchising and leasing arrangements.

(c) The gearing ratio is the relationship between the debt and the equity in a company.

$$\text{Gearing ratio} = \frac{\text{External debt}}{\text{Capital base}} \times 100$$

The gearing ratio measures how much of the capital of the business is held by lenders and how much is owned by shareholders. A gearing ratio of 80-20 would be highly geared since only 20% of the business is actually owned by shareholders.

There are two important implications for a company with a high gearing ratio.

(i) Firstly, a change in interest rates is likely to have an immediate impact of the share price. If interest rates rise, debt charges rise, reducing the interest cover, which is the ratio between profit and interest payable.

(ii) Secondly, a highly geared company is more susceptible to the risk that it will have to default on its loans at a time of rising interest rates and/or falling profits.

31   FINANCE SOURCES

> **Pass marks**. Long-term funds for UK companies are mainly generated internally, from either retention of profits (constrained by pressure for dividend payments); or a policy of depreciation charges which allows for asset replacement. External funds come mainly from share issues and the issue of loan capital. Equity (share) capital normally provides permanent funds, helping stability. Loan capital, though introducing constraints, can be the means of enhancing the return to shareholder funds. Possible effects on control of the company need to be considered.
>
> **Examiner's comment**. Although this was not a popular question, it posed no great problems and was quite well answered by most candidates who attempted it. Weaker answers often ignored retained profit as a source of long-term funds and could provide only brief outlines of loan and equity finance.

(a) In relation to finance, 'long term' is normally taken to mean a period of at least three years but can mean ten years or more. **Long-term finance** is usually intended for and expected to be used for commitments involving a lengthy pay-back period, such as the purchase of fixed assets or the setting up of a product research and development capability.

In the UK, the chief source of long-term company funds is from funds generated **internally**. These have **two main sources.**

(i) Cash from retained profits, ie the company's profits for the year after payment of interest on borrowed funds, corporation tax and dividends to shareholders.

(ii) The funds which are retained within a business to *replace* capital assets which are worn out or from obsolescence. Normally a depreciation charge will have been made against profits over the years, so facilitating the retention of funds.

The relative importance of this source of funds will depend upon the asset structure of each firm. In heavily capital-intensive firms this will be a major source of funds, though in principle it allows only for asset replacement.

Overall, the scope for reliance on **internal financing**, particularly for expansion purposes, will depend upon the effective pressure from **shareholders** for dividend payments. Boards of directors of **companies quoted on a stock exchange** recognise the consequences of a depressed share price and therefore the danger of a takeover bid for the company. **Unquoted companies** have rather more freedom in setting dividends and therefore in determining the level of profit retention.

Externally, funds can be obtained from the following sources.

(i) **Issue of shares.** This could be in the form of a **rights issue** which is offered to existing shareholders in proportion to their current holding. Alternatively (under certain conditions) the company might offer shares to the public. In the latter case, any 'private' company would need to change its status to that of a public company. It might also apply to become a 'quoted' company, which could open its shares to a wider market.

(ii) **Borrowing.** Securities could be issued in the form of debentures or loan stock (nowadays often termed 'corporate bonds'). A debenture is normally secured, this taking the form of a legal charge on one or more of the company's assets. The scope for doing this is dependent upon the asset structure of the company and the specific form of the assets: in some instances only land and buildings are acceptance. The debentureholders will be entitled to receive interest payment each year and will have priority for repayment of the loan should the company go into liquidation.

Corporate bonds are similar to debentures but are often issued unsecured on the company's assets: **unsecured loan stock.** Owing to the higher risk involved, such loans would carry a relatively higher rate of interest.

Borrowing could be by means of a **mortgage**: the title deeds of freehold or long leasehold property could be placed as security with a lender, the loan being repayable over or within a specified period.

A **term loan**, possibly up to 12 years, might be negotiated with a bank. This may be secured on the company's fixed assets, or the bank might accept personal guarantees from the directors or other reputable guarantors.

A company may also enter into a **leasing arrangement** by which capital assets are available for use and are paid for over a specified period.

(b) **Equity capital** is normally a permanent form of financing. This is because there is no obligation to repay the funds raised if no profits are available to repay them. This makes it well suited to the financing of long-term capital projects. Also, there is no legal obligation to pay a dividend on equity shares, though of course share market pressures may necessitate a payment wherever possible. This (legal) discretion as to dividends is important when cashflow is tight or when the future of the company is under threat.

Equity shareholders usually have voting rights in the company. If a rights issue is fully taken up by present shareholders, there is no change in the balance of power. If this is not the case or if an 'open' issue of shares is made, there is a changed spread of ownership, and with it can come a dilution of control. This can be especially important for smaller, previously family dominated companies.

The **transaction costs** in the issue of shares, especially issues open to the public, can be high. This may involve meeting accounting, legal and advertising requirements, while underwriting charges may need to be met. These costs can be especially severe for small companies.

Conditions are not always opportune for raising equity capital. The company needs to be able to offer reassuring prospects and external conditions outside the company's control need to be favourable. In any case, the 'success' of a share issue depends upon the perceived downside risk of that particular company. This will vary greatly between companies. Generally, small newer companies will have more difficulty in issuing equity shares than will large, well established companies.

Long-term debt, eg by the issue of debentures, can be easily arranged as long as the borrowing company has suitable security to offer. Borrowing is not subject (directly) to the movements of the share market, though a borrower needs to have regard to the level of and likely movements in interest rates, especially if borrowing at a rate of interest fixed over the term of the loan. The transaction costs of borrowing tend to be comparatively low. With inflation and therefore the falling value of money, the eventual repayment of the loan will cost less in real terms: the cost of funding is being borne partly by the lender. Interest payments on a loan can be charged as an expense before tax, whereas dividend payments on shares are made out of post-tax profits. Borrowing can be a means of raising the return to shareholder funds: any return on assets in excess of net borrowing cost is attributable to shareholders.

Loan stockholders normally have no **voting rights** in the company so that borrowing does not result in a dilution of control. An exception to this would be if the borrowing terms provide for a share issue as compensation for any default in meeting the borrowing terms.

A key disadvantage of borrowing is that **interest payments have to be met** regardless of the conditions of the company at the time. The terms of any secured loan may entitle the lender to force the company into liquidation should interest payments not be duly made. It is therefore essential that the proportion of borrowed funds to total funds (**gearing**) is kept within a limit appropriate to the company's business and market risks. This is a major constraint on further borrowing.

32 CAPITAL MARKETS

> **Pass marks**. In part (a), the main point is the difference in the period over which funds are borrowed and hence the liquidity of the two markets. It is also important to have a good idea of the institutions involved. Part (b) is about 'why' rather than 'how', despite the use of that word in the question. Some candidates discussed financial instruments themselves rather than why they were used.

(a) Both the money market and the capital market are sources of credit for borrowers. Each is made up of a number of financial intermediaries, some of whom operate in both markets. The principal distinction between the two markets is the period for which finance is provided; money market dealings would extend from overnight up to one year, while capital market funds would normally have a much longer period to maturity.

Dealing on the money market is principally in the form of wholesale lending and borrowing by the commercial banks, usually for sums in excess of £50,000. The financial instruments used are extremely liquid and there is a very narrow margin between lending and borrowing rates. The Bank of England deals on the money market when it carries out open market operations to influence interest rates. Other institutions using the money market include finance houses, larger commercial companies of all types and local authorities.

The principal institution in the capital market is the Stock Exchange, where longer term securities are issued and traded. Long term capital can be raised either by the issue of equity in the form of shares or by borrowing by issuing debentures. The Alternative Investment Market, which is regulated by the Stock Exchange, is also part of the capital market, as are major financial institutions such as insurance companies and pension funds, which provide most of the capital.

(b) Companies which deal directly with these financial markets would use the money market for short term finance and the capital market for longer term funds.

Short term funds are required in varying amounts from day to day as working capital, for instance to smooth the irregular flow of receipts and allow payments to be made when required. Working capital is also required to finance stock and to allow the provision of credit to customers.

The capital market is used to raise longer term capital, particularly to fund investment in land, buildings, plant and machinery. Regular investment in equipment is necessary if a firm is to obtain the benefits of new technology. The capital market can be used to obtain new capital by a fresh issue of securities to all investors or a rights issue to existing shareholders. The tradability of listed securities means that investors may be able to take some of their income in the form of capital growth: this permits the firm to retain cash for re-investment. Finally, many takeovers are financed by share exchanges rather than money payments.

(c) The government will use the capital market to fund part of the public sector borrowing requirement (PSBR) or to pay back part of the national debt – a public sector debt repayment (PSDR). Longer term government financial instruments are known as 'gilt-edged' stock or simply as 'gilts'.

A PSBR is much more common than a PSDR since spending more than is raised in taxes is a common method of raising aggregate demand in order to stimulate output and growth and reduce unemployment. A PSBR can also arise when the economy enters a recession. Receipts from taxes will fall as business turnover shrinks and incomes fall. At the same time, government spending on welfare will increase.

33   COMMERCIAL BANKS

> **Pass marks**. Note that for part (a), it is services for business customers you should be concerned with.
>
> **Examiner's comments**. Some candidates ignored the distribution of marks in part (b) and produced unbalanced answers.

(a) **Commercial banks** are often referred to as primary banks or retail banks but within the UK financial system, they are better known as **clearing banks**.

The clearing banks are dominated by the so-called Big Four comprising Barclays, Lloyds, Midland and National Westminster, which are the familiar high street branches of banks that many of us use on a daily basis.

A very large amount of transactions pass through the **cheque clearing system** of these banks. Each day, a large number of cheques are written by individuals and companies on current account transactions, and accounts are debited and credited. The cheque clearing system is administered on every weekday through the Bank of England, where each commercial bank keeps an account in order that customers' transactions may be met.

Apart from cheque clearing, the commercial banks offer a **wide range of services** for business customers. It is now sometimes difficult to draw clear boundaries between the activities of commercial banks, merchant banks and building societies since they are each now moving into each others' territory to some extent.

The commercial banks provide money transmission services which assist a business in dealing with its receipts and payments.

As well as providing **current account** facilities, the banks offer **deposit accounts** or facilities for investing sums short-term on the **money markets**. Such facilities enable businesses to make best use of their cash surpluses.

Commercial banks provide **loans** to businesses, either in the form of an overdraft or a term loan (for a fixed period of time).

The banks offer various other services which can help a business to trade, including:

- (i) provision of financial advice
- (ii) acceptance of commercial bills
- (iii) insurance services
- (iv) foreign exchange facilities
- (v) international payment facilities

(b) (i) Banks create money when they lend because most of the money lent will find its way back into the banking system as new customer deposits.

When a loan is made, the customer is likely to deposit the major part of his loan with the bank, and the firms to which the customer makes payments are similarly likely to deposit the payments with the banking system.

As a result, the bank only needs a relatively small cash reserve to support a given level of deposits. The proportion of the reserve that it is deemed to retain is known as the '**bank deposit multiplier**'. For example if 10% of the deposit is retained, this represents a multiplier of 10.

(ii) If it wishes to control commercial banks' ability to create credit, the central bank must control the banks' liquidity, as this forms the basis of the banks' ability to create credit. There are the following control methods.

Open market operations. This involves the central bank (The Bank of England - 'the Bank') selling government securities on the open market. The securities will be purchased with cheques drawn on the commercial banks. These transactions will be settled by reducing the operational deposits that the banks are obliged to keep with the Bank. As a result, the banks' cash reserves are diminished, and the growth in the money supply is inhibited.

Interest rate policy. A rise in interest rates - the cost of borrowing - will make customers less willing to take on loans, and so less money will be created.

Direct quantitative controls. The central bank might impose specified levels of liquid reserves that the commercial banks must keep. This will reduce the size of the monetary base for the purposes of lending. 'Special deposits' might be required from the banks, set at a specified proportion of the total liabilities of commercial bank. Such deposits must stay with the central bank, and so cannot form a part of the credit creation process.

Moral 'suasion'. The Bank may use exhortation or moral persuasion to discourage banks from engaging in particular kinds of lending.

Thus a credit multiplier of 5 would mean that the most amount of money that could be created out of an initial deposit of £100 would be 500. So if the central bank wanted to restrict the amount of credit created, it would raise the reserve ration which would reduce the credit multiplier.

34   DATA RESPONSE QUESTION: BANK ASSETS

Pass marks. The risks faced by a bank need to be appropriately classified. Minimising risk requires holding a suitable spread of assets. You should mention the importance of phasing of maturity dates of loans and advances.

Other points. A bank is *secure* only so long as it can meet valid claims upon its funds. Means towards achieving this are: 'capital adequacy'; and ensuring that a high proportion of loans to customers are made against formal security. The ability to meet claims also depends upon adequate *liquidity* within the bank's assets. Yet for *profitability* banks need to have as high a proportion of assets in longer-term advances as is prudent.

Examiner's comment. The best answers showed a good grasp of the meaning of the terms involved and could provide a sensible discussion of the notion of risk, its sources and how banks might minimise risks.

(a) (i) **Security** involves maintaining the bank's financial stability and confidence in the bank's ability to meet valid claims upon it by depositors and others as they arise. Banks help to make themselves secure by ensuring formal security, ie collateral, in respect of most loans advanced by them. The security of banks also requires the maintenance of a sizeable base of capital reserves as protection against bad debts and operating losses ('capital adequacy').

(ii) **Liquidity** is the ability of a bank to meet due claims upon it as they arise. The bank must be able to convert a sufficient amount of its assets speedily into cash without sustaining a capital loss. Under normal banking conditions, funds will be needed to provide cash for withdrawal by depositors as well as to provide for the settlement of amounts owing to other banks. Supplementary liquidity will be required to deal with exceptional demands upon the bank. This may be provided by borrowing in the inter-bank market or by the issuing of certificates of deposit. In practice, banks keep a significant part of their assets in near-liquid form which can be converted into cash as necessary.

(iii) **Profitability**. As commercial institutions owned by shareholders, the banks also have a need to be profitable. A sufficient return on capital needs to be earned to allow for an acceptable dividend to be paid to shareholders and to minimise the threat of takeover. Banks also need to increase their capital reserves in order to allow for inflation and to improve their security. Funds may also be needed to finance strategic development in a competitive global economy.

The assets of a bank range from already liquid cash to longer-term, somewhat illiquid loans. Generally, the more liquid the asset, the lower the return which will be earned by the bank. To help profitability, banks endeavour to keep as high a proportion of assets as is prudent in non-liquid form such as advances to customers. Such advances generally earn for the bank the highest rates of return.

(b) Banks face the following risks of losses.

(i) **Credit risk**: the possibility that debts owed to the bank will not be repaid on the due date at their full value (eg individuals being unable to repay loans made to them) or that a firm which has obtained an advance from the bank might go into liquidation and be unable to clear the loan.

(ii) **Investment risk**: that investments held as assets by a bank will fall in realisable value below their purchase price or book value.

(iii) **Forced sale risk**: the risk that the market may be so unfavourable as to make it necessary to sell the asset below book value.

To meet or minimise such risks, the banks maintain an array of assets, including cash and highly liquid assets. The banks also phase their loans and advances, such that loan repayments are spread over time and not unduly concentrated on certain points in time. Care should be exercised in relation to individual risks and commitments. In addition, the Bank of England capital adequacy requirements stipulate against over-exposure to any one form of debt.

(c) The biggest profits of a bank usually come from lending at higher interest rates than the bank pays its depositors. Usually longer-term lending will earn higher rates of interest than short-term lending. Lending to higher-risk customers will be at higher interest rates than lending to low-risk customers. Cash, as the most liquid of assets, earns zero return. Market loans, eg to discount houses, are short-term (sometimes as short as overnight) and also very secure; therefore they tend to earn lower rates of interest. Investment in gilts provides a higher rate of return but there may be delay in turning them into cash. Loans to individuals and businesses generally will earn the highest rates of return but such loans may be for several years and borrowers may default on repayment.

Although collateral may have been obtained, its effectiveness may be subject to sharply falling asset values (eg real property, plant and machinery), as in an economic recession. Thus, the more profitable an asset, the less liquid or secure it is likely to be.

In reality, the banks endeavour to maintain a **balanced portfolio of assets** reflecting the mix of liquidity, security and profitability considerations.

35 CENTRAL BANK ROLE

> **Pass marks**. Arguments for and against central bank independence must bear in mind the need for monetary policy - the central bank's concern - to be consistent with wider economic policy. The overall system needs to ensure accord between monetary and fiscal policy.
>
> **Examiner's comment**. It seems that less well prepared candidates were attracted to this question because they perceived, incorrectly, that part (b) was an invitation to a general discussion requiring no prior knowledge of the recent debate on the merits of an independent central bank. As a result only a few candidates gained more than one or two marks for part (b).

(a) A **central bank** typically has as its main function the **regulation of money and credit** in an economy. The range of functions carried out by central banks varies considerably but many of them are not the necessary functions of a central bank and could be carried out by other organisations. Thus, the issue of bank notes could be carried out by another government department or by privately owned banks, as indeed it is in Scotland and some other countries. Nevertheless there are many activities which are common among central banks. The functions of the Bank of England, the central bank of the UK, will be outlined by way of illustration.

The **Bank of England** ('the Bank') is banker to the government. Virtually all government revenue, whether from taxation or borrowing, is paid into the Exchequer Account held at the Bank. This account is then drawn upon to pay the various government expenses. The Bank also maintains the National Loans Fund out of which loans are made to local authorities and other public bodies.

In periods when central government expenditure exceeds revenue, the Bank makes 'ways and means' advances to the government to cover longer term budget deficits, and the bank arranges the issue of securities such as Treasury Bills (typically for 3-month periods) and gilts (usually for periods of several years). This in turn involves administering the National Debt: issuing securities, periodically paying interest to the holders of securities, and repaying loans on maturity dates.

The Bank is also responsible for the control (printing, issue and withdrawal) of bank notes.

The Bank is responsible for managing the UK's gold and foreign currency reserves. In this capacity, on behalf of the Treasury, it manages the Exchange Equalisation Account. The Bank uses the foreign currency holdings in this account to intervene in the foreign exchange markets to influence the value of sterling against other currencies.

The Bank is banker to the banking/financial system. All banks and licensed deposit takers have to hold operational deposits at the Bank upon which they can draw as necessary. Through these balances differences are settled by daily 'clearing' between the various banks.

In its relationship with the banks, the Bank is able to implement government monetary policy. It uses **open market operations**, involving the sale and purchase of government securities. This helps determine the liquidity of the banks, and thus affects their power to make loans and advances. The Bank can also exercise **persuasion** upon banks and other licensed deposit takers to restrict lending or to favour, in their lending, certain business categories (eg exporters).

The central bank is used in mixed economies for implementing and in some cases developing monetary policy. It may use direct interventionist methods which are often discriminatory in effect. Thus it may place ceilings on the level of bank lending, require the placing of special deposits by commercial banks at the central bank, or may facilitate more favourable borrowing terms for exporters. For some years, the Bank of England has tended to move away from such direct means and, at the behest of the government, has depended very much upon interest rate policy. It has the role of setting interest rates at a rate compatible with the government's inflation target. The mechanism for achieving this is the sale and purchase of government securities. If wishing to reduce liquidity and the demand for money, the Bank will raise interest rates by restricting the supply of securities. It will then ease any shortage of funds by lending - as 'lender of last resort' - to institutions at higher interest rates.

Many central banks, to varying extents, also have a role as **supervisor of the country's banking system**. Broadly this is concerned not only with financial stability but also with the reputation of the country's banking system.

(b) **Advantages**

Full or a high measure of **independence** for central banks is argued for on the grounds that this can prevent the worst monetary excesses, in some cases resulting in **hyperinflation**. The highly independent Bundesbank owes its origins to the economic (and political) experiences of Germany in the 1920s. High levels of existing public expenditure commitments combined with electoral pressures (along with other factors) build in strong underlying inflationary pressures. An independent central bank is seen as an essential counterweight to the potentially reckless decisions of politicians. As well as avoiding the worst excesses, a strong central bank is regarded as vital for the shorter term stability of domestic prices and of the currency, and so is important to overseas trade. Any government wishing to reduce an already high rate of inflation will however have to listen carefully to the advice of its central bank if it is to have any real success.

All of this does not mean that the central bank does or should set the bounds and main objectives of government economic policy. This remains the province of government. Thus, the government might establish a target for inflation and the central bank would then develop monetary policy accordingly.

Disadvantages

Arguments against independence for the central bank are that it is an unelected body and therefore does not have the open responsibility of politicians. This, however, is only partly true. The largely independent Federal Reserve Bank of the USA is very conscious of its public profile and wishes to maintain its professional reputation. Danger in this respect is minimised by the formal publication of decisions and recommendations of the central bank.

It is also argued that in practice the central bank would be setting the parameters of **monetary policy** and thus effectively removing this from government control. Further, it is claimed that central bank views on monetary policy could be in conflict with other economic objectives of the government. A central bank may, for instance, be concerned mainly with achieving a low level of inflation while the government is concerned also with economic growth and reducing the numbers of those unemployed. Excessively strict pursuit of monetary policy could result in prolonged recession and heavy under-utilisation of resources.

Conclusions

The case for and against independence turns largely on what in practice 'independence' actually means. Formal independence could be much diminished by the way in which the appointment and re-appointment of top bank officials is made, or through failure to publish the bank's recommendations. Monetary policy must be coordinated with other aspects of macroeconomic policy. Failure to do this could mean, for instance, that inflation targets are being undermined by inappropriate or ill-timed tax cuts. The existence of an independent central bank can only go some way to ensuring effective economic management.

36   MONEY SUPPLY

> **Pass marks**. Money can be a very complex and difficult topic, but this question illustrates the fact that there are easy marks in all questions. In part (b), your explanation should include a discussion of those assets which count as money. Talking about the standard monetary measures like M_0 and M_4 should lead into this naturally.

(a) Money acts as a **medium of exchange,** permitting economic transactions without the use of barter and allowing the giving of change. Barter is clumsy as it depends on the existence of two complementary cases of supply and demand at the same time and place. The use of money for exchange **stimulates economic activity** by making buying and selling more convenient.

Money may be used as a **unit of account,** providing an agreed standard measure of valuation by which the relative exchange values of goods can be established. A system of prices **facilitates transactions** and permits a fair and transparent system of **taxation.**

The use of money values can be extended so that money acts as a **standard of deferred payment.** This enables credit to be given and contracts entered into for future discharge at known values. Money must maintain its value over time if it is to be acceptable as a standard of deferred payment.

Money provides a **store of value**. Not all stores of value are money, however. Money is distinguished as being completely liquid and of precise and acknowledged value. It must maintain its real purchasing power if it is to be useful as a store of value.

Anything which performs these four roles may be regarded as money. Gold, a commodity, is still used; in developed economies, most money exists only as entries in bank ledgers, accessed with cheques.

(b) The money supply is the **total amount of money in the economy** and is also referred to as the money stock. It may be measured by '**monetary aggregates**', such as M_0 and M_4 in the UK. There is no single definition of what constitutes money and aggregates are usually set up to measure either '**broad money**' or '**narrow money**'. M_0 consists of notes and coin in circulation plus banks' till money and operational deposits with the Bank of England. It thus uses a fairly narrow definition of money and shows what is available for **immediate spending**. M_4 includes notes and coin in circulation plus private sector deposits with banks and building societies and certificates of deposit. This is a much broader definition of money and shows what is available for **spending at short notice**. It is very much larger than M_0

If an economy grows its money supply must grow also, to enable the increased volume of transactions to take place. Ideally, the two would grow at the same rate. However, there is no completely automatic mechanism to ensure that this takes place. Monetarist economists suggest that excessive growth in the money supply leads to inflation as it stimulates demand for goods and the real growth in output cannot keep up. Keynes felt that a surplus of money would be invested and its easy availability would cause interest rates to fall. The growth of the money supply is thus **fundamental to monetary policy**. Most governments subscribe to the monetarist approach to some extent and thus seek to control the growth in the money supply as part of their **inflation policy**.

(c) The money supply can normally be expected to expand through the mechanism of the **credit multiplier** as banks lend in order to earn interest. Government restrictions on the growth of credit would lead to a reduction in the money supply as part of an anti-inflation strategy. Credit restrictions would affect a manufacturer of consumer durables in two ways.

First, its own **borrowing would be constrained**, which would limit its ability to make further investment in new product development, stocks and customer credit. It would either have to limit its volume of business or accept higher working capital costs.

Second, its own **customers would be affected** by the reduction in the money supply. Their **disposable income would be reduced** by the increased cost of existing borrowing such as mortgages and they would find **new credit was more difficult to obtain and more expensive.** Many consumer durables are bought on credit. They also tend to have a high income elasticity of demand. These effects would **reduce demand** for the firm's products and reduce its turnover.

37 **DATA RESPONSE QUESTION: MONEY SUPPLY AND INFLATION**

> **Pass marks.** It is generally worth defining terms in a question, like 'money supply' and 'rate of inflation' before you address the substantive issue.
>
> **Examiner's comment**. Many candidates who attempted this question appeared to have at least a sketchy idea of the quantity theory of money and hence had difficulties with virtually all parts of the question. There was a minority of good answers which combined evidence of both knowledge of the quantity theory and an ability to interpret the data given.

(a) The **money supply M0** comprises cash in circulation with members of the public or in bank and building society tills, plus the balances of the banks held with the Bank of England.

Inflation is an upward movement in absolute prices. The **Retail Prices Index** (RPI) is a weighted average of price rises, geared to some base year, on a typical 'basket' of goods and services purchased by households in the UK. The RPI is published monthly.

Looking at the data on M0 growth and the annual percentage rise in RPI between consecutive years we can note the following about *changes* in the rates of growth in M0 and prices.

M0 growth	RPI rise	No of years
up	up	3
up	down	6
down	up	8
down	down	2
		19

Monetarist theory suggests that as money supply growth comes down, so should inflation, and *vice versa*. In only five out of 19 of the years shown has this been true.

Comparing the growth of money supply and inflation, we also observe that:

(i) the rate of increase in money supply and the rate of inflation have come down since the late 1970s and early 1980s;

(ii) the downward path has not been consistent;

(iii) in no year were there decreases in either the money supply or prices (deflation).

(b) The **quantity theory of money** can be expressed as Fisher's classical equation:

Money stock × velocity of circulation = price level × number of transactions

ie $M \times V = P \times T$

If we presume that the **velocity of circulation** (the number of times money turns over), and the number of transactions stay constant, then M must equal P. In other words there is a direct relationship between the money supply and prices: increase money supply and prices will rise.

The velocity of circulation could be assumed constant if it is determined by institutional factors. If the economy is assumed to be at full employment, the volume of transactions remains constant.

V & T may however *not* be constant, for example if there are big swings in employment levels due to recession and expansion, something Fisher failed to take into account.

As MV equals expenditure, PT must equal spending and as expenditure equals spending then $MV = PT = GDP$ (Gross domestic product).

(c) Assuming V, T *and* the level of savings are constant, we can say that the data given are not in line with the predictions of the quantity theory of money at least in 14 of the 20 years. Only in four years, 1976, 1984, 1987 and 1992 has there been a reasonably **close relationship** between the rise in M0 and the rise in inflation. In 1977, the rise in RPI was 4.5 points above M0, while in the next year 1978 the rise was 5.9 points the other way round. In each of the last three years 1993, 1994 and 1995, inflation was 4.6 points below the rise in money supply. In 1990, in the summer of which the UK economy took a deep dive into recession, inflation was running 7.1 points above the increase in money supply.

The position was similar in 1981, when again the UK economy went into recession. In that year inflation was running 8.5 points ahead of the money supply.

We can identify two **peaks of inflation**, 1980: 16.9% and 1990: 9.8%. In 1980 there were three years at an average money supply rise of 3.9% before inflation came down to a level of 4.2% in 1983. Likewise with the 1990 peak, there were three years at an average money supply rise of 4% before inflation came down to 1.4% by 1993. This suggests that reducing money supply growth can reduce inflation, but from high peaks of inflation it seems to take two or three years to work.

It also appears to take about two years of high money supply growth, for example in 1977, 1978 and 1979, to feed through to high inflation, in this case in years 1979, 1980 and 1981. Yet, slower M0 growth in 1985, 1987 and 1992 did not produce deceleration in inflation in 1987, 1989 and 1994 respectively, suggesting that any **lagged relationship** is only approximate.

Differences in the definition of the money supply will affect predictions made on the basis of the Fisher equation. There are several measures of 'money' reflecting different levels of liquidity. Narrow money reflects immediate spending (the so-called monetary base, now M0) while broad money (now M4) includes funds held for investment purposes. M0 may not adequately reflect the true amount of money in circulation.

(d) Here we need to consider the **transmission mechanism** by which changes in money affect income, output and prices. The extent of the effects depends on whether a Keynesian or a monetarist stance is taken.

Monetarists believe that an increase in money supply increases not only the price of goods and services, but also the price of **financial assets**. That part of the increased money supply spent on financial assets will not only increase their price but will also lower their interest rate.

Monetarists also believe that the demand for money varies with level of **national income** not the rate of interest. Idle balances will not change because the demand for money is not elastic with respect to interest rates. According to the monetarists, a fall in interest rates will not only increase the demand for consumer goods but will also increase the demand for investments. In the short run, money supply increases will lead to extra spending and hence rising prices. Producers will respond to the higher demand and output will rise.

In the long run, output will revert to the natural employment level of national income: any additional increase in money supply will only raise prices without leading to gains in output.

Keynesians take a different view. They believe that money is like any other product or service. So, when its price, that is the rate of interest, is low, more people will want to 'buy' it. In other words, they say that money is interest-rate elastic. They also believe that financial assets, many of which are close substitutes for money, will increase in value as the money supply is increased. As the value of financial assets goes up, the rate of interest comes down. This reduces the **opportunity cost of holding idle balances** producing a more than proportional increase in the demand for money, but because of the high elasticity of demand for money there will be a *less than* proportional fall in the rate of interest.

The **rate of interest** will eventually settle at equilibrium when the supply and demand of money equate. The Keynesians argue that changes in interest rates produce a less that proportional change in expenditure. They say that an increase in money supply has little effect on aggregate demand and therefore there will be little increase in the GNP. What increase there is in demand will be met by spare capacity in the short run, so that output will rise without inflation. In the long run, further demand increases may cause inflation, but the effect will be less than that predicted by the monetarists.

38   CONTROL

> **Pass marks**. Note that monetarists and Keynesians treat the importance of the money supply differently. For the monetarists, the money supply is the key instrument of their policies.
>
> **Examiner's comments**. Most candidates could give a reasonable definition of the money supply and many could distinguish between 'narrow' and 'broad' money measures. Most of candidates identified inflation as the principal reason for governments' wish to control the growth of the money supply, but fewer used the quantity theory of money to explain this. Part (c) gave most difficulty but even here many candidates were able to identify the main instruments of monetary policy used to control the money supply.

(a) **Money** can be defined as something which is generally accepted as a means of payment. The 'money supply' is the total stock of money in an economy.

Narrow measures of the money supply stress money's function as **a means of exchange**.

In the UK, the most narrow definition of the money stock is M0, the 'monetary base', which consists of notes and coin in circulation, including banks' till money and banks' operational deposits with the Bank of England. M0 is a very narrow definition of the money stock because it comprises the means of immediate payment and the most liquid store of wealth.

The concept of **broad money,** as it name implies, is one which includes more elements than narrow money. In particular, as well as current account balances, broad money includes items such as savings accounts:

(i)   which are not generally a means of making payment for transactions; and

(ii)   which are a less liquid store of wealth than items which would be classified as narrow money.

Broad money therefore includes what might be called 'quasi-money' and stresses money's function as a store of value with a reasonable degree of liquidity.

In the UK, **M4** is the most important definition of broad money because it is used in monitoring monetary conditions in the economy. M4 is a **broad** definition of money, consisting of:

(i)   notes and coin in circulation with the private sector;

(ii)   the private sector's sterling deposits at UK banks and building societies.

Financial assets come in varying degrees of liquidity and usability as means of payment. As the existence of different definitions of narrow money and broad money shows, it is not possible to specify precisely what the concepts 'narrow money' and 'broad money' mean.

(b) The main reason why governments attempt to control money supply is to **control inflation,** in accordance with monetarist theories. **Monetarist theories** assume that money is held primarily in order to purchase goods and services. If we start from a position of equilibrium in transactionary holdings of money, a rise in the supply of money will tend to be spent on goods an services. Monetarist theories assume that the economy is at full employment, and so output cannot rise in the short term. The result is inflation, with 'too much money chasing too few goods'.

Control of inflation by changing interest rates is based on the idea that the demand for money, like any other commodity, falls away the more expensive it becomes. The expense in this context is the rate of interest.

The above view is an over-simplification because the demand for credit depends on considerations other than its price. Confidence of borrowers about the economy and future rates of inflation plays an important part in the demand for credit.

It is also difficult to judge just how interest-elastic is the demand for bank credit. There is some evidence that it is not very elastic at all.

The Bank of England was in 1997 given the power to change interest rates to keep inflation under control, but only time will tell whether controlling interest rates alone will achieve desired levels of inflation.

The Treasury, as the controller of the money supply, tends to underpin the changes in interest rates by increasing or decreasing money aggregates.

Another reason why governments believe it is important to control the money supply is to stabilise the foreign sector, that is the balance of payments. In the UK there is a high propensity to import foreign goods and therefore governments have to keep credit in check to make sure that we do not bring in to many imports.

(c) One means of seeking to control the supply of money is through what are called **open market operations**. The **Bank of England** lends money to the banking system through the discount markets. It is able to supply cash to the banking system on days when there is a cash shortage by buying eligible bills and other financial instruments from financial institutions, and to remove excess cash at other times by selling bills to the institutions. These open market operations, in influencing the supply of money, enable the Bank of England to exert an influence on short-term interest rates.

Apart from open market operations, the Bank of England can affect the volume of cash in the market by:

(i) imposing a **Minimum Lending Rate**, indicating its willingness to act as a lender of last resort at the chosen rate; or

(ii) instructing banks and other institutions to place **non-operational special deposits** with the Bank, with the objective of restricting the availability of credit in the economy.

The Bank of England makes use of open market operations to provide a signal to the market of the interest rates which it, acting as the agent of governmental monetary policy, would like to see.

Despite recent calls for the introduction of a requirement for special deposits by the banks to restrict credit growth, the UK government has resisted such controls, which are however used by the German Bundesbank. Arguments used against such controls include the argument that such restrictions could themselves drive interest rates upwards, and therefore may not act as a viable alternative to interest rate policy. A further argument is that such restrictions would simply cause foreign money flowing into the country to be used to satisfy credit demand, unless exchange controls were enforced.

A policy option directed at the same target of restricting credit by putting pressure on commercial banks' reserves is known as **monetary base control**. This seeks to control the monetary base on the supply side by imposing limits on the Bank of England's own assets, thus controlling the Bank's liabilities and preventing the Bank from supplying unlimited funds to the banking system.

Under the Competition and Credit Control policy in the UK (1971-1981), banks were expected to maintain minimum ratios of reserve assets to total assets. Reserve assets are short-term liquid assets, and by requiring that banks hold a certain proportion of these in their asset portfolios, the authorities would hope to reduce the volume of bank loans and therefore the volume of bank deposits.

In more recent years, the UK government has rejected reliance upon most methods of seeking to control the supply of money and has instead sought to influence its demand through the policy instrument of the **interest rate**. Measures designed to influence the supply of money have been rejected as much on doctrinal grounds, since they are seen as interfering with the market mechanism, as on pragmatic grounds. It is argued that if monetary expansion is excessive and credit growth is out of control, then money should be made more expensive. Higher interest rates should act as a disincentive to borrow and will thus curb credit growth through the mechanism of the market.

High interest rates can potentially exert effects on inflation, by cooling domestic demand, and on the exchange rate, possibly avoiding depreciation of a weak currency.

A government's own **budgetary policy** also exerts an effect. By financing its borrowing requirement in a neutral way, the government may be able to avoid causing interruptions in the money supply.

39   DATA RESPONSE QUESTION: MONETARY THEORY

> **Pass marks**. In (a), bear in mind that the term 'expenditure by firms' covers more than investment expenditure. The different significance of movements in long-term and short-term interest rates is also important. The MEC curve can provide only a basic and limited explanation of the effect of interest rate changes. A danger in (b) is to provide a dismissively short answer, stating the MV = PT relationship.
>
> *Other points*. In (c), be careful to make the distinction between the return on long-term real investment, ie profit, and that on moveable funds, ie interest rates. There is a world-wide structure of interest rates and relative changes in interest rates are as important as absolute changes.
>
> **Examiner's comment**. Better scripts showed a clear understanding of the relationship between changes in interest rates and expenditure by firms and individuals and could provide economic theory to explain the relationship. In response to parts (b) and (c), the better scripts showed a clear grasp of the basic theory involved and could use the theory to explain the economic processes involved.

(a) (i) **Interest rates** represent the **cost of borrowing funds**. According to the **loanable funds theory**, the demand for funds is inversely related to movements in interest rates.

At interest rate r_1 in the diagram below, the demand for funds is Q_1. At the lower rate of r_2, the demand for funds is Q_2.

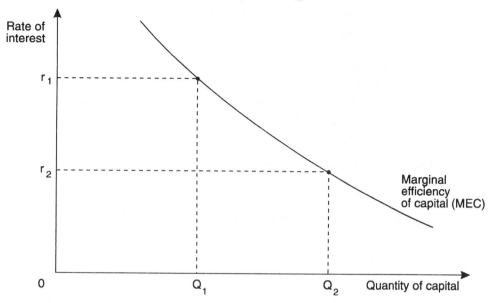

Figure 1

The curve shown represents the **marginal efficiency of capital** (MEC) - the return on funds available to the borrower of funds. At a lower borrowing cost, the productivity of capital rises, as a higher return overall is obtainable. The demand for funds in the private sector comes from firms as well as from consumers.

The impact of changes in interest rates on the expenditure of firms will be various. Capital expenditure decisions are more likely to be affected by movements in longer term interest rates, especially long-term projects. However, in times of financial stringency changes in the cost of shorter-term funds will be of importance in some investment decisions.

Decisions on stock levels may also be affected by movements in short- to medium-term interest rates. If interest rates were to rise substantially, the additional borrowing costs and the wider effects on the demand for sales could lead to fewer concessions on wage demands.

Interest rates are one of several factors which need to be considered in investment decisions. Forecast consumer demand, selling price levels, inflationary effects, and general business confidence will also be taken into account.

(ii)   Interest rates changes will also influence **consumer expenditure**. This may be through the effect on mortgage interest rates, hence affecting the demand for housing as well as for all the wide range of products and services associated with residential property. For those on existing mortgages, a rise in monthly interest rates will mean less income available to spent in other sectors.

Generally, higher interest rates will tend to **encourage saving** and to **discourage borrowing** or entering into hire purchase contracts in order to buy consumer durables. Again, the relationship or response is unlikely to be direct or automatic. In a period of rising incomes, and general business confidence, substantial rise(s) in interest rates may be necessary to reduce consumer demand. Conversely, if consumers are wary from the bitter experience of a recession, a fall in interest rates may, in itself, do little to stimulate consumer demand.

(b) The monetarist theory that changes in the money supply affect mainly prices was stated by Irving Fisher in the **quantity theory of money**. The nucleus of the relationship is expressed in his **equation of exchange**:

$$MV = PT$$

where
- $M =$ the quantity of money in the economy
- $V =$ the velocity of circulation of money, ie the speed at which money moves through the economy over a given period
- $P =$ the general price level
- $T =$ the total number of transactions over a given period

Since M is the quantity of money and V is the number of times that each unit of money is used on average over a given time period, it is clear that MV equals the total value of expenditure during that time period. Since P is the average value of each transaction and T is the volume of transactions during a given time period, it is evident that PT equals the total value of expenditure during the time period. MV must equal PT.

The **Fisher equation** is definitionally true: it shows two different ways of measuring the same group of transactions. It begins to have practical value when valid assumptions are made regarding the variables. Thus, if it is assumed that the velocity of circulation is constant and the volume of transactions is fixed, it follows that any change in the quantity of money will be matched by a change in the price level. Changes in M bring about changes in P, with V and T unchanged.

$$M\overline{V} = P\overline{T}$$

The contention is that at least in the **short run**, V is constant or at any rate predictable: it is determined by institutional factors such as the payment intervals for wages or business accounts. T, the volume of transactions, is determined by the productive capacity of the economy, and a further assumption of monetarist theory is that an economy tends naturally towards **full employment**.

Given that V is a constant and that T is fixed, at least in the short term, the consequence of a change in M must be a change in P. Thus, an increase in the money supply under conditions of full employment will impact on prices rather than on output, provided that the velocity of circulation is unchanged.

(c) A given **exchange rate** is determined by the **demand** for and, **supply** of that country's **currency** on the foreign exchanges.

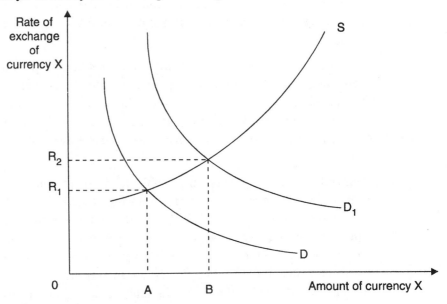

Figure 2

A rise in the demand for currency X, from OA to OB in Figure 2, pushes up the rate of exchange from R_1 to R_2.

In practice, there is a world-wide structure of **interest rates**. Any change in interest rates in the UK, unless matched by similar changes in interest rates in the other main trading and financing nations, will affect the relative position of the UK economy. Thus, a rise in the UK interest rates, unmatched abroad, would encourage portfolio-type investment into the UK as well as money looking for marginally high or short-term returns ('**hot money**'). This would lead to a rise in the value of sterling as the demand for sterling to place within the UK increases. In point of fact, much of this rise in sterling might already have taken place through speculation in sterling on the foreign exchange markets, the markets having anticipated the rise in the UK interest rates. Any fall in the value of sterling would have the reverse effects.

The **effect upon longer term investment** into the UK could be quite different. Such investment is looking for a return by way of profits rather than the reward of interest. It may not be deterred by shorter term movements in interest rates. On the other hand, it may be discouraged if, for instance, the rise in interest rates is part of a package of deflationary measures: setting up or operating costs within the UK might rise and selling markets there might be depressed.

There could be less direct effect upon the value of sterling from an initial rise, say, in UK interest rates. The initial rise in the value of sterling would raise the effective price of British exports. This would make exporting more difficult. Any consequential fall in the demand for UK goods/services would, in turn, have some downward effect on the value of sterling. Any major effect upon the UK economy resulting from the initial rise in interest rates could, in turn, lessen UK demand for imported goods, so tending to result in an upward movement of the value of sterling as the balance of payments deficit is lessened.

40   TUTORIAL QUESTION: VOLUME OF PRIVATE INVESTMENT

> **Examiner's comment**. There were many creditable attempts to explain this aspect of the Keynesian analysis. Most candidates were able to provide a partial answer, giving an adequate explanation of either the rate of interest or the marginal efficiency of capital, but rarely of both.
>
> Definitions of investment were not always accurate. Where diagrams were provided they tended to be accurate in themselves but not satisfactorily explained in the text. Many candidates omitted the essential observation that investment will only continue as long as the marginal efficiency of capital is greater than the rate of interest.

In economic analysis the term **investment** refers to physical investment, in other words, capital expenditure on the purchase of physical assets such as plant, machinery and other types of equipment (the fixed capital of the enterprise) and on stocks (working capital). Such physical investment creates new assets so adding to the country's productive capacity.

Much investment is made with borrowed money. It will pay a firm to borrow money to finance its investment projects as long as the return on the investment exceeds the rate of interest (cost of capital). The entrepreneur will know the current price of the capital goods and the current price of loans (the rate of interest) but will not know, since it lies in the future, the yield or returns to be obtained on the investment. In order to arrive at an estimate of the expected stream of net earnings (expected revenues minus expected variable costs), the entrepreneur has to forecast the demand for his final product over future years.

Discounted cash flow techniques are used to obtain the present value of the expected future stream of income. In using this type of technique, the businessperson has two possible methods to choose from.

(a) The **market rate of interest** can be used to discount the expected net profits of the investment project. The present values of these returns can then be compared with the supply price of the capital goods (ie the current costs of the capital). If this present value exceeds the supply price, the investment would be profitable.

(b) Alternatively we can find the rate at which the future stream of income must be discounted in order to make the present value of the expected profits exactly equal to the supply price of the capital. If this rate of discount exceeds the current market rate of interest, the investment project will be profitable. The rate of discount which equates the present value of the expected profits with the cost of capital was defined by Keynes as the **marginal efficiency of capital** (MEC).

Both of these approaches make the level of planned investment dependent upon the rate of interest. Businesses will choose to invest if the potential earning power of the investment project, as measured by the MEC, is greater than the cost of the funds required to finance the project, in other words the rate of interest. The **demand curve for capital** will, therefore, relate the rate of interest to the quantity of capital demanded. For the following various reasons, it is to be expected that the demand curve for capital will slope downwards from left to right:

(a) the extra output resulting from successive small increments in the capital stock, ie the **marginal productivity of capital**, will tend to diminish as more and more capital is combined with some fixed amount of the other factors of production;

(b) the prices of the goods produced with the capital will tend to fall following the increased output of such goods from the extra capital investment;

(c) the supply price of capital might rise as the demand for capital increases.

All of these developments would tend to reduce the net revenues expected from further investment. Hence the demand curve for capital will have a normal shape as shown in the diagram below.

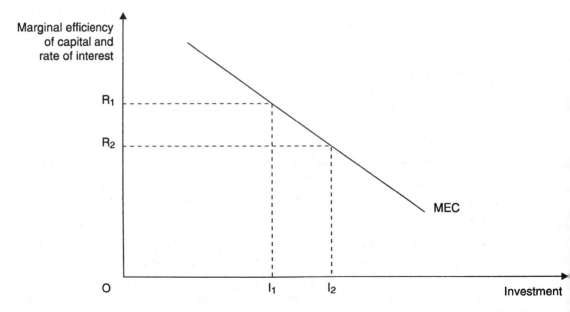

The demand curve for capital illustrated is, in fact, a curve representing the **marginal efficiency of capital** (MEC). The aggregate quantity of capital demanded depends on the relationship between the MEC and the market rate of interest. The equilibrium level of private investment is that level at which the market rate of interest is equal to the marginal efficiency of capital. When the rate of interest is R_1, the level of investment will be I_1. A fall in the rate of interest to R_2 will lead to an increase in the volume of investment to I_2. Investment will only take place up to the level at which the MEC exceeds the rate of interest. As the rate of interest falls, projects with lower expected returns will become profitable. Entrepreneurs will purchase capital, ie invest, up to the point where the marginal efficiency of capital is equal to its cost, the rate of interest. Hence a basic aspect of the Keynesian analysis of the determinants of investment is that investment is a function of the rate of interest.

Given this relationship, Keynesians argue that the **demand for investment** is very **inelastic with respect to the rate of interest**. In other words, the volume of investment demand tends not to be particularly responsive to changes in the rate of interest. Large businesses, for example, usually engage in long-range planning which calls for an investment programme spread over several years. Hence short-term movements in the rate of interest are not likely to disturb these investment plans to any significant extent.

It is also likely that the MEC schedule will be very unstable. The calculation of the MEC, being based on the future revenues obtained from the sale of the firm's product, will therefore depend on **forecasts**. Rising optimism on the part of businesspeople will produce expectations of higher returns which will shift the MEC schedule to the right. Conversely, a collapse of business confidence will cause a downward revision of the estimates of future returns and the MEC schedule will shift to the left. Given this instability in the investment demand curve, it becomes extremely difficult to predict the level of investment demand at any given rate of interest. Keynes particularly stressed the importance of expectations in the determination of the rate of planned investment.

Expectations are closely related to movements in the level of national income. According to the **accelerator theory** of investment, when income is increasing it will be necessary to invest in order to increase capacity to produce consumption goods and investment will also be high because business expectations based on the rising trend of sales are favourable. On the other hand, when income is falling, it may not be necessary even to replace capital equipment as it wears out, and also expectations may be favourable because of the falling trend of sales, hence investment expenditure is likely to be low. According to the accelerator theory therefore, investment is a function of changes in the level of national income. In conclusion Keynesians argue that there are a number of influences on investment demand. Although investment is a function of the rate of interest the extent of its influence is not considered to be great as the demand for investment is thought to be interest inelastic. Keynesians tend to stress expectations as a major determinant of short-term movements in the rate of investment.

41   CIRCULAR FLOW OF INCOME

Pass marks. A truly brief answer to part (a) would provide an explanation of the household-firm flow of income in a simplified economy. A fuller explanation would include explanation of investment/savings, withdrawals/injections, ie their effect on income flow. The use of diagrams reinforces the explanation. In relation to part (b), a narrow money-based interpretation of the term 'standard of living' should be avoided.

Examiner's comment. Virtually all candidates attempting the question did well in part (a), giving a clear explanation of the circular flow. The best answers included a brief outline of the importance of injections and withdrawals in determining the level of national income. The best answers to part (b) dealt confidently with issues relating to the measurement and international comparison of national income levels and with the problems in drawing conclusions about living standards from such data.

(a)   Initially, the economy can be regarded as containing only two elements, **firms** and **households**. It is a closed economy, with no exports or imports. In addition, it is assumed that there is no government sector, so there are no taxes or government spending.

In this simplified economy, households fulfil two functions. They purchase goods and services from the firms; secondly, they provide firms with labour. Firms also fulfil two functions: they produce the goods and services; secondly, they provide income to households in return for the labour services.

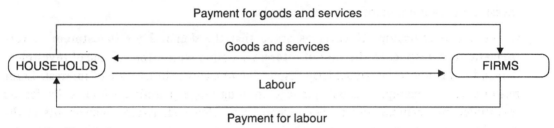

Figure 1

This process is termed the **circular flow of income**, describing how money flows around the economy. Households receive income from for providing labour which they can spend on goods and services. This provides firms with the means to employ labour to produce more goods and so provide further income. Some of the income is saved, thus diminishing the amount spent on consumption. Saving is termed a 'leakage' or 'withdrawal' from the circular flow of income. In effect, money has been taken out of the system. There will also be an injection into the system in the form of investment, ie spending on **capital formation (investment).**

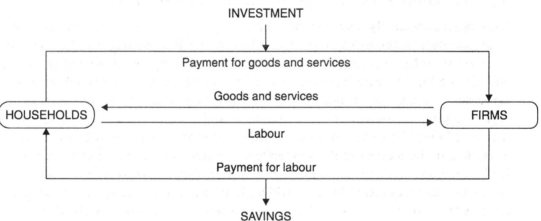

Figure 2

The economy will now be in equilibrium so long as the amount of investment equals the amount of savings. If, however, the level of **investment** exceeds that of **savings,** there is a net inflow of money into the system and national income will increase; and conversely.

The **government sector** and **overseas trade** can now be incorporated into the model. Amounts paid by households in taxes will reduce the amount available to be spent on consumption: taxes therefore are a withdrawal from the circular flow of income. Spending on imports will also take money out of the economy; hence imports are also a withdrawal.

On the other hand, any expenditure by the government is an injection into the economy. Exports are also an injection, there being an inflow of money into the economy from abroad.

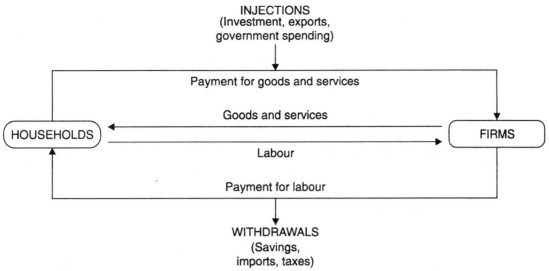

Figure 3

If **withdrawals** (savings, imports, taxes) equal the amount of **injections** (investment, exports, government spending) the model will be in equilibrium.

(b)   In considering the problems involved in using national income data to compare the living standards in different countries, it is important to recognise that while comparison of money incomes is a major factor, **quality of life** factors must also be taken into account.

The following are factors to consider.

(i)   There are **differences in trading structures/processes**. The more advanced economies generally have a relatively high proportion of trade passing through formal market channels which are included in official national income data. In less advanced economies, trading (eg through barter) is often not reported. The effect is to understate income.

(ii)   With each country measuring its national income in its own currency, official exchange rates are commonly used to translate these into a **common measure** - generally US dollars. But exchange rates result from trade in internationally exchanged goods and do not reflect the relative prices of goods/services confined to domestic/home markets.

(iii)   There will be differences in the **collection of data** and in the **reliability of source data**. There may be a significant 'black economy' in which income is not declared to the authorities: the indications are that the relative significance of this varies greatly between countries.

(iv)   The **distribution of income** may vary markedly between countries, therefore invalidating straight per capita comparison of living standards.

(v)   **Government services**, for the purpose of measuring national income, are usually valued at cost. The relative importance of the State in the provision of services such as health and education may vary widely. If such services are provided privately, they will be valued at market price and hence the national income figures will be boosted.

(vi)   The output of some countries may in part provide items that do little or nothing to improve living standards, eg **spending on armaments**. This would contrast with spending on hospitals which directly improves quality of life.

(vii)   The **needs and commitments of countries** vary considerably. Arising from demographic differences, some countries need to devote more resources to supporting dependants (young or elderly), hence depressing living standards for the non-dependant sector. Some countries will need to divert considerable resources into activities such as flood prevention or earthquake defences.

(viii) The **pattern of spending over past years** will affect current living standards. A country which over recent years has invested heavily in education and training, or in infrastructure and the improvement of (worthwhile) public facilities is likely now to benefit in its quality of life as compared with a country which, for several years, has applied most of its income to current consumption.

(ix)   Some countries now are paying a severe penalty for, in the past, living beyond their means: by **borrowing heavily** they are burdened with hefty payments of interest to creditor countries. Other countries, for various reasons, have managed their financial affairs more beneficially.

(x)   The costs of economic growth can be high in **quality of life** terms. The countries which take steps to prevent further amenity loss must expect to pay a price in the present (temporarily depressing recorded levels of national income); other countries will merely 'live for the day'.

(xi)   To be meaningful, national income figures need to be adjusted for the **effects of inflation**. The basis of adjustment for inflation may vary between countries, affecting the interpretation and comparison of income figures.

Viewed as a whole, the term **national income** can mean different things. Unless adequate allowance is made for the depreciation of capital assets, officially reported figures of income may be noticeably misleading. How provision is made varies between countries.

42   METHODS

> **Pass marks.** This was a technical question on national income accounting, not just about the circular flow of income. Note that part (b) was worth 14 marks and is not just concerned with problems of the black economy.

(a)   National income can be defined as Gross National Product (GNP) at factor cost less depreciation. The Gross National Product is a calculation of the overall level of activity in an economy.

Three sets of statistics can be used to calculate GNP. Firstly, it is calculated by measuring the total **expenditure** in the economy by households, firms and the government. This figure is adjusted to take into account imports and exports: exports are merely expenditure in the economy by foreign consumers, and imports can best be considered as negative exports. Income from property abroad refers to rewards paid by foreigners to domestic households for the use of domestic factors of production. Expenditure-based GNP measures what the spending agents in the economy have paid out for the goods and services they have consumed; consequently, since goods and services are sold to spending agents gross of indirect taxes, expenditure-based GNP will include an indirect tax element. To make expenditure-based GNP comparable to other methods of GNP calculation, it is necessary to adjust the figures to remove the indirect tax element (and also, conversely, any element of subsidy). With-tax GNP is known as GNP at market prices and GNP net of tax as GNP at factor cost (ie GNP adjusted to represent that portion of expenditure received by firms).

Secondly, GNP is calculated by measuring the total **income** received by households and firms. Since all expenditure in an economy which does not go out to pay for imports must be received by participants in that economy, income based GNP should have the same value as expenditure based GNP. There is no need to adjust income based GNP for indirect taxes and subsidies since the government will already have collected its indirect taxes from expenditure before it is received by households and firms as income. Imports can be wholly ignored since income cannot naturally include monies paid out to foreign countries (and expenditure based GNP takes imports out of consideration by deducting them from exports).

Thirdly, GNP is calculated by measuring the **output** from firms in the economy. Since expenditure in the economy less any amounts spent on imports and to pay indirect taxes must be paid to firms in exchange for goods, we would expect the total amounts of goods sold to be equal to expenditure based GNP except for the fact that the latter also takes into account income from property abroad.

(b) The three approaches for calculating GNP generally do not produce the same results in practice, and can only be reconciled by the introduction of **residual errors**. There are a number of difficulties in collecting the statistical information, as follows.

(i) Some of the definitions are arbitrary, for example:

(1) production only includes goods and services paid for and not work done by an individual for his own benefit; and imputed or 'notional' value is usually assigned to such work;

(2) goods which have a serviceable life of several years are included in national income at their full value in the year in which they were bought, despite the fact that they will render services over a number of years;

(3) government services which are not paid for (eg the police) are included in national income at cost.

(ii) Much of the raw data is anyway incomplete and inaccurate; income-based GNP, for example, is compiled partially from tax returns; other data is based on estimates.

(iii) There is a serious danger of double-counting: if a firm buys vegetables from a farmer to produce soup, both the output of the vegetables by the farmer and the output of the vegetables by the firm in the form of soup will be included in output-based GNP.

(iv) Although transfer payments (ie the transfer of income from one person to another, eg from a taxpayer to a person in receipt of social security) do not affect national income, net transfer payments from abroad increase the total size of a nation's income and efforts must be made to calculate them.

(v) National Income includes a rise in the value of stocks; since this does not reflect real income, such a rise should not be included.

43   INJECTIONS AND WITHDRAWALS

> **Pass marks**. Note that investment is *not* the same as saving. Investment is used to produce goods and services in the future. Note that the rectangular circular flow of income drawn here presumes a closed economy in which there are only households and firms.
>
> **Examiner's comment**. Most candidates coped well with part (a). Many produced useful diagrams of the circular flow model and gave clear explanations of the nature of injections and withdrawals. The best answers gave a clear explanation of the concept of equilibrium and of the role of injections and withdrawals in achieving equilibrium. Weaker answers were characterised by poor and mislabelled diagrams, and by a failure to relate injections and withdrawals to the circular flow mechanism. For part (b), few candidates worked through the model to show the effect on the level of national income and the ultimate amount of saving. The weaker answers were often characterised by the mere listing of points.

(a)   Below is set out a simple model of the **circular flow of national income** showing only two groups, **firms** and **households**. Households earn their income from firms as **rent, wages, interest** and **profits** from selling to firms and households **land, labour, capital** and **entrepreneurship**. Firms earn their income from households as consumers' expenditure by selling goods and services to households.

The circular flow of income

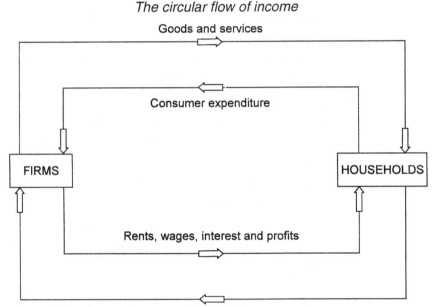

The circular flow diagram illustrated presumes that households spend all the money they earn and that firms sell all of the goods and services (output) they produce.

The circular flow model shown will correspond more closely to reality if we include government and the external economy (ie international trade), and if we drop the assumption that all income is spent. To do this, we need to introduce the concept of injections into and withdrawals from the circular flow. An injection adds to the income of domestic firms not resulting from an increase in households' spending.

Injections into the economy comprise '**G**' for **government expenditure**, '**I**' for **investment** and '**X**' for **exports**. In other words, they consist of expenditure by government, business and foreigners. We can also refer to the **fiscal sector**, the **private sector** and the **foreign sector**. These are all supplementary to, that is they do not include, household expenditure.

Government spending. Something like 42p in each pound spent every day in the UK is spent by the government. That is £220 billion a year out of all spending or national income of £530 billion, on things like education, social services, defence, transport, trade and industry, environment and agriculture.

Investment. This is spending by business on things like office furniture, plant and equipment, vehicles and buildings. It involves adding to or replenishing capital stock.

Exports. These are goods and services sold overseas.

Sometimes called leakages, **withdrawals** comprise 'T' for **taxation**, 'S' for **savings** and 'M' for **imports**. Withdrawals comprise income not passed into the circular flow of national income.

Taxation. Examples are **direct taxes** like income tax, corporation tax, capital gains tax, inheritance tax and petroleum tax, and **indirect taxes** like VAT oil duties, excise duties on alcohol and tobacco and oil duties. Included in other taxes are council taxes, road tax, television licence and airport taxes.

Savings consist of income not spent on consumption.

Imports. This is the purchase of goods and services from overseas.

Included in both exports and imports in the basic national income model are net capital transfers, overseas profits and speculative money flows.

The circular flow of income will be in **equilibrium** provided that **total injections equal total withdrawals**. If one is greater or less than the other national income will rise or fall accordingly. All of this affects the capacity of the nation's resources. For example, if injections exceed withdrawals, planned spending will now exceed available output, and producers will respond by expanding output. As national income rises, so will withdrawals, ie extra savings, taxes and imports. When the rise in withdrawals equals the original increase in injections, equilibrium will be restored but now at a higher income level.

(b) **Savings,** as we saw above, are a **withdrawal** from the circular flow of income. Therefore a **rise in the savings ratio** implies a lowering of the level of household consumption. With reduced consumer spending, the income of businesses falls and businesses find that demand does not match the output levels which they had planned. Firms will react by allowing their stocks to fall, which is equivalent to a dis-investment or lowering of investment.

All of this is exacerbated by the **multiplier effect**, that is the number by which a change in investment is multiplied to achieve the change in the equilibrium level of national income. The fall in output will result in a fall in employment and income levels.

The level of national income will continue to be driven down until equilibrium, that is the point at which planned withdrawals equal planned injections, is restored. With a new lower level of national income, firms will be operating in a downturn of the business cycle.

An increase in savings will also have the effect of putting more funds into the hands of **financial intermediaries**. The price of money, that is **interest rates**, will tend to fall, according to the **loanable funds theory**. A higher level of funds available more cheaply may boost investments. This *may* restore all or part of investments, depending on other determinants, including the confidence which businesses may have about the future, particularly the prospect of growth or otherwise of national income. Contraction of the national income may **lower business confidence**, so that the boost in investment does not occur.

44   DATA RESPONSE QUESTION: CONSUMER EXPENDITURE

> **Pass marks.** Part (a) of this question is asking for *description*, so you should not seek to *explain* the trends until you start part (b).

(a) The table shows the component parts of consumer expenditure in the UK between 1970 and 1990 expressed at 1985 prices. This means that the increases shown are real increases in consumer expenditure. Expressing the figures using a common base year removes the effect of inflationary price rises on consumer expenditure in money terms.

Total consumer expenditure rose by 73% over the twenty years to 1990. The largest rises were recorded for consumer durables (196%), other services (124%), other goods (101%) and clothing and footwear (97%). Rises below the average were recorded for energy products (42%), and rent, water and rates (42%). The slowest growing categories were drink and tobacco (18%) and food (14%). For inferior goods, consumption falls as incomes rise. The fact that all sectors showed positive growth indicates that no sector was inferior overall, in this technical sense.

As a result of these changes, by 1990 the **other services** sector had grown to 33.3% of total expenditure compared with 25.7% in 1970 and consumer durable goods made up 10.2% of the total compared with 5.9% in 1970. The share of total expenditure represented by food, drink and tobacco declined from 30.9% in 1970 to 20.7% in 1990.

Working

	Increase on 1970		Percentage of total		
	1980 %	1990 %	1970 %	1980 %	1990 %
Consumer durable goods	65	196	5.9	7.9	10.2
Food	5	14	18.4	15.4	12.2
Drink and tobacco	23	18	12.5	12.3	8.5
Clothing and footwear	34	97	5.7	6.0	6.4
Energy products	20	42	9.1	8.8	7.5
Other goods	32	101	9.6	10.1	11.2
Rent, water and rates	23	42	13.1	12.9	10.7
Other services	29	124	25.7	26.6	33.3
Total expenditure	25	73	100.0	100.0	100.0

(b) The period from 1970 to 1990 was a period of **rising real incomes**, together with some **reduction in levels of direct personal taxation**. There was therefore a rise in real disposable incomes after tax over the period. As well as having more to spend from income, people had increasing confidence to borrow more, and there was an expansion of consumer credit and a decline in the personal savings ratio over the period. Individuals' confidence was encouraged by rising levels of employment and rises in asset values, particularly in the case of owner-occupied housing.

The pattern of expenditure is influenced by the **income elasticities of demand** for different types of product. Income elasticity of demand is a measure of the responsiveness of demand to changes in income. Food, drink and tobacco have relatively low income elasticities of demand. There is a limit to the amount of these products which individuals can consume, and so in a country where almost everyone has enough to eat, it is only by substitution of cheaper foods with more expensive goods that expenditure on food will increase significantly. The rising share of consumer durables and other services reflects the fact that households consume more of these as income rises, and therefore income elasticity of demand is high. As incomes rise, households are able to acquire more durable goods and to buy more services to deal with tasks they might previously have carried out themselves.

Consumer durables also have a **high price elasticity of demand**, and so falls in real prices of these goods resulting from cheaper production methods would be expected to have led to an overall increase in expenditure on them. Additionally, the process of technological advance has expanded the market for consumer durable products over the period.

Expenditure on energy products has risen over the twenty years to 1990, although their share of total expenditure has fallen. This reflects the development of more energy-efficient products, such as in domestic heating, over a period when the real price of oil and other fuels has risen.

(c) **Food** represents a relatively stable constituent of **household expenditure**, and this is reflected in its relatively low income and price elasticities of demand. This is because food is regarded as an essential and, in a relatively affluent country, there is no need for people to go without enough food. As incomes or prices rise or fall, households will not change their expenditure on food by very much, and there will therefore be relatively stable demand.

Consumer durables are different in that their income and price elasticities of demand are higher. They often represent major items of expenditure, such as a television set or a dishwasher, and many are considered to be luxury items. If real incomes fall in a recession, households will readily postpone expenditure on consumer durables until they feel that they can afford them. As the trade cycle moves on to the recovery phase, people will feel more confident and will make purchases which were previously postponed. They may also have increased confidence to make new major purchases out of borrowings. The trade cycle can thus lead to relatively large fluctuations in the demand for consumer durables.

45   AGGREGATE MONETARY DEMAND

> **Pass marks**. To tackle a question like this you must have an appreciation of the way the main aspects of the macroeconomy relate to one another. It is essential that you are able to describe the basic theoretical connections between unemployment, inflation, demand, interest rates, the exchange rate, growth and the money supply. Clearly, this is a huge field of study, but do not be put off. You should be able to grasp the basics from your study manual or even from this kit.

(a) An economy's **aggregate monetary demand** (AD) is the total value of all the purchases of domestically produced goods and services made by firms and households during a given reference period, usually one year. It has **four components. Consumption** (C) consists of purchases by households for their own private use. **Investment** (I) is spending by firms on the creation of capital goods for use in their businesses. **Government expenditure** (G) includes investment in fixed assets, such as roads, payment of public sector salaries and expenses and welfare payments. Finally, **net export demand** (X-M) consists of purchases of domestically produced goods by firms and households in other countries minus purchases by domestic firms and households of goods and services produced abroad.

(b) (i) An **appreciation in the exchange rate** means that **each unit of domestic currency can be exchanged for a greater amount of foreign currency than previously** and, conversely, each unit of a foreign currency may only be exchanged for a smaller amount of domestic currency. If export prices in domestic currency remain the same, they will be more expensive in term of foreign currency, while imports priced in foreign currency will be cheaper in terms of domestic currency. As a result, **imports** (M) are likely to increase in volume and **exports** (X) are likely to fall, assuming that demand is price elastic. **Net export demand** will be **smaller** and therefore **AD will be reduced.**

(ii) The propensity to save is the proportion of household income which is saved rather than spent on consumption. If this proportion were reduced, the amount spent on consumption would rise and so AD would increase.

(iii) The level of business confidence reflects firms' collective expectations about future economic activity. If confidence is rising, firms are expecting turnover and profit to increase. Their expectation of increased demand will lead them to increase production, build stocks and po'ssibly to invest in extra productive capacity. This spending increases AD, as do any extra wages paid, up to the limit of the marginal propensity to consume.

(c) The principal long term goal of economic policy is a high but sustainable rate of **economic growth** since this is likely to improve the material well-being of the population in terms of both individual wealth and services provided by government. An important short-term goal is the **avoidance of high levels of unemployment**, which both wastes a productive resource and creates a range of social problems. The control of **inflation** is often considered to be an important policy goal because it has undesirable side effects and high levels of inflation can hamper growth. A country which is committed to a fixed exchange rate will a seek to maintain **stability in its balance of payments**, while a country with a floating exchange rate will wish to minimise its fluctuations.

If the economy is in **recession** or, in Keynesian terms, there is a **deflationary gap**, a rise in AD should reduce the resulting **demand-deficient unemployment**. Firms would expand output and take on more employees. However, an increase in AD will not reduce frictional, seasonal or structural unemployment. When demand-deficient unemployment has been reduced to low levels, further increases in AD will create an inflationary gap and inflation may follow.

However, economic growth requires continuing buoyant demand to encourage firms to invest in increased capacity. If this investment takes place, non-inflationary long term growth may follow. For this to happen there must either be an increase in the size of the available labour force or an increase in productivity. The **natural increase in the population** and an increase in the **participation rate** can provide more labour to enable growth to continue.

A rise in AD is unlikely to contribute to the control of inflation and may cause it to increase. This is likely to happen when there is full employment and an inflationary gap. **Scarcity of labour** will force wages up and the increasing costs will be easier to pass on than when demand is low.

A rise in AD is likely to affect the balance of payments and the exchange rate. If domestic production cannot expand fast enough, goods destined for export will be diverted to domestic consumption and more imports will be sucked in. If inflation rises, exports will become more expensive and imports cheaper, emphasising the adverse effect on the balance of payments. A fixed exchange rate will come under pressure and a floating rate is likely to fall unless interest rates are raised to attract capital flows into the country.

46   DATA RESPONSE QUESTION: TRADE CYCLE

> **Pass marks**. The question requires an explanation of what is *meant* by the 'trade cycle'. From the mark allocation it would seem that a full discussion of the possible causes is not required. Explanation of the accelerator principle is helped by an example.
>
> *Other points*. The indirect effects of interest rate investments may be as important as the direct effects. The is true in interpreting the data. A high correlation between interest rate changes and changes in the level of business investment does not make interest rate changes the sole, unqualified causal factor.
>
> **Examiner's comment**. Answers were often rather thin and lacking in economic analysis. Candidates found part (b) the most difficult; few seemed to have any real knowledge of the accelerator model of investment. Parts (a) and (c) were better answered, but the answers often lacked any real depth.

(a)   **Trade cycle** is the term used to describe the phenomenon of periodic alternating **booms** and **slumps** in a national economy or throughout the world, showing major imbalance between supply and demand. These were experienced quite regularly in the 19th century. In the relatively prosperous 1950s and 1960s the average duration of 4-5 years was short compared with the prolonged depression of the inter-war years.

In the **slump** or **depression** there will be a low level of both demand and capital utilisation, together with heavy unemployment. Generally profits and business confidence will be low. A recession is an extreme of a fall in real national income (normally measured as negative notional income for two quarters in succession).

In the **recovery phase** or **upswing** there will be rising consumption, expanding production and the replacement of old machinery, and prices will start to rise. In the boom phase, prices will be rising rapidly, and investment will be high with increased capacity being installed. There will be key labour shortages and wage rates will be rising. There may be production bottlenecks.

From the data, cycles can be identified as follows.

A moderate **boom** in the UK economy peaked in 1979: GDP for that year shows a falling off in the growth rate. It is believed that the cycle which started in 1979 would have lasted until about 1984 but for the Falklands War which acted as an external factor to stimulate the UK economy into a GDP growth figure for 1983 of 3.7%. The GDP figure for 1984 (2.0%) reflects the return to 'internal' influences and suggests the recovery phase. The boom peaked in 1988 (GDP growth 4.9%) and then moved into a deep and prolonged recession. In 1993 recovery was underway and was well established in 1994. The figures show the UK economy to be in recession in 1980-81 and again in 1991-92.

(b)   The **accelerator principle** is about the effect of the **rate of change in national income** upon the **level of investment in the economy**. It can be explained as follows. When income is increasing, it will be necessary to invest in order to increase capacity to produce goods for consumption. In a boom period, expectations will be high and therefore will favour much more investment. Conversely, when income is falling it may not be necessary to replace capital assets as they wear out. The outlook will then tend to be highly adverse, so further deferring replacement decisions. Investment expenditure might then fall heavily.

When income is constant, it is necessary merely to replace existing machinery as it wears out. If income starts to rise and product demand rises with it, it will be necessary to expand production capacity. Each £1 increase in income is likely to lead to an increase of more than £1 in investment expenditure: plant and machinery is normally intended for an earning life of several years. The ratio may, for instance, be £5 of investment for every £1 to be added to annual output. As spending increases, the multiplier effect increases national income much more. This in turn brings the accelerator into operation.

In the following illustration the initial increase in consumption lifts demand in each of years 2 and 3. A ratio of 5:1 is assumed for capital expenditure to the addition in annual output.

Year	Demand (C)	Total investment required	Change in investment (I)		Effect on national income (C+I)
	£m	£m	£m		£m
1	10	50	-		10
2	12	60	+10	(12 + 10)	22
3	16	80	+20	(16 + 20)	36
4	16	80	0	(16 + 0)	16
5	14	70	−10	(14 − 10)	4

In year 4, demand fails to increase; therefore no extra investment is required. The fall in new investment results in a reduction in national income. In consequence, consumption falls also. The accelerator then goes into reverse.

The data provides evidence of the accelerator effect. The big increase in business investment in 1978 follows a relatively strong rise in GDP from the mid-1970s to 1978. The falling off of increase in GDP in 1979 led to a fall to +3.4% in business investment. The recessions of 1980 and 1981 led to negative business investment in both years. The rise in GDP in 1982 is larger than at first appears (ie moving from − to +). The increase in business investment in 1982 (+ 8.4%) follows the cut-back in the two previous years. The large increase in GDP in the later 1980s brought about a major acceleration in business investment in 1987 and 1988. The subsequent decline in GDP, into recession, brought about a reduction in business investment through 1990-92. In 1993 and 1994, business investment responded to the upswing in GDP.

(c) **Interest rates** represent the **cost of borrowing funds**. According to the **loanable funds theory**, the demand for funds is inversely related to movements in interest rates.

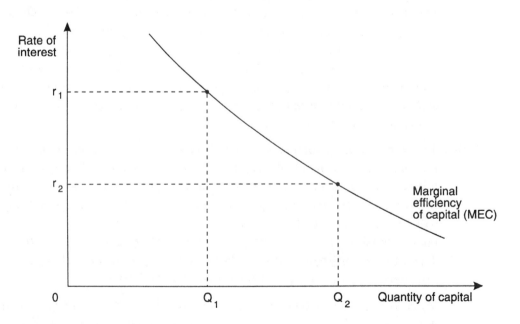

At interest rate r_1, the demand for funds is Q_1. At the lower rate of r_2, the demand for funds is Q_2. The curve represents the marginal efficiency of capital: the return on funds available to the borrower of funds. At a lower borrowing cost, the productivity of capital rises, as a higher return overall is obtainable.

The basic explanation of interest rate changes on capital investment decisions is that, with increases in interest rates, capital investment will fall; whereas with falls in interest rates, capital investment will rise. This, however, is simplistic as an explanation.

The impact of changes in interest rates on the expenditure of firms will be various. Capital expenditure decisions are more likely to be affected by movements in longer term interest rates, especially long-term projects. However, when financial conditions become acute, the cost of shorter term funds will also influence project decisions. Decisions on stock levels will be affected by movements in short to medium-term interest rates.

A high proportion of **capital investment in the private sector** is financed from retained profits, insulating firms to some extent from interest rate changes. Moreover, investment projects already under way cannot easily or economically be curtailed.

Interest rates are one of several factors which need to be considered in investment decisions. Forecast consumer demand, selling price levels, inflationary effects and general business confidence will also be taken into account. The indirect effects of interest rate changes on these factors may be as important as the direct influence of such changes.

The data shows a high **correlation between interest rate levels and changes in business investment**. Thus, the substantial rise in interest rates in 1979 and 1980 was followed by the heavy fall in business investment through to 1981. The modest fall in interest rates in 1982 in itself would hardly account for the dramatic rise in business investment in that year; perception of the likely future downward path of interest rates was a more likely contributory factor.

The fall in interest rates to 1988 appears to have brought about a major rise in investment in 1987 and 1988. The subsequent rise in interest rates in 1989 and 1990 correlates with the heavy fall in investment. The fall in interest rates from 1991 correlates with the improvement in the level of business investment. However, statistical correlation does not necessarily mean that the changes in interest rates were the dominant or sole causal factor. The whole context in which the interest rate changes took place would need to be taken into account.

47   TUTORIAL QUESTION: GOVERNMENT EXPENDITURE

There are essentially two means by which a government may finance its expenditure. These are the **raising of revenue from taxation** and **from borrowing**. It is customary to distinguish between direct taxation and indirect taxation. In the UK, **direct taxation** is collected by the Inland Revenue and direct taxes are mainly levied on incomes and transfers of capital. The main direct taxes are personal income tax, corporation tax, petroleum revenue tax and capital gains tax.

Indirect taxes can be either specific or *ad valorem*. Specific taxes have a fixed money value, whereas *ad valorem* taxes are levied as a percentage of value. In this case, the amount paid in tax varies directly with the value of purchases subject to taxation. The main indirect taxes levied in the UK are VAT (value added tax), and the excise duties on tobacco, oil and alcohol. When planned government expenditure exceeds planned revenue a budget deficit exists. This is financed by borrowing. The public sector borrowing requirement (PSBR) is the total amount the public sector needs to borrow from the private sector and from overseas for the year ahead. It therefore consists of borrowing by the central government (ie the Central Government Borrowing Requirement (CGBR)), by the local authorities and by the public corporations. The National Debt is the total accumulated sum of all outstanding government debt.

Taxation is more than an instrument for raising revenue, as taxes have a number of effects on the economy, as follows.

(a) **Fiscal policy**. The government is by far the economy's largest spender and can exert a powerful influence on total spending by variations in its own expenditure. Where a **deflationary gap** exists (ie at the full employment level of income there is a deficiency of aggregate demand), an increase in government spending without any changes in taxation will, via the multiplier process, raise the equilibrium level of national income. Alternatively the government might decide to leave the level of public spending unchanged and reduce taxation. Cuts in the rates of taxation on incomes and expenditures will raise the levels of real disposable income and lead to an increase in consumption spending. A reduction in the rate of corporation tax may serve as a stimulant to investment spending. All these changes in the rate of spending will have multiplier effects on income. A reduction in taxes will also increase the level of saving, as some of the increase in disposal income will be saved.

Alternatively if the government wished to **reduce the level of aggregate demand**, one way would be an increase in taxation aimed at reducing consumption and investment spending. The level of spending would not fall by the amount of the increased tax revenue because there would be some fall in savings.

(b) **The distribution of income and wealth**. One view is that a major function of the budget should be to reduce the inequalities of income and wealth which result from the operation of market forces. The main instruments for achieving this aim are **progressive taxes** on income and wealth and the redistribution of this revenue in the form of benefits (in money and in kind) which will help the poor far more than the rich. For the UK it seems that the impact of the tax system as a whole is broadly neutral and the progressive element in public finance is provided by the benefits system, the rich getting back in services much less than they pay in taxes, with the opposite applying to those who are least well off.

(c) **Incentives to work**. Taxation of income may act as a disincentive to work effort. The effects on effort may be analysed by looking at the income and substitution effects on income taxes. Taxing income from work makes the worker worse off in that he can afford to buy less. The effect of the tax might therefore be to encourage him to do more work in order to restore the level of his disposable income. This is the **income effect**. The imposition of the tax also, however, reduces the opportunity cost of leisure, ie leisure is now cheaper. Less income is now lost by working less hard than would be the case without the tax. Thus there might be a **substitution effect**, encouraging the worker to take more leisure, and to work less.

The income and substitution effects pull in opposite directions, hence economic theory is ambiguous with respect to the impact of direct taxation on work effort. Empirical evidence on the matter is not conclusive but there is no strong empirical support for the contention that direct taxation acts as a disincentive to work.

(d) **Effects on saving, investment and enterprise**. Although a tax on income reduces the ability to save, its effects on the willingness to save are far from clear. The tax will have two effects: a relatively high rate of income tax might reduce the incentive to save because it will substantially reduce the income (interest) on savings. However, someone saving with the object of attaining some given future income (for example a retirement pension) will have to increase his rate of saving if the rate of income tax is increased.

An income tax may also act as a **disincentive to risk-taking and enterprise**. A tax on profits will make the expected returns from new investment appear far less attractive than the gross returns. Any disincentive effects will be greater where the tax is progressive. In addition to its effect on the incentive to invest, a tax on profits will reduce the ability to invest. Retained profits provide a large part of the funds which finance new investment, so that a tax on corporate income will tend to reduce a firm's ability to save.

(e) **Effect of taxes on wealth and capital.** A tax on wealth may encourage its more productive use. It will oblige the holders of wealth to move their resources out of assets which earn no income and into income earning assets. A wealth tax may, however, lead to large scale avoidance and encourage the movement of wealth out of the country. The price of wealth held in the form of real assets may be driven downwards if people are forced to sell assets in order to meet their tax liabilities.

(f) **Effects of indirect taxation.** Indirect taxes can be used to discriminate between different goods and services and hence affect the allocation of resources. So, for example, an attempt to divert particular goods to export markets might be supported by imposing taxes on these same goods when sold in the home market. Also where the social costs of producing a good are considerably higher than the private costs, the imposition of an indirect tax might be justified as a means of raising prices to a level which fully reflects the social costs of production.

Effects of borrowing. An important aspect of the PSBR is its effect on the money supply, and in particular its relationship with M4. In practice, the effect of an increase in the PSBR on the money supply is uncertain since its impact on M4 may be offset in whole or in part by a change in any of the other components which make up M4. Nevertheless, the authorities remain convinced that there is a central link and thus that a rise in the PSBR leads to a rise in the money supply. This particularly concerns the present government because its monetarist perspective leads it to argue that an increase in the money supply will lead to an increase in the rate of inflation.

The **National Debt** may impose a burden on the economy. It is often argued that a burden is imposed via the community being taxed to meet interest payments on the debt and to redeem part of the debt. However, to the extent that the National Debt is held internally, there is simply a redistribution of income within the community: the generation which receives interest payments from holding the National Debt is also the generation which pays taxes to meet those interest payments. Taken as a whole, the community is neither better off nor worse off.

It is possible, however, for the National Debt to impose a burden on present and future generations. To the extent that the National Debt is held externally (ie the government borrows from abroad), interest payments on the debt and its redemption give foreigners claims on domestic output which can only be met from exports. Hence what the domestic economy is able to consume will be less than domestic output. A burden has therefore been transferred to future generations who must cut their consumption because of debts incurred in the past. Finally, there are costs of administering the National Debt which are paid out of current tax receipts. If the National Debt did not exist these costs would not be incurred and taxation might well be lower, and hence any economic consequences of taxation would be less than otherwise.

48   MAIN OBJECTIVES

> **Examiner's comment.** The majority of those attempting this question scored relatively high marks especially for part (a). This demonstrates that where candidates have acquired a good understanding of an area of economic theory, the explanation of that theory and its application presents no great difficulties. Weaker answers often merely listed the objectives of macroeconomic policy and made no real attempt to explain them.

(a)   The overall fundamental objective of economic policy in a democratic country is to enhance the welfare or well-being of the community. Towards this end there are or need to be certain key objectives.

   (i)   **The maintenance of 'full employment'.** Full employment may be defined as the full utilisation of all factors of production. The existence of persistently high unemployment of labour is objected to on the grounds of the resulting under-utilisation of national resources and the consequential loss of output and unnecessarily depressed living standards.

   It is now generally recognised that to be economically sustainable, the level of employment must be compatible with a low and stable level of inflation. Artificially maintaining or even raising employment levels, eg by over-manning or by public handouts, would only work against other economic objectives, for example through its effect on efficiency.

   An important aim is to improve the level and quality of training and therefore of skills, to overcome the common mis-match between job vacancies and the numbers unemployed.

   (ii)   **Price stability.** The government is concerned not merely with stability of prices as such, but also with the level of inflation, the expectations of what the general level of prices will be in the future, and the effects of this on confidence. Major upsurges in inflation require government intervention and inevitably result in wasteful under-utilisation of resources in the ensuing period of deflation.

   (iii)   **Equilibrium in the balance of payments over time.** A deficit on the balance of payments current account cannot be sustained indefinitely. The aim will not be to achieve the maximum possible surplus as this can work against the achieving of other economic objectives, through an exceptionally high exchange rate. In practice, the objective is likely to be to achieve a modest surplus on the balance of payments.

   (iv)   **Economic growth.** The preceding objectives are really subsidiary to the prime objective of achieving and maintaining a reasonable, acceptable rate of growth, ie an increase in real national income. This can allow a widespread increase in living standards and makes possible the achievement of wider welfare objectives, eg maintaining the quality of the environment.

(b)   **Fiscal policy** involves the direction of the economy through public financing and public expenditure. Public financing includes government borrowing and taxation. It is thus concerned with the overall relationship between government expenditure and income.

   Governments may pursue a policy of **fiscal deficit,** with government expenditure exceeding its income. Often this is forced upon governments through high levels of expenditure commitments. When pursued out of choice, it could be in order to regenerate an economy later in a recession, ie to reduce unemployment and to get back on a path of economic growth. The aim would be to raise aggregate monetary demand, achieved possibly by means of tax cuts. A reduction in income tax, for instance, would have increased spending power in people's hands which the government would hope would be spent to add to the flow of national income. Increased spending within the UK on consumer goods could then raise the level of investment expenditure, so raising the level of national income. A problem there could be the high marginal propensity of UK consumers to buy foreign-made goods, resulting in harmful side-effects on the balance of payments.

Alternatively, a government could aim for a **budget surplus**. This would mean that revenue from taxation exceeds government expenditure. This would result in a fall in aggregate monetary demand. This could be applied at some stage in an attempt to deal with an over-heated economy and to combat a high level of inflation. Often, though, in such a condition there is already a large budget deficit and the immediate effort will be concerned with reducing that rather than actually moving into surplus.

A budget surplus could also have the intended effect of reducing a balance of payments deficit. It would be hoped that the reduction in consumer spending power would diminish the demand for foreign goods. UK experience, however, shows general deflation to be a very blunt weapon to be used for this purpose.

Fiscal policy could be used more specifically to achieve economic objectives. Increases or reduction in taxes or government subsidies could be used to attempt to influence **employment** (eg reduction in employer national insurance contributions or the payment of an employment subsidy), to influence the level of **training** being provided (a subsidy to employers), or to raise the level of **private sector investment** (through investment allowances or less directly through a reduction in corporation tax).

(c)   The broad aim of **supply side policies** is to remove the obstacles which prevent or discourage people and firms from adapting quickly to changing conditions of market demand and changing techniques of production. The emphasis on supply side policies stems from a belief that if markets can be made to operate more efficiently, this will encourage economic growth and employment without adding to the risk of inflation.

There are various policies which the government might adopt in an attempt to improve the supply side of the economy. Measures to **improve training**, both for school leavers and for those already in work, can be used to assist the operation of the labour market, and labour mobility can be improved by providing better information on job opportunities and financial assistance to those people considering moving to take up a new job. Other measures may be aimed at trade unions and other restrictive practices which cause inflexibility in the labour market.

A number of policies can be implemented to **improve the efficiency of capital markets**. For example the abolition of exchange controls, which took place in the UK in 1979, removes the restriction on the flow of funds into and out of the country. The government can attempt to make its policies tax-neutral in respect of different savings schemes. The aim is to improve efficiency by allowing savings to go where the best combination of risk and return is deemed to be. Financial markets can be deregulated to encourage competition in the seeking and allocation of capital funds. Competition has been encouraged in the UK by the Building Societies Act 1986 allowing the building societies to compete more effectively with the retail bank and by changes in the Stock Exchange rules to permit dual-capacity trading and to abolish fixed brokers' commissions.

The government's **taxation policy** is regarded as an important aspect of supply side economics. It is claimed that cuts in the rates of personal taxation, for example, and increases in the tax threshold can be used as an incentive mechanism to encourage people to enter employment or to work harder. Similarly, it is claimed that dependence on state support can be reduced by cutting welfare and unemployment benefits or by making them taxable. The broad aim of all these measures is to ensure that, in general, people are better off in work than out of work. Cuts in corporation tax rates can also be introduced to encourage firms to invest in more productive capital by reducing the taxation of profits.

The government can make its **competition policy** more rigorous, remove unfair restrictions on trade and break up monopolies. This should encourage competition in the market place which, in turn, should improve economic performance. This was the basis of the Competition Act 1980, giving the Monopolies and Mergers Commission the powers to investigate firms suspected of anti-competitive practices, and the programme of privatisation and deregulation which took place during the 1980s and early 1990s.

In general, supply side measures concentrate on **encouraging entrepreneurship and self-reliance**. The aim of the government is then to create an **environment conducive to enterprise and risk-taking** in which individual initiative is rewarded as the basis for increasing economic efficiency.

49   PRODUCTION POSSIBILITY CURVE

> **Pass marks**. Correct drawing of the diagram is important here.
>
> **Examiner's comments**. The best scripts showed a good grasp of the production possibility curve and the concept of scarcity of resources which underlies it. The poorer scripts contained less clear explanations of the curve and often produced mislabelled diagrams.

(a)   A **production possibility curve** (PPC) show the different combinations of goods possible to be produced in an economy bearing in mind, (a) the resources available (b) the use of the best technology, (c) maximum employment and (d) the most efficient combination of all of these.

An illustration of the PPC is shown below.

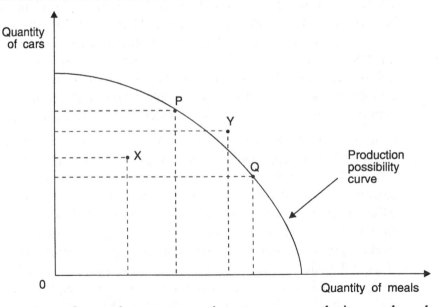

Let us suppose that we have a two-product economy, producing meals and cars. Combinations like X within the curve are inefficient. Here, we are not bringing in all the resources available to us. Likewise, combinations like Y, lying outside the curve, are impossible to achieve because we have insufficient resources.

What we have to do is reallocate resources into an optimal efficient mix which is *on the curve* itself. This will mean moving resources back and forth between the 'meals' industry and the 'cars' industry until we achieve the best mix, that is when they are on the efficiency curve.

Once on the curve, this two-product economy can then move along the curve to rest at *any point* to reflect the different volumes of meals and cars desirable at any one time. If you have more meals, you have fewer cars and if you have fewer meals, you have more cars.

Many problems arise from the scarcity of resources.

One is that it may not be possible to move production out, say from position X, to the possibility curve. Another is that there may be a scarcity of a particular **material resource** essential for a particular product: this might be fuel for cars, without which the steel for car bodies may lie unused. Another scarce resource may be **skilled or well-educated labour**. This may keep an economy down to subsistence level while other economies flourish.

Entrepreneurial skills are another resource that will keep production well within the PPC.

(b) **Economic growth** would push the productivity curve upwards and to the right. Total production would increase and consumers could have, in this case, more meals and cars as well. Instead of the **opportunity cost** being (say) either one extra car per 4000 meals, there may now be the choice of having one car per 5000 meals. In other words the *shape* of the PPC may change, giving a change in marginal rate of transformation between cars and meals.

Economic growth is dependent on a number of factors. Firstly, demand must be sufficient to utilise the capacity of the system. This may come from **domestic demand** as well as from **overseas demand** for exports.

On the other hand, **imports of foreign goods** lessen the utilisation of domestic resources. At the same time, the demand must be relatively stable whilst growing in line with increase in capacity.

Supply needs to be facilitated by an **adequacy of natural resources**, suitably applied to economic development. Any country lacking in these has to compensate by excelling in some other way. The availability of natural resources by itself is not sufficient to ensure growth: they need to be utilised with full efficiency.

Investment in capital (eg plant and machinery) is fundamental to economic growth. It can provide the extra capacity but any given investment expenditure, through the multiplier, has a much larger effect on economic activity than the amount of initial outlay. However, surveys over different countries show that there is no full correlation between the level of investment and the rate of economic growth. Investment is a necessary but not sufficient factor towards economic growth. The quality and type of investment are all-important, there not being a constant capital/output ratio. The new capital must be of the right kind at the right time: business systems together with the skills, organisation and motivation of the workforce must match up to the potential of any new equipment. There is the danger of diminishing returns being experienced, as more and more investment is applied to an already large stock of capital. This can be counteracted by the introduction of new technology which might then take an economy into a further path of growth.

Technology enhances economic growth through improved productivity. New materials, processes and techniques can all allow greater growth of output from a given stock of factors of production. Technological progress will be enhanced where there is greater expenditure on research and development.

The **quality of the workforce** is of undoubted importance, indeed in many industries today it is the cardinal factor. To make its due contribution to growth, the labour force needs to be suitably skilled, organised and motivated. Creativity, inventiveness and disciplined intellect are vital elements in business development. Growth in a economy requires not merely producing more but also deriving better value from domestic resources, so improving the terms of trade with other nations. This in turn requires an economic system that works with allocative efficiency, free of forces (eg major monopoly; restrictive practices) which retard adjustment to changed circumstances. It means moving industry on into higher added-value goods and services, thus raising the average real value of products in which the country trades.

In turn, the **ability to compete** with other countries on both price and quality is fundamental to enhancing economic growth. This increases exports and tends to lessen imports, thus promoting domestic activity.

Economic growth may be hindered by the **diversion of resources** from investment and from providing the necessary education and training of the workforce. Such diversion could arise from the **population structure**, for example an increasingly dependent population (old or young). It is claimed that an ageing population might inhibit economic growth through being more cautious and less risk-inclined, but it is difficult to prove. If the **participation rate** (the proportion of the population that is economically active) is low, this might require a relatively small working population to support a relatively large dependent population; resources might then be significantly diverted from industrial development.

A **stable optimistic environment** favours economic growth. Booms and recessions undermine the confidence of both investors and consumers and tend to lead to a short-termist approach to business activity. Major industrial and technological advances, fundamental to sustained economic growth, are undermined. Much diversionary expenditure becomes necessary in a recession, for example unemployment benefit, and investment decisions are deferred or dropped altogether. More favourable economic conditions are a balance between aggregate demand and aggregate supply, a high level of capacity utilisation (= low unit costs), together with an environment which facilitates business forecasting and therefore is conducive to optimal investment decisions.

50 DATA RESPONSE QUESTION: ECONOMIC TRENDS

Pass marks. This question is not complex, and paying attention to how marks are split between the sections will help you to secure the highest mark you can. In part (b)(i) it is acceptable to calculate the real rate of interest by subtraction, as we have done.

(a) **Interest rates** are the cost of borrowing money or the rates of return that are earned by lenders.

In the table, there are four different types of interest.

(i) The **bank base rate** is a 'benchmark' lending rate which is set by the clearing banks. It is the rate by reference to which bank overdrafts are normally set. Most borrowers would be paying a rate which is above base rate. A major 'blue chip' company like ICI might pay 1% over base. An individual might pay 5% over base, to reflect the higher risk of the loan.

(ii)   An **instant access account deposit rate** reflects the rate of interest which the bank pays depositors. Since banks make a profit out of lending, they pay depositors a lower rate than the base lending rate.

(iii)   A **90-day access account deposit rate** is also a rate paid to depositors but will offer a higher rate than an instant access account because a 90-day notice is required to withdraw money.

(iv)   The **mortgage rate** is the interest rate charged by banks and building societies on long-term loans in properties, and will tend to move broadly in line with bank base rates.

(b) (i)   The **nominal rate of interest** is the actual rate of interest in monetary percentage terms, as quoted, while the **real rate of interest** takes into account inflation.

Real rate of interest = Nominal rate of interest *less* inflation rate.

(ii)   Real rate of interest★

1992	1993	1994	1995	1996	1997
4.5%	5.4%	3.2%	3.3%	3.1%	3.3%

★Calculated as: Bank base rate *minus* RPI inflation rate.

Both **inflation** and **nominal interest rates** were low over the period resulting in low real rates of interest, especially between 1994 and 1997. The lower real interest rate from 1994 onwards indicates a less restrictive monetary policy in this period. It is also more stable than the nominal rate.

(c) (i)   The **FTSE 100**, referred to as the 'Footsie', is an index of the shares of the 100 largest companies (in terms of the total value of the company's shares) quoted on the London Stock Exchange. The base value of the index is 1000 at January 1984. The composition of the index changes as companies' total share values ('market capitalisations') change. The 'Footsie' gives an indication of how share prices in general are rising or falling.

(ii)   Share prices can be affected by a number of factors, as follows.

(1)   **Speculative buying.** This takes place when investors believe shares are undervalued, for example in terms of the dividends and profits they are likely to generate in the future.

(2)   **Speculative selling.** This takes place when investors believe shares are overvalued.

(3)   **Political stability.** The market will be more confident in share price valuations if the government is politically stable and is pursuing favoured economic policies.

(4)   **Interest rates.** When interest rates rise, this is normally associated with a fall in share prices because borrowing becomes more expensive, increasing companies' borrowing costs.

(iii)   Two factors that may have contributed to the fall in share prices in 1995 are the **rise in bank base rates** and the **rise in inflation** from 2.3% to 3.5%.

A rise in interest rates makes borrowing more expensive, which will affect companies that are **highly geared**.

An increase in inflation will undermine **confidence in the economy** and may be thought to make future interest rate rises more likely. It may also see investors switch from financial assets such as shares into real assets such as land.

As a consequence of both of these influences, there will be a reduction in the demand for shares that will lead to a fall in share prices.

51 PRIVATISATION

> **Pass marks**. Bear in mind that privatisation is wider in meaning than just the sale of shares in publicly owned utilities to private investors. The economic arguments in favour are based on improved allocative efficiency, for which a more competitive structure may be necessary; and X-efficiency, which may be helped by a change of culture.
>
> **Examiner's comment**. Answers to part (a) were often developed insufficiently given the allocation of marks to it. The best answers outlined the range of meanings attached to the term 'privatisation' from the outright sale of public assets to the contracting out of services in some parts of the public sector. These answers also explained why things like a change of ownership could bring economic advantages such as improved efficiency. In part (b) the better answers explained how the utilities might have monopoly power and hence competition could not be relied upon to ensure benefits for customers.

(a) **Privatisation** is regarded as taking any of three main forms.

   (i) **Transfer of ownership of assets from the state to private investors**. This usually has meant the government offering for sale to individual and institutional shareholders the shares in the big public corporations such as British Telecom, British Gas, British Airways or British Steel. In some cases, the government might, for a while at least, retain a smaller shareholding in the institution concerned. It has also meant the sale to the public, or sometimes by **private placing**, of a partial government shareholding in an industrial company, eg BP and Amersham International.

   (ii) **Contracting-out of work to private firms,** ie work previously carried out by government or local government employees, such as refuse collection, cleaning and catering in the health service, or the running of prisons or prison services.

   (iii) **Deregulation of industries and markets** to allow private firms to compete against state-owned businesses, as with the deregulation of bus and coach services. Such competition had not previously been allowed.

This process is beginning to be extended through the privatisation of merit goods such as education. This might be achieved through 'back door' privatisation (or privatisation *de facto*) as with the provision of free vouchers for the purchase of places in privately run nurseries instead of (the further) setting up and running of publicly owned nurseries.

The economic **arguments in favour** of privatisation may be considered as follows.

   (i) So far as the privatisation increases competition, there might be a **reduction in allocative inefficiency** where the organisation has been run with prices higher than marginal cost. Competition may force an organisation to be more cost-conscious, making it easier for changes in work practices to be introduced and enforced, both operationally and in the management of the organisation. X-efficiency, ie internal efficiency, should therefore improve, resulting in reduced unit costs and scope for price cutting.

   (ii) Where privatisation results in the breaking of a state monopoly, so that a number of competing enterprises are able to operate, **consumer choice** may be enhanced. This in turn would compel the competing firms to be 'on their toes' to identify and respond to consumer demand: quality of service should be improved and innovation encouraged in both products and the means of their production and distribution.

(iii) Privatisation can change the **culture of the organisation**. The often narrow vision of directorate and management and the supply orientation of the organisation can be replaced by a much more commercially aware enterprise. Restraints can be removed on financing and product or market diversification. Links with other companies (eg joint ventures) can be developed and the business can become internationally engaged, as with the development of BT. The resources of each company can thus be more fully utilised.

(iv) It is claimed that the private sector operates **more efficiently** than the public sector. Lower unit costs can then result from the contracting out of services.

(v) There can also be **public financing advantages**. External borrowing by previously nationalised undertakings is switched from the category of 'public expenditure', reducing the pressure on the PSBR. The government also raises funds from the sale of shares in the newly privatised companies. Therefore the government has more latitude in the financing of other areas of the public sector, such as growth in health service provision, or for tax cuts. In the first case, economic and social welfare can be enhanced. In the second case, the tax cuts might result in beneficial incentive effects.

(b) A fundamental for the achievement of the possible benefits of privatisation is the **creation of a competitive market**. This would involve the substitution of a number of smaller producer/suppliers for the single dominant supplier. Generally, in the cases of privatised utilities, this has not happened and private monopoly has replaced the publicly owned monopoly. The reason for this is that utilities tend to be natural monopolies and there have been economic and technological arguments for keeping them as single suppliers.

A **natural monopoly** presents disadvantages for society. The lack of competition may result in a failure to improve efficiency. The fact that a utility is providing an essential service will have tended to make it supply-oriented. Prices could be raised, to the detriment of both industrialists and consumers. This would have consequences for other sectors of the economy, eg if fuel costs were to rise. Supernormal profits could be earned and because of the high barriers to entry (eg exceptionally high setting up costs) this could endure for many years. There is also the danger that safety considerations could be neglected, while uncontrolled negative externalities could have wider harmful effects.

In anticipation of problems resulting from the setting up of privatised monopolies, the UK government has established **regulatory bodies**. Thus Oftel regulates BT, Ofgas regulates British Gas and Ofwat regulates the water industry. The emphasis has been upon using price controls as a substitute for competition: the extent of price increases has been restricted and in some cases price cuts have been imposed. The introduction of capital investment targets has also been proposed.

It has become clear that the potential **competitive gains** from privatisation have generally not in fact occurred and therefore the regulatory bodies are requiring the introduction of more competition. British Gas is required to reduce its share of the commercial market. BT is having to face more domestic competition, in the telecommunications market.

52   DATA RESPONSE QUESTION: UNEMPLOYMENT AND INFLATION

> **Pass marks**. For part (d), you could alternatively discuss the rise in the value of sterling, or the impact of tax rises in a deflationary Budget.
>
> **Examiner's comment**. Many weak answers resulted from not reading the passage with sufficient care.

(a)   The main reasons for the recent **fall in UK unemployment** are as follows.

   (i)   The UK economy has recovered from recession, bringing an upturn in the trade cycle.

   (ii)   Increased consumer spending caused by windfall gains as building societies became plc's has helped to boost aggregate demand.

   (iii)   There has been a slowing down of the annual rate of increase in wages and earning, and so firms can afford to employ more workers.

   (iv)   There have been various government programmes helping to take people off the unemployment register.

(b)   (i)   Recent **Budget measures** contained significant tax increases, which reduces disposable income and so might dampen down consumer expenditure, and therefore employment.

   (ii)   The **strength of sterling** makes UK exports expensive in international markets, making it more difficult for UK exporters to sell abroad. Also, imports would be made cheaper. This could dampen demand and slow the growth in employment.

(c)   The **Phillips curve** was devised by A W Phillips who studied the UK economy over an eighty-year period and concluded that there was an inverse relationship between the rate of inflation and the level of unemployment. As unemployment falls, this leads to an increase in demand and the economy might begin to suffer from demand-pull and cost-push inflation.

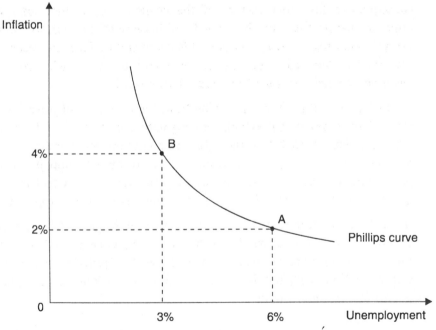

Suppose the economy is at point A in the diagram above, where there is 6% unemployment and 2% inflation. **Keynesian** economists would argue that you could get to point B (3% unemployment and 4% inflation) by increasing some component of aggregate demand - usually government expenditure - and so the government could reduce the level of unemployment. Full employment could be achieved but the opportunity cost would be higher inflation.

The Phillips curve assumes that labour market demand is a key factor. As unemployment levels fall, firms need to compete for labour and wages are pushed up. When the demand for labour is high, trade union power increases and higher wage demands can more easily be passed on by employers when demand is rising.

(d) One of the factors that are operating to ease inflationary pressures in the UK economy is a fall in the annual rate of increase of **wages** and other earnings. Wages are one of the key costs of production and if they rise faster than the productive capacity of the economy then there will be cost push inflation. However, if wage increases are lower, this will reduce inflationary pressures.

A possible reason behind this is the **structural changes in the UK labour market** which have weakened trade union power considerably.

53   PERSISTENT INFLATION

> **Pass marks.** Part (a) is quite simple, but parts (b) and (c) require some knowledge. You must know what is meant by the three phrases used in part (b); the savings rate, for instance, is not the interest rate. Part (c) again requires a grasp of the basics of macreconomics.
>
> **Examiner's comment.** Many candidates appeared to rely on general knowledge rather than bringing economic theory to this question.

(a) Inflation may be defined as a continuing increase in the general level of prices. Prices of individual goods may rise or fall but the overall effect is a persistent year on year increase. The effect is that money gradually loses its purchasing power.

Inflation is measured by price index numbers. In the UK, the retail price index (RPI) reflects changes in the prices of a wide of consumer goods. RPI adjusted to remove the effect of changes in mortgage interest rates (RPIX) is the Government's favoured overall inflation indicator. There are other indices, including those for house prices, manufacturers' inputs and manufacturers' outputs. The Tax and Price Index was established to show how disposable income is affected by changes to both prices and taxes.

(b) (i) Inflation reduces the effective value of given sums of money. Borrowers whose incomes are compensated for inflation benefit at the expense of lenders and those on fixed incomes. This discourages saving and encourages borrowing and spending.

(ii) A country whose inflation rate is higher than those of its trading partners is likely to find its exchange rate under downward pressure. Its exports will become more expensive and therefore less attractive, while imports will become cheaper and will therefore increase. This cannot last long as the balance of payments on current account will be in deficit. Devaluation may well result, or interest rates may have to be raised to encourage the inflow of capital to balance the current deficit. Either course of action is likely to depress the economy.

(iii) As outlined above, inflation can discourage saving and encourage spending. This effect is exaggerated when the rate of interest is less than the rate of inflation and there is thus a negative real interest rate. However, if real interest rates remain positive, this effect is minimised. Also, much saving is contractual, in the form of life insurance and pension premiums, and is likely therefore to continue.

(d) Raising taxes reduces disposable income and hence aggregate demand (AD). The fall in AD will have a deflationary effect as firms will reduce output and reduce prices to move stock and defend market share. However, the fall in output is likely to increase unemployment as firms move to cut costs.

Deflation caused by tax increases is likely to reduce the rate of economic growth. Investment in productive capacity is unlikely if AD is depressed. Also, higher taxation may have a disincentive effect on both work and risk taking, since it reduces the rewards available to both workers and entrepreneurs.

Higher taxes will themselves inevitably feed through into inflation. Indirect taxes affect prices immediately while direct taxes cause higher pay demands. Firms recover the cost of increased pay by passing it on in the form of higher prices.

54   UNEMPLOYMENT

> **Pass marks**. Note that structural unemployment arises from structural change within the economy brought about by fundamental changes in demand, greater foreign competition or changes in technology. Cyclical unemployment is related to the phenomenon of the trade cycle and tends to be more widespread throughout the economy than structural unemployment. 'Demand deficient unemployment' in Keynesian terms may denote a longer term problem which requires state intervention.
>
> *Other points*. Supply-side policy assumes the market, left to itself, to be a self-regulating, self-adjusting mechanism. Any intervention or involvement by the State should be directed towards facilitating the working of that mechanism. A 'natural' level of unemployment is accepted. Reflation by the authorities is therefore regarded as an anathema.
>
> **Examiner's comment**. There were some excellent answers to this question, but most failed to achieve very high marks, especially in part (b). Weaker answers were often unclear about the different types of unemployment and showed very limited knowledge of supply side policy.

(a) **Structural unemployment** results from a structural change in the economy. This may be due to changes in demand, including the introduction of new products into markets, or resulting from the emergence of overseas competitors who are able to produce at much lower unit costs. It may be due to slowness to adapt to changed conditions of supply. Much structural unemployment in the UK in the inter-war years and post-1945 was in the staple industries such as textiles and shipbuilding. The problem was mostly concentrated in the traditional industrial areas and created a regional unemployment problem. In more recent years, structural unemployment has been more widespread as, firstly, whole areas of industrial activity have suffered decline and now financial and distribution services are undergoing rapid change. The South of England, largely insulated for a long time from the adverse effects of industrial change, is now suffering much structural unemployment. The effect is often upon localities and districts rather than whole regions, where, for example, a main employer closes down. A regional or locality multiplier can operate to compound the decline in spending. The situation clearly is much worse where there are few new, substitute employment opportunities.

Technological unemployment is a particular form of structural unemployment. It occurs when the introduction of new technology reduces the demand for labour. Unfortunately, those made redundant are often not equipped - for a while at least - to take on new jobs.

Cyclical unemployment, according to the view of classical economists, was related almost entirely to business cycles: the 'trade cycle', ie alternating boom and slump. Apart from these periodic disturbances, the market mechanism, according to their viewpoint, was sufficiently self-adjusting to ensure that demand would be sufficient to take into new employment those temporarily displaced. According to classical theory, any deficiency in demand is short-lived. The problem is essentially self-correcting; in a depression the adjustment will take rather longer.

Keynesian theory challenged this approach and saw demand deficiency as a longer term phenomenon. The problem was not necessarily self-correcting and intervention by the State might be necessary to deal with the problem. Fundamental to this was the **paradox of thrift**. At times of low consumer/business confidence, people may decide to save more of their income. This then creates a deficiency in demand and so affects employment opportunities. The deficiency in demand could exist for a very long time indeed. This was essentially at variance with the classical view. Saving, regarded by individuals as a virtue, can have seriously harmful effects for society. Furthermore, if real wages were to be cut, this would make things far worse. The intervention of the state to overcome this problem would include, for example, the central government financing infrastructure projects. The concept of the multiplier was central to this: a certain amount injected into the circular flow of national income would radiate through to have a much larger total effect over a period of time. The need for pump-priming was likely to be greatest in a major recession, though the need could exist at other times as well.

The effects of **cyclical or demand-deficient unemployment** can vary greatly according to local conditions at the onset of, say, a recession. Different industries can also be affected differently by a recession. A prolonged recession may make structural unemployment more likely.

(b) **Supply side policy** starts from the premise that the economy is self-regulating: there are 'natural' competitive forces in the economy and problems arise when these are prevented from operating. The blame is put on **state interference**, including various forms of welfare support, and restrictive practices by trade unions as well as within and by firms. The emphasis is placed on costs of production (the origin of the term 'supply side'): by reducing costs, inflation will be better controlled and the longer term effect will be to increase employment opportunities.

Central to supply side policy is that there is a **natural level of unemployment** (including **transitional unemployment** and those who are '**unemployable**'): by excessively trying to reduce this, inflation will be fostered. Subject to that, it is desirable for economic growth that the economy operates at a higher level of employment as is economically possible. Reflation in itself does not deal with problems of economic inefficiency: it is likely to lead to inflation rather than an increase in output.

More specifically, supply side policy includes the following means towards reducing the level of unemployment.

(i) **Reducing the power of trade unions and abolishing minimum wage agreements.** It is contended that trade union power has resulted in wage rates, in some instances, being set above the equilibrium rate. In the diagram below, through trade union bargaining, the wage rate has been set at W_1. At this rate the demand for labour is OL_1, far below the supply of labour OL_2. Without trade union intervention, the wage rate would drop to OW and the demand for that category of labour would rise to OL. The lower wage rate would allow higher-cost producers to enter the industry and so raise the level of employment.

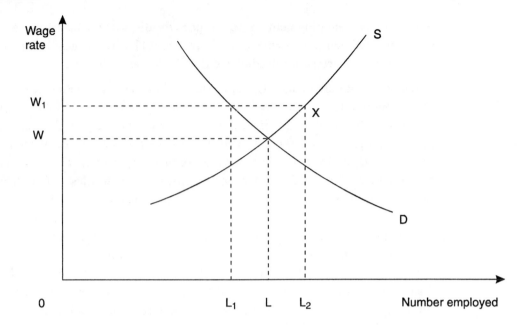

Supply side policies would also be aimed at improving productivity and reducing unit costs throughout, diminishing trade union power. This might be achieved through eliminating restrictive practices, abolishing demarcation agreements and reducing over-manning.

(ii)   **Reducing disincentives to work.** This would include revising various state benefits. It is contended that these may be set at a level which is above the equilibrium wage rate in the lower paid labour markets. The incentive for people to find work is then substantially removed. For those people only temporarily out of work the cuts in benefit might not be so severe but it would be harsh for those in long-term unemployment.

Supply-siders would also argue for revision of the tax system to ensure that income tax rates and allowances do not reduce the incentive to work.

(iii) **Encourage positive incentives to both employ and find employment.** The incentive to employ people could be improved by, for example, cutting employer's national insurance or by temporary subsidies to take on staff. Individual employers could be encouraged to provide, wherever possible, employment arrangements that show a possible avenue of future advancement that may induce people to make a greater effort to seek employment.

(iv)   **Training.** More effective and more widespread training should make labour more efficient and so raise productivity. This would shift the demand curve for labour to the right. Retraining facilities should also be available for those displaced from jobs.

The emphasis from society's viewpoint should be on ensuring the development of basic transferable skills. Workers thus become more adaptable and there may be considerable economies in later periods of re-training. This, however is not always seen by individual employers to be in their own interest. The development of basic skills in school years is, of course, essential for an effective labour force in an advanced economy.

(v)   The **provision of information** and advice on job opportunities.

(vi)   The **provision of relocation facilities and assistance.**

(vii) **Regional policy** directed to improving the infrastructure within a depressed region, to serve also as a catalyst to growth.

(viii) **Reducing public expenditure**, so lessening the '**crowding out**' of private investment. This should also lessen the cost of borrowing generally.

Such measures as a whole would be directed to making businesses more efficient, thereby reducing costs, as well as enhancing incentives both to employ and be employed.

55   FISCAL POLICY AND MONETARY POLICY

Pass marks. The key word in part (b) of the question is 'means'. Firstly, the government needs to ensure that economic conditions are favourable for (ie can make possible) a successful expansionary policy. Open market operations and interest rate reductions would follow. Transmission of that policy into the 'real economy' requires additional demand and that is dependent on business and public confidence.

Examiner's comment. Better answers had no difficulty in distinguishing between fiscal and monetary policy and could give relevant examples of each. Part (b) tended to generate more difficulties, but the better answers identified increasing the money supply or reducing interest rates as the main elements of an expansionary monetary policy. The best answers described the means by which the monetary authorities could bring this about.

(a)   **Fiscal policy** is the management of the economy through public expenditure, taxation and public borrowing. The key aspect is the relationship between **government spending** and **taxes**. Government expenditure operates as an injection into the circular flow of national income; taxation as a withdrawal from it. If, in a given year, the government spends more money than it collects in taxes, this is termed a budget deficit. A deficit has an expansionary or inflationary effect upon the economy. This might be considered appropriate if there is much unemployment. If the government collects more in taxes than it spends this is referred to as a budget surplus. A surplus has a restraining or deflationary effect upon the economy. This would be considered an appropriate policy at a time of significant inflation.

For any given year, the application of fiscal policy may lead to a quite different outcome in respect of both expenditure and taxes than had been planned. The government might have become committed to unexpected areas of expenditure, while tax revenue might be more or less than was expected.

In the 1950s and 1960s, with **Keynesian demand management policies** being pursued, fiscal policy was at the forefront of government economic policy. Thus fiscal policy was the main means of attempting to deal with inflation, often involving frequent changes in public expenditure and taxation. However, the **maintenance of full employment** was given a higher priority than combating inflation, and a brief period of fiscal tightening with limited impact on inflation was likely to be replaced by another expansionary period. As monetarist ideas came to the forefront in the 1970s, fiscal policy became subordinated to the pursuit of monetary policy.

Monetary policy, broadly, is the management of the economy through controlling the quantity of money available and the price of money - the rate of interest to be paid by borrowers. If the quantity of money is expanded, this should lower the rate of interest. As a result spending should be stimulated. This would be expansionary or inflationary. If however the quantity of money is restricted, the rate of interest would rise. This would have a deflationary effect on the economy. In reality, monetary policy is directed to maintaining the stability of income and prices, ie to keep the rate of inflation under control. The ultimate aim is to facilitate economic growth, by providing stability and avoiding economic depressions and slumps.

Monetary policy, in practice, ranges over concern with the following.

(i)   Growth in the money supply

(ii)   The level of, and movements in, interest rates

(iii)   The volume of credit, and growth/contraction therein

(iv)   The volume of expenditure in the economy

(v)   The exchange rate

Official targets may be set for these and performance is closely monitored against the targets.

For much of the 1980s, control of the money supply, through various measurements, was at the forefront of economic management. Considerable difficulties were however encountered in selecting and effectively utilising monetary aggregates in influencing changes in the money supply. Interest rate changes became the central means of control.

Movements in the exchange rate and the **interdependence of interest rates and the exchange rate** are fundamental to monetary policy. If the exchange rate rises, this lowers the cost of imports and so lessens the need for interest rate rises. Through consequential rises in the prices of exports it will also have an unfavourable effect on the balance of payments. If the exchange rate falls, this will cause a rise in the cost of imports, and a fall in export prices, which may necessitate a rise in interest rates. Movements in interest rates, both at home and abroad, will have an effect upon the exchange rate, eg a fall in domestic interest rates will tend to depress the exchange rate, as short-term investment funds are moved to other countries.

(b)   To conduct a successful **expansionary monetary policy**, economic conditions first need to be favourable. If existing inflationary pressures are not first brought under control, the increased money supply will lead to inflationary pressures which may be very difficult to control. Any marked growth in the money supply must first be brought under control. Spare capacity in the system is also desirable, to allow for the expansion in demand without inflationary results.

Fiscal policy also needs to be consistent with monetary management. This may involve diminishing public expenditure: to avoid the **'crowding out' effect** (public expenditure squeezing out possibly more productive private sector expenditure) as well as to lessen inflationary pressures. If this is not done, fiscal policy may be undermining monetary policy.

Monetary policy would then need to operate on **immediate targets,** eg interest rates or the liquid assets held by the banking system. Thus, interest rates could be used to influence the demand by the general public to hold money balances (so affecting the stock of money) rather than other financial assets. Alternatively, if the authorities are able to control the liquid assets of the banks, control could be exercised over total bank deposits and therefore over the money supply.

Open market operations may be used for expansionary purposes. The Bank of England could buy securities from the general public, paying for the gilts with cheques or drafts drawn on itself. The cheques would, in due course, be paid into the general public's deposits in the clearing banks. The money supply thus rises. The banks' cash ratios also are higher than is necessary for prudent banking. The banks therefore expand total lending and deposits towards the acceptable limit in terms of cash and liquid ratios. In effect, there is a secondary rise in the money supply which is a multiple of the initial increase.

Open market operations may have a much greater effect on interest rates than on total bank deposits and the money supply. The buying of gilts affects long-term interest rates. In addition, the Bank of England can influence short-term interest rates by buying bills and other financial instruments in the money markets. These operations do not affect the size of a bank's liquid asset ratio, but through changing the proportions of cash and bills held by the bank, they affect the composition of the liquid assets.

Government buying of securities should lead to a rise in their price levels and therefore a fall in the rate of interest. The cost of borrowing thus falls, hopefully bringing about an increased demand for borrowed funds and therefore increased consumer and investment expenditure.

The lower rate of interest would result in a relatively lower exchange rate. This is potentially expansionary through an increased demand for exports. In the shorter term, through the **J-curve effect**, the consequences for the balance of payments could be adverse. Such an exchange rate effect could, however, be constrained by interest rate movements and foreign exchange speculation in other major financial centres.

In the earlier 1980s, **money supply control** was used to influence the rate of interest. In more recent times, the rate of interest has been the policy instrument for influencing the money supply, which has become a policy objective. Further, with the opening up of UK banks and other financial institutions to foreign competition, the British government has ceased to exercise direct control over their financial ratios. This, therefore, has placed an even greater burden on interest rates as a means of control. Experience has shown that, in the shorter term at least, the demand for money is not always closely sensitive to movements in interest rates. The importance of general public and business confidence should not be under-rated.

56   IDEAL TAX SYSTEM

> **Pass marks**. Adam Smith's four canons of taxation are still valid. This was the basis for the expected answer. Part (b) is about price elasticity of demand.

(a)   **Tax revenues** are used to provide goods and services that the market economy either does not provide at all (for example, defence) or will not provide in sufficient quantities (for example, education) and to pay for the upkeep of government administration. The four principles on which a system of taxation should be based were set out by Adam Smith in *The Wealth of Nations*.

     (i)   **Equity**. The burden of taxation should be distributed according to people's ability to pay. Smith thought that proportional taxes would satisfy the criterion. A tax is **proportional** when all taxpayers pay the same percentage of their income, wealth or expenditure in taxation. Today however it is generally accepted that progressive taxes are the most equitable type of tax. A tax is **progressive** when the marginal rate of tax is greater than the average rate. The purpose of a progressive tax system is to ensure that the higher income groups and the more wealthy individuals not only pay more tax than the less well-off but pay a greater proportion of their income and wealth in taxation. The justification for taxing the rich more than the poor rests on the assumption that the law of diminishing marginal utility applies to additional income. This would mean that an extra £1 would give less satisfaction to a rich person than to a poor person, so taxing the rich does not involve as great a hardship as taxing the poor.

         A tax which takes a higher proportion of the income of the less well-off is called a **regressive** tax. Value added tax (VAT) - an **indirect tax** - is generally regressive, because the less well-off spend a greater proportion of their income on consumption of goods subject to VAT.

(ii) **Certainty**. The taxpayer should know how much tax they have to pay, when it must be paid, and how it must be paid. He should be able to assess his tax liability from the information provided and should not be subject to arbitrary tax demands. The British system of taxation satisfies these requirements in theory as all of the necessary information is available to taxpayers. The tax laws have become so complex, however, that it is sometimes difficult for the average person to be certain of his tax liability actually is.

Not only should a taxpayer know exactly when and where to pay tax, he should find it difficult to evade payment. In this respect, **indirect taxation** is preferable to **direct taxation**. Normally, too, the Chancellor of the Exchequer should be able to estimate the yield of a tax with a fair degree of accuracy.

(iii) **Convenience**. Taxes should be collected in a convenient form and at a convenient time. The payment of tax should ideally be related to how and when people receive and spent their income. The Pay as You Earn (PAYE) system for **direct taxation** is a convenient method of tax collection because tax is deducted when wages are paid - taxes on wage payments arc not levied some time after the income has been received. The payment of VAT by consumers is also convenient because VAT is charged and paid for at the time the goods are bought.

Taxes are paid in money and in general this is the most convenient form of making tax payments. Some difficulties may arise, however, when taxes are levied on wealth, as the wealth may be held in forms other than money. This leads to problems in making valuations of different assets and often in realising these assets so that payments can be made in money. For instance an auction may have to be held in order to sell wealth held in the form of paintings or other works of art.

(iv) **Economy**. The costs of collection should be small relative to the yield. By this criterion the UK car road tax is probably an inefficient tax. The economy requirement often conflicts with that of equity. The fairest or most equitable system of taxation would involve casting the tax net so widely and so carefully that collection costs would be disproportionately high.

Although Smith's canons of taxation are a sound basis for a system of taxation, a modern tax system should have regard to a number of other attributes.

(i) It should be **easily adjustable**. A tax should be capable of variation so that rates may be altered up or down, according to changes in government policy.

(ii) It should operate as an **automatic stabiliser**. One objective of taxation is to vary, through fiscal policy, the level of aggregate demand, for example by affecting the level of disposable income. The Chancellor is able to make a *deliberate* adjustment in tax rates at the time of the budget; it is helpful, however, if taxes operate automatically in the required direction. To some extent the UK tax system operates in this way: thus when money incomes fall so does the yield from both income tax and VAT, so helping to maintain the level of aggregate demand. The opposite occurs when money income rises.

(iii) It should **encourage initiative**. The way in which taxation affects initiative is a controversial topic. It has been suggested that relatively high rates of **income tax (direct taxation)** reduce the incentive to work. The evidence on this matter is inconclusive, however, and it is just as possible that relatively high rates of taxation provide an incentive to work as people may work harder to achieve a target post-tax income. It has also been argued that taxation reduces the net return from investment and so might discourage enterprise and risk taking.

(iv)   It should **avoid distortion** of resource allocation. In the long run under conditions of perfect competition, where only normal profits are earned, the price of a good will be equal to its marginal cost. Also consumers will have allocated their consumption to expenditure according to their preferences, so that consumers' marginal utility will be reflected by the price of the good. An **indirect tax** on a particular good will cause the price of the good to rise which will lead consumers to buy less of the taxed good and relatively more of untaxed goods. This means fewer factors of production will be used in the production of the taxed good and more factors of production will be used in the production of the untaxed goods. Hence the imposition of an **indirect tax** could result in resources not being allocated according to the underlying preferences of consumers.

(b) (i)   The imposition of an indirect tax is shown in Figure 1. This has the impact of shifting the supply curve to the left (S_1 to S_2), making the new equilibrium Q_2P_2 compared to Q_1P_1. An increase in tax raises price and lowers output.

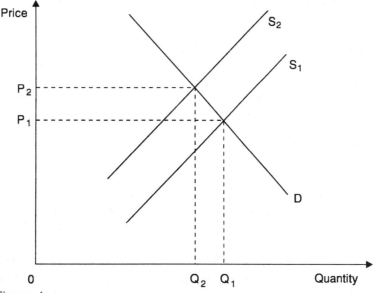

Figure 1

The relative effect on price and output depends upon the **price elasticity of demand (PED)** for the product. The higher the PED, the greater will be the fall in sales. The company will try to absorb some of the tax itself rather than pass on the full rise to the consumer, in order to prevent too serious an effect on sales.

(ii)   An increase in income tax on consumers (Figure 2) will **reduce aggregate monetary demand**. We can show the effect on consumers' demand for a product as a shift from D_1 to D_2, leading to a new equilibrium Q_3P_3 compared to Q_1P_1 previously. An increase in income tax reduces both price and output.

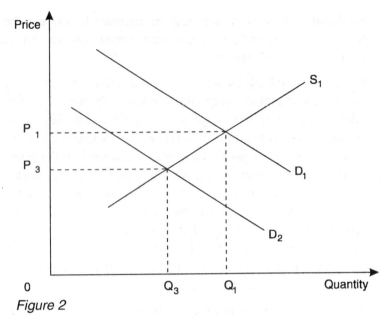

Figure 2

The extent of the drop in sales from an increase in income tax will depend on the **income elasticity of demand (IED)** for the product. Luxury goods, with high IEDs, may suffer a greater fall in demand than basic items such as foods.

57   DATA RESPONSE QUESTION: TAXATION

Pass marks. Remember that direct taxes can be levied on profits (corporation tax) as well as on income (income tax); also, more exceptionally, on wealth. Progressiveness/regressiveness in taxation is about the proportionate burden of tax in relation to income levels. Incentive effect and motivation are both difficult to measure. Questions concerning the incentive effect of taxation need to be answered with some caution.

Examiner's comment. The best answers dealt accurately and clearly with the explanations of direct/indirect and progressive/ regressive taxes and could cite examples in each category. Most candidates coped well with part (c) and identified the switch from direct to indirect taxation as the principal issue. Many candidates coped reasonably well with the incentive effects of direct taxes but fewer could analyse the income distribution effects of a shift from income tax to VAT.

(a)   **Direct taxes** are levied on income and profits, or on wealth. The impact (or formal incidence) of a direct tax and its burden (effective incidence) are borne by the same person. The party on whom the tax is levied also has to pay the tax (although it may be argued that in some instances the burden can be passed on elsewhere by compensating wage/salary increase or higher product prices). Thus they cannot be avoided other than by evasion or the assertion of monopoly power. In the table, the examples of direct taxes are income taxes, social security taxes, corporation tax, capital gains tax and inheritance tax.

Indirect taxes are levied on expenditure. Mostly they are collected by the revenue authority, eg Customs & Excise, from an intermediary, eg a supplier of goods or services, who then passes on the tax (or part of it) to consumers in the price of the goods or services. In the table, the examples of indirect taxes are value added tax, excise duties and other expenditure taxes. Motor vehicle duties (part of 'other expenditure taxes') are normally collected directly from existing vehicle owners. Indirect taxes, to a large extent, are avoidable: other than where a tax is imposed on a basic commodity/service, as with VAT on domestic fuel, people can in theory choose not to pay the tax by not buying the goods or services.

(b) A tax is said to be **progressive** because it takes proportionately more from those with higher incomes or, possibly, greater amounts of wealth. An example from the table is **income tax**. Overall it is progressive, as the rate of tax rises in stages according to the level of taxable income.

Corporation tax incorporates an element of progressiveness: companies with taxable profits below or above a certain level are subject to different rates of tax. **Capital gains tax** also has a progressive element in that the rate of tax is determined by the highest rate of income tax to which that person is subject within a given tax year.

A **regressive** tax takes a lower proportion of income or wealth as the level of income or wealth increases. From the table, value added tax and excise duties are forms of regressive tax, since poorer people will pay a higher proportion of their income in these taxes than richer people.

(c) An important feature over the years 1979 to 1993 in the UK was a **reduced progressiveness** in the system of taxation, superimposed on a situation of more unevenly distributed pre-tax income. The decline in the progressiveness of taxation was partly the result of a reduction in the highest marginal rates of tax. Furthermore, there was a highly significant switch from direct to indirect taxation. Thus, income tax fell from 34.1% to 30.0% of total tax revenue, while VAT rose form 14.7% to 22.9% of total tax revenue during the same period. A fall in the percentage of tax-take of 'other expenditure taxes' only partly offsets this. Within the indirect taxes, VAT now makes a much greater contribution than it did in 1979. This switch of revenue raising from income tax into VAT has further diminished the progressiveness of the tax system as a whole.

(d) Direct taxes, which generally are more progressive, were reduced over the period 1979 to 1993, while indirect taxes as a whole (which tend to be regressive) were increased. It is often claimed, especially by **supply-side economists**, that lower levels of income tax act as an **incentive** because of the resulting increases in disposable income. People will thus work harder. All of this will increase productivity and create more employment. Entrepreneurial risk-taking may be encouraged by the higher after-tax returns. The increased post-tax income will make possible increased saving by both individuals and firms, so making available the funds for increased investment. Real national income consequently will rise, so raising the level of tax revenue.

It can be argued that income-receivers are likely to be well aware of any income tax cut which takes place, whereas they may be less aware of any increases in indirect taxes - especially if they are spread among a range of indirect taxes or are not fully passed on by producers or distributors. If that were to be the case, the **incentive effect** of reductions in direct taxes could outweigh any incentive effect from increase in indirect taxes. The incentive effect of a reduction in direct taxation is likely to vary between different groups of individuals. Some may work less, so as to maintain the same level of post-tax income, after a decrease in direct taxation. In many cases however, the pace of work and the number of hours worked, among other things, are determined by factors outside the control of the individual. Various studies suggest that any possible incentive effect of income being increased is often short-lived.

The diminution in the role of direct taxes and the increased importance of indirect taxes has reduced the progressiveness of the tax system and increased the regressive element. As a consequence, lower income groups have been required to assume a greater burden of taxation. In addition, as mentioned earlier, pre-tax incomes have moved in favour of higher income groups. Hence, the distribution of income after taxation has become less equal in the UK.

58   **BUDGET BALANCE**

> **Pass marks.** In part (a), emphasise the balance between government expenditure and revenue. The impact of the trade cycle and the Keynesian theory of aggregate demand are the key issues in part (b). Note that part (c) is about financing a deficit, not about correcting it.

(a)   The fiscal year in the United Kingdom revolves around the **Budget** announced by the Chancellor of the Exchequer. Like households, the government also has income and expenditure and if expenditure exceeds income then there is a budget deficit. The main source of income for the government is taxation and examples of expenditure include health, education and social security. If the amount of money that the government spend is equal to the amount they collect in taxation, there is a **balanced budget**.

(b)   A budget deficit occurs where expenditure exceeds income and a budget surplus occurs where expenditure is less than income.

In a **mixed economy** like that of the United Kingdom, the level of economic activity fluctuates depending upon where we are in the trade cycle. During the **upturn** in the trade cycle production is rising, firms and individuals earn more profits and wages so the government should collect more revenue. Unemployment should also fall during this period, and so government expenditure should fall. At this stage of the cycle, the budget may be in surplus.

During the **downturn** of a trade cycle, the reverse applies. Profits and incomes fall and government revenue falls, but unemployment rises and government expenditure on unemployment benefit rises. There is then more likely to be a budget deficit.

Keynes suggested that budget deficits should be used to help an economy out of recession. According to Keynes, unemployment was caused by a lack of aggregate demand in the economy. So if the government increased its expenditure, this would raise aggregate demand.

Using Keynesian policies, a government may plan a budget deficit to boost aggregate monetary demand. Increased government expenditure might be on infrastructure such as roads, schools or the health service. Alternatively, taxes could be cut to increase consumers' disposable incomes. The objective would be to close the 'deflationary gap' that is seen to be preventing the economy reaching a level of full employment. Thus, variations in the budget balance can be the result of deliberate government budgetary policy.

(c)   If a government has a budget deficit it is said to have a **public sector borrowing requirement (PSBR)**. There are a number of ways in which a budget deficit can be financed.

The government can borrow money in the short term by issuing short-term bonds including Treasury bills via the money markets. Short and long-term government securities may be sold to the private sector (individuals and financial institutions), to overseas investors and to banks. In order to encourage people to buy bonds, they have to offer an attractive rate of interest. Long-term bonds can be offered for a period of up to thirty years.

Since the government controls the money supply through the central bank, it can print money but such a policy is likely to have inflationary consequences.

59   TUTORIAL QUESTION: TERMS OF TRADE

A country's **terms of trade** show the rate at which a country's exports exchange against its imports. In other words the terms of trade mean the quantity of another country's products which a nation gets in exchange for a given quantity of its own products. So, if the terms of trade move in the nation's favour, it means that it gets a larger quantity of imports for a given quantity of its own exports. This has happened because the prices of goods imported have fallen relative to those exported.

Assume, for example, that a country exports only washing machines and imports only cocoa. If it exports 10,000 washing machines at a price of £500 each, the value of its total exports is thus £5m. If the price of cocoa is £20 per ton it can import 250,000 tones. If now the price of the washing machines remains unchanged but the price of cocoa falls to £16 a ton, the result is that it is now possible to import 312,500 tons in exchange for the same number of washing machines. Alternatively the same amount of cocoa as previously can be imported but only 8,000 washing machines need be exported. Thus either an extra 62,500 tones of cocoa or 2,000 washing machines can be consumed at home. This occurs not because of an increase in productivity but because the terms of trade have moved in favour of the washing machine manufacturing country.

In practice, it is not possible to compute the terms of trade as so much of one product for a particular amount of another. Instead, the terms of trade are measured as the **ratio of an index of export prices to an index of import prices multiplied by 100**. So for any particular year the value of the terms of trade is:

$$\frac{\text{Index of export prices}}{\text{Index of import prices}} \times 100$$

In the base year, because the value of both indexes is 100, the terms of trade will be 100. The terms of trade are said to move favourably when the value of the terms of trade index rises and unfavourably when the terms of trade index falls.

Movements in the terms of trade are caused by **changes in relative prices**. A favourable movement can occur in one of three ways:

(a)   export prices rise and import prices fall;
(b)   export prices rise by more than import prices rise;
(c)   export prices fall by less than import prices fall.

A **rise in export prices** may be the result of **changing exchange rates**. For example, if the value of sterling rises against the US dollar, the prices of exports from the UK to the US will rise in terms of the US dollar. It will now require more dollars to buy the same goods. This can have the effect that, *ceteris paribus*, demand for UK exports will fall in volume because they will be made less competitive than other countries' exports.

Movements in exchange rates may occur as the result of **speculation pressures** rather than as a reflection of underlying economic strength. Such movements will nevertheless change trading conditions for exporters and importers. In 1990, speculative flows of money into the UK prior to sterling's entry into the European Exchange Rate Mechanism kept sterling's value high and made conditions more difficult for exporters than they would otherwise have been.

The net effect of changes in the terms of trade on the trade balance of a country will depend upon the relative elasticities of demand for imports and exports. If demand for a country's exports is relatively elastic, an improvement in the terms of trade could have an adverse effect on the economy. Less exports will be sold and revenues will diminish. If demand for a country's exports is relatively inelastic, then an improvement in the terms of trade will result in an improvement in the balance of trade. A good example here is that of oil. Oil price rises lead to trade surpluses for the oil exporting countries.

Less favourable terms of trade will improve demand for export goods for which demand is elastic, since it will be possible to sell the goods more cheaply abroad.

Many Third World countries remain highly dependent on the export of **primary commodities** which exhibit a high degree of price volatility. Prices of commodities exported by such countries may fall significantly while the industrial imports which the economy requires remain fairly stable in price. This kind of situation can lead to serious balance of trade difficulties for developing countries.

60 TRADE BENEFITS

> **Pass marks.** Attempting a question on trade theory requires use of the theory of comparative advantage.
>
> **Examiner's comment.** International economics remains the least well-answered section of the syllabus. Trade deficits cannot be financed through taxation.

(a) **International trade** arose because of the diversity of conditions between different countries: it enabled countries to obtain resources/goods which they were unable to produce for themselves, for reasons of climate or resource differences or from the absence of skills or know-how. It also enabled them to obtain goods more cheaply from abroad than they could be produced at home. International trade depends not just upon this absolute advantage but, more importantly, upon comparative advantage.

Within a medical research organisation the leading research scientist might happen also to be the organisation's best computer operator. It is evident that the research scientist's **comparative advantage** is greater in research and so he should concentrate on that. This enables him to provide a relatively rarer capability and so enhances the value of the organisation, and someone else should be employed as a computer operator. Applying this principle at the international level, countries should specialise not at what they are absolutely best at but what they are relatively best at. Earlier in this century, the USA, with its almost complete self-sufficiency in natural resources, could produce most products more cheaply than all other countries. Yet it was to its overall benefit to import a range of goods and to concentrate its efforts on those products in which its relative advantage was greatest.

Comparative cost relates to the **opportunity cost** of producing goods. Hence, expressed in alternative terms, each country should specialise in the supply of goods and services in which it has the lowest opportunity cost ratio. The countries so operating will all benefit and total output will be higher than otherwise would be the case. Maximum mutual benefit will occur when the rate of exchange of one good for another lies between the respective opportunity cost ratios of any two trading countries.

Comparative advantage and the process of international trade work to the advantage of the greater number. There may thus be some individual losers. Thus, agricultural workers might become unemployed as a country switches trading emphasis and resources into economically more advantageous industrial products. In the longer run, the greater number of people are likely to benefit from the change of trading emphasis, given the existing opportunity cost ratio.

It could be that, as one country specialises in the production of A, economies of scale reduce the cost of a unit of A. This would mean improved efficiency in the use of resources, so reducing output costs and making possible lower selling prices.

Given the high minimum efficient scale in many industries, closed domestic markets would result in much supply being in the hands of monopolists. International trade stimulates competition, leading to improved operating efficiency, innovation in the means of production and supply, and perhaps also better quality of output.

For the potential benefits of international trade to be realised, there must also be a free movement of investment funds between nations, with funds being attracted to those activities which offer the greatest return.

Constraints on economic activity arising from resource mis-match between countries can also be overcome by international trade. A country with resource shortages, eg certain raw materials, might be obliged to suffer limitations on industrial activity, unless it can make good the deficit from abroad. Those countries in surplus in those resources can export them to those countries in need.

Consumers benefit from world trade. There is a resulting increase in the choice of different goods, as well as increased diversity available within each product group. There can be greater innovation in product design. Furthermore, any cost reductions resulting from specialisation should benefit the consumer.

(b) The maintenance of a healthy **balance of payments**, at least over the medium to long term, is one of the more important macroeconomic objectives. For a country suffering from a persistent deficit on its trade with the rest of the world, such a deficit can result in severe economic difficulties.

A current account deficit implies that the country is 'living beyond its means' in that it is consuming imports at a greater rate than it is exporting. There may be an improvement in the standard of living in the short run, while in the long run increased inward investment may increase growth prospects.

The current account deficit may indicate that the country's goods are uncompetitive on world markets. If there is significant import penetration, domestic employment levels may suffer and there will be a resultant loss in living standards. For a country like the United Kingdom, this has led to de-industrialisation, which gradually erodes our manufacturing base.

Apart from the fact that in the short-term a country will need to finance these deficits by borrowing, it will have a negative impact on **other macroeconomic objectives** such as high employment and low inflation. In addition, the country may have to use macroeconomics policies such as fiscal and monetary policy to help reduce the deficit, which may conflict with domestic macroeconomic objectives.

61   TRADE AND IMPORTS

> **Pass marks**. Absolute advantage and comparative advantage are often confused with one another. Briefly explaining absolute advantage helps in outlining the comparative advantage model. The model is necessarily based on simplistic assumptions, eg as to the mobility of resources, and takes no account of social and political considerations.
>
> **Examiner's comment**. Better answers provided an explanation of the comparative advantage principle emphasising the concept of opportunity cost. In part (a), many candidates resorted to 'general knowledge' approaches to the benefits of trade rather than explaining and using the comparative advantage model. Part (b) was nearly always well answered with candidates distinguishing between tariff and non-tariff barriers. Part (c) was often less well answered but most candidates identified industrial protection as the main reason for the use of trade barriers.

(a) The **comparative advantage model** shows the possible **benefit obtainable from international trade**. Given limited resources, the cost of producing goods is the opportunity cost of not being able to produce the goods which alternatively could have been produced. One country has a comparative advantage over another country in a particular product if it has a lower opportunity cost of production in terms of the production foregone of another product.

To illustrate, suppose there are two countries, A and B. With the same total resources available, each country devotes half of these resources to wheat production and half to the production of motor vans. The following annual units of output are recorded.

	Wheat	*Motor vans*
Country A	80	200
Country B	240	120
World total	320	320

Country A is more efficient at producing motor vans than wheat while Country B is more efficient in the production of wheat. B has an **absolute advantage** in motor vans while B has an absolute advantage in wheat production.

If each of the countries now **specialises** in the product in which it has an absolute advantage then, given constant returns to scale, Country A would produce 400 units of vans and Country B would produce 480 units of wheat.

This increase in total production demonstrates the theory of absolute advantage: if each country has an absolute advantage in the production of a given product, total output will increase if each specialises in that product.

Specialisation and trade can also benefit both countries even if one country has an absolute advantage in both products. The following shows the output of countries X and Y before specialisation, with half of each country's resources being devoted to each product.

	Wheat	*Motor vans*
Country X	240	240
Country Y	80	60
World total	320	300

Suppose that Country X is more efficient at producing both wheat and motor vans. However, the competitive advantage is greater in the production of motor vans. It is three times as efficient as Y in the supply of wheat but four times as efficient in the production of motor vans.

If Country X now specialises in the production of motor vans and Y specialises in wheat production, the following output will result.

	Wheat	*Motor vans*
Country X	-	480
Country Y	160	-
World total	160	480

The outcome is an increase of 180 motor vans but a fall of 160 in the output of wheat. Provided that the relative values of wheat and vans in value terms fall within a certain range, the increased output of motor vans in value terms will exceed the fall in the output of wheat. If 160 units of wheat was insufficient to meet world demand, it is possible that country X would only partially specialise in the production of motor vans.

Certain **qualifying factors**, in practice, need to be taken into account. Thus, transport costs, which in the basic theory are ignored, might lessen the possible benefits of exchange. Nevertheless, application of the comparative advantage model in international trade has the potential for maximising economic welfare through permitting production to be carried out where it can be done most efficiently and furthermore facilitating the exploiting of scale economies. Apart from that, international trade makes possible a wider distribution of resources: a country with a surplus of a certain resource can exchange it with those countries lacking that resource. Consumers throughout the world consequently have available to them a much wider choice of products. If trade is freely conducted internationally, the danger of domestic monopolisation of supply will be much less.

(b)   Governments might use the following methods to restrict international trade.

      (i)   **Tariffs**. These are government imposed taxes on goods entering a country. The tariff may be applied across a wide band of imported goods or may be applied selectively on particular categories of goods. The effect is to raise the price paid for the goods by domestic consumers and normally leaves unchanged the price paid to the foreign suppliers. A tariff may be applied as a percentage of value (*ad valorem*) or as a fixed tax per unit (a *specific* duty).

            The overall effect of the tariff will depend upon the price elasticity of demand for the product. In some cases, the introduction of a tariff will make little or no difference to the volume of demand for those goods: the beneficiary would then be the government with the increased tax revenue.

      (ii)   **Import quotas**. These restrict the quantity of a product or product category which can be imported into the country over a given period. The restricted volume of supply on the domestic market will tend to raise the price of the good(s). This higher price benefits both domestic and foreign suppliers, to the detriment of consumers.

            Normally, to be effective, import quotas require a licensing system by which sub-quotas are allocated to importing firms. This may distort the market, for example if some sub-quotas are not fully taken up and may favour established importers as against possible new entrants to the market.

            No revenue is derived by the government from the use of a quota system; indeed, quotas can be costly to administer.

      (iii)   An **embargo**, or total ban, may be placed on particular imports or on imports from a particular country. This is usually done for social reasons, eg a ban on the import of certain narcotics/drugs. Exceptionally, there may be a total ban on imports from a country for political reasons.

      (iv)   **Hidden or indirect means** might be used by a government to restrict important and to protect home industries. This can include such as special safety standards being stipulated for imported goods, or complex import regulations and documentation. Subsidies to home producers will reduce the effectiveness of foreign competition and so tend to diminish the volume of international trade.

            Devaluation of the currency, by raising the price of imports, may depress the volume of imports. This would depend upon the price elasticity of demand for imported goods. However, this could be more than offset by the increase in the volume of exports.

(c)   The comparative advantage model considers the economic effects of free trade on an international scale. It is necessarily based on simplistic assumptions and therefore cannot be other than a starting point for analysing and assessing actual economic and trading situations. Governments need to take into account social, political and economic factors relating to their own country. The more protectionist stance adopted by the Democratic administration in the USA in the later part of President Clinton's first term in office is one example of their impact of politics on national trade policy.

Resources are often relatively immobile or not easily adjusted in the shorter term. Labour has limited mobility if serious social consequences are to be avoided. Such social effects have economic implications for a country. The greater part of business is conducted through organisations which have been built up over a long time. These are complex entities which are not easily replaced should they fail through trading slumps, sometimes outside their control. For an economy to be dynamic and expansive, it needs to be open to foreign competition. Yet governments are aware that to encourage people to accept the need for change, economic conditions must be kept reasonably stable. At times, restraint might need to be placed on what is considered 'excessive foreign competition'. Some countries are at a relatively early stage in industrial development and it is therefore not surprising that official policy is then even more protectionist.

More specifically, the following factors may encourage governments to restrict imports.

(i)   It may be said that foreign produced goods, using very low-paid labour, are undermining home industries. It may be contended that although there may be some loss to home consumers from the introduction of import controls, this would be more than offset by avoiding the social effects from a free influx of goods.

(ii)   Some industries which are in decline may need a period of adjustment. Measures can then be taken to develop new employment opportunities.

(iii)   For strategic reasons a measure of self-sufficiency may be sought. This might be official policy, for example in respect of agriculture and the defence industries.

(iv)   It may be claimed that foreign goods are being 'dumped' in the country, these being surplus production sold at economically low prices. This problem is exacerbated by (overseas) governments subsidising the over-production. The effect upon marginal home producers could be severe.

(v)   It may be that 'infant industries' need to be protected. The argument is that protection is necessary in the shorter term to enable newly established industries to become established and so be strong enough to withstand foreign competition. This assumes that there will be a large enough market to justify the extra production.

A positive approach by governments is to encourage the import of capital instead of goods so, in the longer term at least, obviating the need for **import controls**. The imported capital may take the form of overseas companies setting up subsidiary units within the investee country and so providing employment opportunities.

62   EXPLANATIONS

Pass marks. In (b), the terms of trade are affected by movements in the relative prices of exports and imports. A further factor is a change in the composition of exports or imports. In relation to part (c), the key point is the change in the relative elasticities of demand for exports and imports.

Examiner's comment. Common errors included:

- claiming that the terms of trade referred to the volume of imports and exports rather than to their prices;

- arguing that the terms of trade could in themselves be favourable or unfavourable when only movements in the terms of trade can be so defined;

- failure to see that changes in relative export and import prices would affect their volumes and that the resulting impact on the balance of trade would depend on the price elasticity of demand for imports and exports.

(a)   **A free trade area exists** when there is no restriction on the movement of goods and services between countries. This may be extended into a customs union when there is a free trade area between all member countries of the union, and in addition, there are common external tariffs applying to imports from non-member countries into any part of the union. In other words, the union promotes free trade among its members but acts as a protectionist bloc against the rest of the world.

A **common market** encompasses the idea of a customs union but has a number of additional features. In addition to free trade among member countries there is also complete mobility of the factors of production. A British citizen has the freedom to work in any other country of the European Union, for example. A common market may also aim to achieve stronger links between member countries, for example by harmonising government economic policies and by establishing a closer political confederation.

(b)   The **terms of trade** indicate the **rate at which a country's exports exchange for its imports,** ie the volume of other countries' products which a nation can obtain in exchange for a given volume of its own products. It may be measured against any other particular country or in terms of all other countries (in the aggregate) with which it trades.

If country A must produce 1.3 units of goods to obtain 1 unit of goods from country B, then the terms of trade are 1.3 units of A goods: 1 unit of B goods.

If the ratio changes so that 1.4 of A's goods exchange for 1 of B's goods for example, the terms of trade for A have deteriorated.

This, however, is only in terms of the volume of goods exchanged. Exchange also involves prices. Basically, the terms of trade are measured as:

$$\frac{\text{Unit value of exports}}{\text{Unit value of imports}}$$

In practice, the terms of trade are measured as the **ratio of an index of export prices to an index of import prices, multiplied by 100**. The indexes are based on a sophisticated system of weighting for the relative importance of the various goods entering into import and export trade.

Thus, for a particular point in time, the terms of trade can be calculated as:

$$\frac{\text{Index of export prices}}{\text{Index of import prices}} \times 100$$

Movement in the terms of trade, say between 1997 and 1998, would be calculated as:

$$\frac{\text{Price of exports 1998} / \text{Price of exports 1997}}{\text{Price of imports 1998} / \text{Price of imports 1997}}$$

Changes in a country's terms of trade arise from changes in prices of imports and exports, as well as changes in the composition of exports and imports.

A rise in a country's terms of trade could result from:

(i)   export prices rising whilst import prices fall;
(ii)   export prices rising by more than import prices rise; or
(iii)   export prices falling by less than import prices fall.

A rise in export prices relative to import prices could be the result of the exchange rate strengthening. Overseas buyers will then have to use more of their currency to buy UK goods. This could arise from an increased volume of demand for British goods which is forcing up the price of sterling. It could be that there is speculation in favour of sterling. Alternatively, it could be that the authorities are pursuing a high exchange rate policy and are using the reserves and higher interest rates if necessary to support the domestic currency.

An alternative price effect could be through a rise in the price of imported commodities. The result would be to depress the terms of trade.

Over a period of time there could be a change in the composition of exports so that more higher-value goods and less low-value goods are being exported. Alternatively, country A could have become more self-sufficient in high-grade, high-price products so that the average price of imports has fallen.

(c)   The **effect on a country's balance of trade of a fall in its terms of trade** would depend on the **price elasticity of demand** of the goods traded.

A fall in the terms of trade indicates that import prices have risen relative to export prices. Alternatively the country's exchange rate could have depreciated.

With the fall in the terms of trade the country has become more competitive in world markets. On the face of it, this would result in a rise in the volume of exports and a fall in the volume of imports. The effect on values would depend on respective price elasticities of demand. If the demand for imported goods is price elastic, the volume and value of imports will fall. If the demand for imports is price inelastic, as with raw materials and a wide range of foodstuffs, in volume of demand may fall little if at all and the value of imports will rise. If export demand is price elastic, both the volume and value of exports will rise. If export demand is price inelastic, the total value of exports will fall.

The overall effect on the balance of trade will depend on the **respective price elasticities of demand for exports and imports**. If the sum of these elasticities is greater than unity, a fall in the terms of trade will result in an improvement in the balance of trade.

63   DEVALUATION POLICY

> **Pass marks**. A good answer will explain the meaning of devaluation and will identify balance of payments difficulties as the reason for devaluation, providing some explanation of why such difficulties might arise. It will go on to show that devaluation was only an appropriate measure when these difficulties arose out of a loss of international competitiveness.
>
> *Other points*. For devaluation to be necessary, the currency must have been officially supported at too high a level. The success of devaluation depends upon economic conditions at the time being favourable: the existence of spare capacity in domestic industry, and sufficiently favourable conditions in the main export markets. A significant devaluation is likely, over the longer term, to affect all domestic companies, though in some cases the effect might be indirect, eg rising wage rates due to later inflationary pressures.
>
> **Examiner's comment**. Discussion of the effectiveness of devaluation rarely considered the need for spare capacity in the economy in order for the output of exports to increase. Most answers considered the effect of rising import prices on domestic companies but few considered the change in international competitiveness for different companies.

(a)   If the UK was operating a **fixed exchange rate** and dropped the external price of its currency, eg if the rate moved from £1 = $2.50 to £1 = $1.75, this is termed *devaluation* of the pound sterling. This has the effect of making UK exports cheaper in US dollars and imports from the USA more expensive.

A government might consider **devaluation** if the country is experiencing a major and prolonged balance of payments deficit. This could be because the economy is uncompetitive with the economies of the country's main trading partners.

Alternatively, it could be that the exchange rate has been set at too high a level to reflect purchasing power parity between countries. Devaluation would be intended to improve the relative price position of the country's products. As a result, export sales should rise, imports should fall, and the balance of payments deficit should be eliminated. Devaluation is an **expenditure switching measure**, directed to increasing the volume of exports and encouraging domestic buyers (industrialists and consumers) to switch out of imports into domestically produced substitutes.

For devaluation to be successful, certain conditions must be met. The total earnings from exports will rise only if the demand for exports is elastic; while expenditure on imports will be reduced only if demand for imports is elastic. However, that is not sufficient: the key point is how the relative elasticities of demand affect the balance of payments position. The **Marshall-Lerner criterion** states that devaluation will only improve the balance of payments if the sum of the elasticities of demand for exports and imports is greater than one.

In addition, **total domestic expenditure (C + I + G)** must not be absorbing the whole of the gross domestic product, ie there must be spare capacity in the domestic economy. Moreover, any consequential increase in exports will, through the multiplier, create an increase in national income which in turn will raise the demand for imports.

The **J-curve** effect also needs to be taken into account. According to this, shortly after the devaluation, a deterioration of the balance of payments would take place followed later by the recovery. This would be more likely to apply if insufficient capacity in the domestic system thwarts the effectiveness of the expenditure-switching measure.

In the absence of the necessary spare capacity, **aggregate monetary demand (AMD)** needs to be reduced through deflationary measures. It is preferable that these measures are taken some time before the devaluation as there is likely to be a delay before they become effective. The spare capacity needs to exist at the time the devaluation takes place.

It is essential that the downward adjustment of the exchange rate is sufficient to deal with the disequilibrium. To have to devalue a second time soon after the first one can be disastrous for confidence in both currency and business markets.

Devaluation may not be the appropriate measure. An excess of AMD could be the problem rather than the uncompetitiveness of producers or suppliers. **Deflation** would then be more suitable than devaluation.

The success of devaluation will, in part, depend upon economic conditions in the country's main trading partners being favourable. If some of those countries were undergoing a prolonged recession, this could impede any expansion of exports. Any advantage in importing terms might not compensate for the export disadvantage.

There is also the need to retain any advantage achieved through the devaluation. Rises in the prices of imports could diminish any apparent expenditure-switching advantages. The increased demand for labour and increased working time could increase the pressure for wage increases. These possibilities further underline the importance of the **spare capacity argument**. Appropriate deflationary measures might need to be applied for some while after the devaluation in order to keep inflation in check.

(b) The extent to which domestic companies would be affected by a significant devaluation of the currency would depend basically upon:

(i) their relative **dependence on imports**; and

(ii) the relative **importance to them of overseas markets** in which to sell their products.

Companies dependent upon imported raw materials, components or capital equipment would experience a **rise in costs**. Other companies able to purchase parts or equipment from home manufacturers would be less affected.

Companies with a major part of their output sold abroad could benefit markedly from the **fall in the exchange rate**, as this would enable them to lower their list prices. Any increase in sales volume, however, would depend upon the price elasticity of demand for the products. A company would also need to have the spare capacity to meet the extra demand. Instead of reducing list prices to overseas buyers by the extent of the devaluation, companies could take all or part of the advantage in the form of an increased margin of profit, so gaining an increased incentive to sell in these markets. The scope for doing this would, of course, depend upon the selling power in the given markets at the time. Some of the extra margin of profit could be used for improvements in product quality, marketing, or distribution, so strengthening the market position for the future.

Inevitably the effects of devaluation will **vary greatly** between companies, and sometimes even for companies within the same industry. Many companies now operate to a major extent through subsidiary companies abroad and this may insulate them from some of the effects of devaluation. Thus, for a company sourcing raw materials from overseas manufacturing subsidiaries, there might be no effect on input costs.

Devaluation by one country sometimes is followed by **devaluation by other countries**. This could eliminate any initial advantage/disadvantage in these particular markets. The different spread of overseas markets between companies would result in various effects on companies from the net devaluation process.

Some companies have **little or no involvement overseas**, whether through imports or exports. The consequences of devaluation for such companies could be very limited indeed and perhaps only indirect, from the adjustments that follow in the economic system as a whole.

64 DATA RESPONSE QUESTION: UK TRADE

> **Pass marks**. Read the passage carefully: part (a) offers four marks just for extracting information. When you come to comparative advantage, do not panic. The best approach is via opportunity cost, but a simple numerical example will work. Also, remember that the information given is in percentages not volumes. It gives us information about proportions, not absolute quantities. Do not, for instance, fall into the trap of saying that imports of finished manufactured goods have increased five fold: what has happened is that manufactured goods represent a much larger **proportion** of the total. This may be because exports of this category have increased in volume or because exports of other categories have decreased. In part (f), the question asks for two reasons for change. We have given four: no doubt you can think of more.
>
> **Examiner's comment**. Poor time allocation was very evident in the answers to this question.

(a) The **proportions of two categories of exports have changed significantly**: exports of finished manufactured goods have risen from 48% of the total to 55%, while semi-manufactured goods and metals have fallen from 36% to 28%. There has been a smaller change in the proportion of food and drink, which has risen from 5% to 7% of the total. Even larger changes have occurred in imports, particularly in finished manufactured goods, which have risen from 11% to 55%. The proportion of semi-manufactured goods and metals has fallen from 22% to 27%. These rises are balanced by major falls in food and drink and fuel and raw materials, both down from 33% to 10% and 7% respectively.

(b) The theory of **comparative advantage** is based on the idea of **opportunity cost** and the **production possibility frontier**. Within a country, opportunity cost for any category of product may be established in terms of the next most advantageous use of national resources. If two countries produce different goods most efficiently and can exchange them at an advantageous rate in terms of the comparative opportunity costs of importing and home production, then it will be beneficial for them to specialise and trade. Total production of each good will be higher than if they each produce both goods. This is true even if one country has an absolute advantage in both goods.

(c)

> *Tutorial note.* This is a rather odd question. It is not possible to use the **changes** in the structure of UK trade to illustrate the theory of comparative advantage, since that would require an increase in exports of one category to be balanced by an increase in imports of another category, and this has not happened. The CIMA suggested solution refers to the preponderance of manufactured and semi-manufactured goods in exports at both dates and surmises that the UK has capital and skilled labour which give it a comparative advantage in this area, while its land and climate may not be suited to the production of food. However, imports of food have fallen significantly in percentage terms, and the proportion of imports of manufactured and semi-manufactured goods has increased markedly. The simplest explanation for this is that the economy has expanded but, not surprisingly with a relatively stable population, the absolute quantity of food required has not increased markedly. The growth has been in both the production and consumption of manufactures. If there are any illustrations of comparative advantage, they probably lie within the rather wide categories presented to us and would only be evident if more detailed analysis were available. For instance, textiles manufacturing has certainly declined in the UK while the medical and pharmaceutical products sector has developed. However, even if such analysis were given for comment, it would be very difficult to distinguish the effects of **comparative** advantage from those of **absolute** advantage.
>
> It might also be appropriate to consider the following points:
>
> - The UK's entry to the EU took place between the dates and the UK is now a low wage manufacturer within the EU.
>
> - International trade has grown in most sectors with the general reduction in tariffs and other barriers to trade.
>
> - Services are not covered by the figures given but the UK's balance of payments largely depends on them.
>
> - How should you tackle a question like this? If you are **very** sure of your ground you may choose to write in the terms we have used above. You are probably better advised to give the marker what he or she is looking for, making whatever you can out of the data.

(d) **Any rapid economic change can cause disruption**, especially in the factors of production and particularly in the case of labour. Significant changes in demand, whether for export or home consumption, can lead to surpluses or shortages of goods and, via the mechanism of **derived demand**, surpluses or shortages of the **factors of production**. Labour is slow to respond to changed demand. A reduction in demand will lead to unemployment; in the past, in the UK; this has tended to be regional and long lasting because of the concentration of manufacture in particular regions. Increases in demand may lead to shortages of labour which tend to drive up wages, thus increasing costs.

Rapid changes in international trade may produce problems in the **balance of payments**. An adverse movement must be paid for. Under a fixed exchange rate system, this may involve adverse capital flows, or, if these are inadequate, higher interest rates or outflows of official reserves to support the exchange rate. Ultimately, **devaluation** may become necessary. There may be a decline in a floating exchange rate unless it is supported by higher interest rates. A surplus on the balance of payments is also undesirable since it creates **hostility** among trading partners and may lead to **protectionism**.

(e)   **Exports to the EU have more than doubled** as a proportion of the total, rising from 21% to 58%. This rise has been accompanied by compensating proportional falls in exports to other European countries, both within and outside the OECD. Taken together, these exports have diminished by two thirds, from 24% to 8%. There has been a fall in the proportion of exports going to North America, from 16% to 14%, and the proportion going to the rest of the world have fallen by about half, from 39% to 20%.

(f)   The much increased proportion of exports going to the EU is traceable to the UK's entry, which occurred during the period in question. The EU is a **free trade area** and trade between members could be expected to expand significantly.

A reduction in trade with countries outside the EU would also be expected, as the EU is also a **customs union**, with common tariff barriers against imports. This would tend to affect exports.

55% of the UK's exports in 1995 were finished manufactured goods. Many of these will be **consumer goods** and these have a **high income elasticity of demand**. Income growth in the EU may therefore explain some of the swing of exports to the EU.

The period in question saw the continuing decline of old established manufacturing industries such as textiles and motor vehicles in the UK. The UK had formerly exported much of this type of production to the rest of the world, but increasing competition from Far-Eastern countries led to significant reductions in these exports as the UK's comparative advantage diminished.

65   DEFICIT

> **Pass marks**. There is often confusion about the difference between the two terms 'balance of trade' and 'balance of payments'. Be clear about the difference in your answers.
>
> *Examiner's comment.* Most candidates had little trouble with part (a), although some limited themselves to very brief statements indeed. However, there was a significant minority who made a fundamental error in claiming that a balance of payments deficit was the government budget deficit. For these candidates, parts (b) and (c) made little sense, as did their answers.

(a)   The **balance of payments (BOP)** is a statistical record, in the case of the UK, of debits and credits covering all financial transactions between the UK and the rest of the world recorded in a particular period.

The BOP accounts are in two parts. There is the **current account**, through which the export and import of goods and services are posted, and the **capital account** through which capital flows.

By definition, the balance of payments account must always *balance* overall. Individual sections of the accounts may, however, be in deficit or surplus. In the case of the UK, the **current account deficit** is usually partially offset by **surpluses on the capital account** (ie **transactions in assets and liabilities**). Usually, reference to a balance of payments deficit is intended to mean a deficit on the current account.

(b)   The main factors causing a country to have a **deficit on current account** are as follows.

(i) The **quality of a country's goods** may make it uncompetitive in international markets, limiting exports. Late delivery, poor design, lack of functionality, propensity of goods to break down, wrong or improper position in the market, insufficient marketing advertising and promotion, goods being out of date, poor sales and maintenance support, poor packaging and so on could all make goods unattractive to overseas buyers. Likewise with services, impoliteness, lateness, untidiness, inaccuracies and other deficiencies may restrict demand from overseas.

(ii) The **price of home-produced of goods and services** may be too high for overseas markets. Overpricing may be connected with high costs. This could be the result of overmanning, low levels of capital investment, low economies of scale, small and inefficient premises, incorrect mixture of labour and capital, poor organisation, low levels of automation and robotics, poor and weak management, restrictive practices, or a lack of modern computer technology and software.

(iii) If **inflation at home is greater than among competitor countries** then, other things being equal, business could be lost as overseas consumers switch their purchases to countries in which inflation is lower.

(iv) The **exchange rate** could be overvalued, for example as a direct result of incoming 'hot' money and because of tight monetary control at home with high interest rates. This will make exports relatively more expensive and imports cheaper. If demand for exports and imports is elastic, the current account will move towards a deficit position.

(v) **Lack of competitiveness in home-produced goods and services** can cause our own consumers to have, as in the UK, a high propensity to consume foreign goods. **Insufficient capacity** in a country, particularly in manufacturing, can also shift aggregate demand from home-produced goods to foreign goods.

(c) The process of **financing** is that by which any deficit or surplus on the current account, and this is the part through which trade in goods and services flows, are met or balanced by capital balances in the capital flows section.

The deficit in capital needed over the longer term to meet the deficit on current account has to be met, for example by being:

(i) borrowed from 'official sources' such as the International Monetary Fund;

(ii) taken from a country's gold and foreign currency reserves; or

(iii) borrowed from overseas banks.

These borrowings might be obtained from overseas sources with repayments being made over say 5, 10 or even 20 years. However, the borrowing powers and foreign currency reserves of a country are finite, and so over the longer term a current account deficit is not sustainable indefinitely.

Correcting a balance of payments deficit means reducing the potential deficit to a lower level.

A deficit on current account might be rectified by one or more of the following measures:

(i) a depreciation of the currency (called **devaluation** when deliberately instigated by the government, for example by changing the value of the currency within a controlled exchange rate system);

(ii) **direct measures** to restrict imports, including tariffs or import quotas or exchange control regulations;

(iii) **domestic deflation** to reduce aggregate demand in the domestic economy.

Deflationary measures aim to **reduce expenditure,** while other policies are aimed at **switching expenditure.** For example, devaluation of the currency will make a country's goods cheaper in export markets while imports will become more expensive in the home economy. Such a change in the relative prices of exports and imports should, it is hoped, encourage expenditure switching in favour of the country's products.

As noted above, direct **protectionist measures,** for example in the form of **tariff or non-tariff barriers to trade,** might be used to correct a deficit, although membership of the **World Trade Organisation** will prevent a country taking severe protectionist measures unilaterally.

In summary, measures to **finance** a current account deficit deal with a **temporary imbalance** in trade, while measures to **correct** the deficit try to tackle the **underlying causes** of it.

66 DATA RESPONSE QUESTION: EXCHANGE RATES

> **Pass marks**. Exchange rates are determined by supply and demand. Use diagram to explain. A rise in the exchange rate makes our exports more expensive to foreigners. Changes in interest rates cause capital flows, which change exchange rates. Interest rates are part of monetary policy used to reduce inflation. Opportunity to use international macro-theory, eg terms of trade.
>
> **Examiner's comment**. This question was poorly answered. Candidates who answered part (a) badly were struggling since each part of the question was related to the previous one. Many students could not distinguish the relationship between interest rates and exchange rates.

(a) **Exchange rates** are the 'prices' at which currencies are traded against each other. The exchange rate between two currencies is determined, as for any other competitive market, primarily by conditions of demand and supply in the foreign exchange markets.

Demand for a currency arises mainly from consumers' and firms wishes to purchase commodities from or to make an investment in the country of the currency. **Supply** of the domestic currency on foreign exchange markets depends upon domestic residents' wish to purchase foreign goods or to invest overseas. There are also speculative pressures that can affect foreign exchange trading. The daily volumes of trading in major currencies are huge, reflecting the actions of currency traders seeking to take advantage of speculative opportunities.

If the sterling/deutschmark exchange rate is high, then the price of German goods in sterling terms is relatively low. British people will wish to buy relatively more German products, a process that will increase the supply of sterling. The comparative levels of demand and supply of sterling relative to those of the deutschmark will determine the sterling/deutschmark exchange rate.

(b) UK exporters might be worried by a rise in the exchange rate for sterling because it pushes up the price of their goods in international markets. If the current rate of exchange is £1 = $2, then a UK exported machine costing £100,000 will be $200,000 in the USA. If the exchange rate went up to say £1 = $2.20, then the machine would now cost $220,000 and this might dissuade the importer from purchasing this machine.

On the other hand, the British exporter may seek to stay competitive, and may try to maintain the dollar price of the goods exported in order to avoid losing sales. The effect of this will be a fall in the exporter's profits since the proceeds in sterling terms will be lower. The exporter may now even be making a loss on the transaction.

In either case, the situation becomes more difficult for UK exporters.

(c) A change in UK **interest rates** has an impact in the international economy as well as the domestic one. International investors will place their money where it gives the highest rate of return. If interest rates in London are raised to 10% and interest rates in New York are 7%, then someone investing this money in London would have a 3% higher rate of return. If this money was transferred from New York to London, someone would be selling dollars and buying sterling which would tend to raise the sterling/dollar price. What has happened in this case is that there has been a sterling capital inflow, raising demand for sterling.

(d) Interest rates represent the 'price' of money. A rise in interest rates is an example of using monetary policy to try and achieve a macroeconomic objective. One of the key macroeconomic objectives is to maintain a stable price level by keeping down the rate of inflation. A rise in interest rates makes the borrowing of money more expensive. This may delay or curtail expenditure and investment, and inflation will be kept in check. Higher interest rates also encourage individuals to save rather than to consume, which will again have an anti-inflationary effect.

In the article, it is stated that the growth in broad money supply was well above the government's target for money supply growth. This presents the risk that excessive money supply growth could have an inflationary effect in the future.

(e) There are two ways in which a rise in the sterling exchange rate would tend to exert downward pressure on inflation.

(i) Firstly, there will be **demand effects**. The sterling prices of imports will fall, and more imports will be purchased. This will have the effect of reducing sales of domestically produced goods in the UK market. Sales of exports will be reduced, since their prices in world markets will rise in relative terms. Lower exports combined with higher imports will have the effect of reducing demand-led inflation in the UK.

(ii) As the exchange rate rises, the impact of **cost-push inflation** will be reduced. The UK imports a high proportion of its raw materials as well as consumer goods. Cheaper imports will mean lower production costs, which should feed through to consumer prices as lower inflation.

67   DATA RESPONSE QUESTION: ECONOMIC RELATIONSHIPS

> **Pass marks**. In (a), the word 'explain' signifies that more than a brief statement or description is required. At the same time, answers to this type of question need to be to the point. Answers to both (b) and (c) require reference to the data included in the question. The main statistical movements first need to be identified.
>
> **Examiner's comment**. Better scripts gave accurate definitions and explanations of the concepts in part (a); this indicated a sound grasp of basic macroeconomic concepts. There were many good answers to parts (b) and (c); candidates successfully identified the relationships between growth, the PSBR and the balance of payments and could provide clear explanations for them. These candidates saw that the causal link was from the rate of growth of GDP to the PSBR and the balance of payments, with the former deteriorating when growth slowed and the latter improving.

(a) (i) **Gross domestic product (GDP)** is the term given to the value of output produced within a nation over a given period, normally one year. It includes the value of goods/services produced for export in addition to goods/services produced within the economy for internal use.

Given the basic accounting identity:

Income ≡ Output ≡ Expenditure,

GDP can be measured:

(1) by adding together all of the incomes received from producing the year's output; or

(2) by finding the value of final output, ie applying the 'added value' approach and so avoiding double counting; also including exports but excluding imports; or

(3) by finding the total of expenditures or 'outlays' on goods and services produced by the economy.

'Gross' signifies that no allowance has been made for capital consumption or the depreciation of fixed assets.

(ii) The balance between the income and spending of the whole of the public sector is known as the **public sector borrowing requirement (PSBR)**. Effectively, it is the amount of funds which the public sector needs to raise each year if its expenditure exceeds its revenue. It incorporates the borrowing of central government, public corporations and local authorities. In the UK, the major part of the PSBR results from the government running a budget deficit, with central government expenditure exceeding the total of tax revenues. Government outgoings tend to be heavy in the early months of any tax year (for example, because of European Union contributions) whereas government receipts tend to be loaded towards the later months of the tax year. Thus, the weight of government deficit varies throughout the year. The sum of the accumulated PSBR over a period of years adds to the 'National Debt'. If government receipts in any year exceed outgoings, there is a public sector debt repayment (PSDR) and this, of course, serves to reduce the National Debt.

(iii) The **current account of the balance of payments**, being the international trading account of a country, records the flow of visible and invisible items imported and exported over a given period. Visible items are the trade in goods, and the balance of visible goods - into and out of the country - is known as the 'balance of trade'. Invisibles include services, payments/receipts of interest, dividends, profits, together with governmental and private transfer payments (for example, foreign aid payments and money transfers by people living abroad). The total of visibles and invisibles will result in either a net surplus or deficit on current account. The relative importance of receipts and payments can vary considerably over a year according to trading patterns and settlement arrangements, so that quarterly balance of payments deficits or surpluses are not necessarily indicative of the outcome for the year. Also, adjustments to the figures are often necessary well after the year.

(b) The figures show that the **rate of growth of GDP** in the UK was negative in 1980 and 1981 but then improved (with the exception of 1984), until reaching a peak of 4.9% in 1988. It became negative again in 1991 and 1992, years of recession in the UK economy.

The **PSBR** exceeded £10bn in each of the years 1980 to 1984, with the exception of 1982. From 1985 it declined markedly, becoming negative between 1987 and 1990. In this period, with revenues exceeding expenditures, the government was able to make a net debt repayment, so reducing the National Debt. Expenditure again exceeded revenue in 1991, and the PSBR reached the exceptional figure of £28.9bn in 1991.

The figures show an **inverse relationship** between the growth rate of GDP and the size of the PSBR. High levels of PSBR are associated with low growth rates. If the growth in GDP declines, tax revenues fall while social security payments (for example, to those unemployed) increase. If the economy actually moves into recession, the consequences for the PSBR of this two-way effect may be severe. Efforts then to reduce the PSBR, involving cut-backs in public expenditure, may prolong the period of negative growth. Conversely, as the rate of growth of GDP improves, government tax revenue (eg from VAT, income tax and corporation tax) increases while the outgoings on social security payments tend to fall. This upswing in GDP and fall in PSBR may be slowed, as in the period 1992 to 1995, by employers being more wary in engaging additional labour. Generally, however, as growth rates improve PSBR falls.

(c) During the period of **negative growth** in GDP in 1980 and 1981, the current account of the balance of payments was in surplus. However, during the period of growth in GDP in the mid-1980s, the balance of payments moved into deficit, this becoming substantial by the end of the decade. As the rate of growth of GDP fell heavily and the economy then moved into recession, so the balance of payments showed improvement with the deficit falling heavily. The figures indicate a direct relationship between growth in GDP and the size of the current account deficit/surplus.

The UK has a noticeable **marginal propensity to import**, due in part to an underlying lack of competitiveness, as well as to capacity shortages when demand peaks. As the economy picks up and incomes increase, a rise in imports has tended not to be matched by a corresponding increase in exports. Imports rise due to increased UK demand for overseas goods, as well as from increased need for raw materials, components, and capital equipment. There is also some tendency for goods to be diverted from exports to meet the rising consumer demand. As the economy moves into decline, the reverse tends to take place with, in due course, a noticeable fall in imports.

There are some indications that since 1993 there has been an increased movement into exports, as a substitute for the low level of domestic consumer demand. Significant improvements in productivity in UK manufacturing industry have helped to make UK goods more competitive. These factors at least provide the potential for some modification of the relationship indicated by the data.

68 FIXED OR FLOATING

Pass marks. Even fixed exchange rates are subject to supply and demand and must be managed. Note the terms 'expenditure reducing' and 'expenditure switching' in this context.

(a) A **fixed exchange rate** applies where a country keeps the value of the exchange rate fixed over a period of time in relation to certain other countries.

The first system of fixed exchange rates to be used was the Bretton Woods system, in which participating countries pegged their currencies in relation to the US dollar.

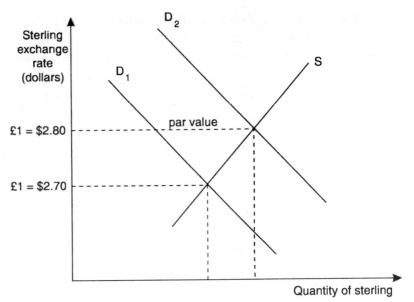

Figure 1

In the example in Figure 1, the par value of sterling is £1 = $2.80. However, suppose that the market value or the rate at which sterling is trading at $2.70m, below the par value. The government would need to go into the market and buy sterling. Demand would consequently rise (to D_2) and the par value and the market value move back into equilibrium. Under a system of fixed or semi-fixed exchange rates, maintaining the exchange rate is an objective of economic policy.

A flexible exchange rate is one that is determined by market conditions. This is the type of system that the UK had between 1972 and 1989, and after 1992 when sterling left the European exchange rate mechanism.

Under flexible exchange rates, if there is an increase in the demand for sterling, the sterling exchange rate will rise against other currencies. The level of an exchange rate is related to the balance of payments. Countries with a balance of payments deficit would experience a downward pressure on their exchange rate and countries with a surplus would experience upward pressure. An advantage of a flexible exchange rate system is that the rate can be adjusted to help the balance of payments, so that the exchange rate is an instrument of policy and not an objective.

In practice, most countries operate a system of managed floating where, by and large, on a day to day basis, exchange rates are determined by market forces. Governments will step in if they feel that the rate has gone too high or too low. This system is halfway between fixed and floating which gives the advantage of stability of fixed rates and flexibility of floating rates.

(b)   Under a system of **fixed exchange rates**, a devaluation is not an option to correct a current account deficit on balance of payments. Exports need to be increased and imports need to be reduced in order to restore equilibrium. Chiefly, **expenditure reducing policies** will be necessary. For example, taxes may be raised or government spending may be cut to reduce aggregate monetary demand. As well as **fiscal policy** measures, the **monetary policy** measure of raising interest rates may also be used. Such deflationary measures may reduce imports, especially where there is a high marginal propensity to import. They may also reduce inflation, making exports more competitive in world markets. Higher interest rates may bolster capital inflows, improving the capital section of the balance of payments.

Another option is to put a **tariff** on imported goods. This will make imported goods more expensive and consumers will switch to domestically produced goods. **A quota** might be imposed, restricting the amount of goods being allowed into the country.

A further option is to give subsidies to industries in export markets, which reduces the price of exported British goods. Typically, where this policy is operated by other countries, it is not known as an export subsidy, but dumping.

Since joining the WTO and the European Union, unilateral tariffs and quotas are not an easy option for the UK. The EU is a free trade area which encourages the movement of goods and services. Such policies would not be accepted by the UK's trading partners. Many tariffs and quotas would also contravene WTO rules.

Under a system of floating exchange rates, the key policy to correcting a balance of payments current account deficit is through automatic adjustment of the exchange rate, which will have **expenditure switching effects**.

A country which has a current account deficit will experience downward pressure on the exchange rate. This will reduce export prices and raise import prices, which should increase exports and reduce imports. A devaluation of 10% will make our exports 10% cheaper but, for the value to rise, the volume increase must be greater than 10%. On the other hand, a devaluation makes imports 10% more expensive and so if the import bill is to fall, the volume of imports must also fall by more than 10%. In other words, the combined elasticities of demand of exports and imports must total more than one (the 'Marshall-Lerner' criterion).

The United Kingdom presently has a balance of payments **deficit on current account** and one of the reasons put forward for this is the **high value of sterling**. However, the balance of payments is also concerned with the capital account and inflows of money into the UK have meant that sterling is a currency that international investors want to hold. Thus, although a reduction in the value of sterling might be the appropriate policy to reduce a current account deficit, market conditions are making it difficult to do so.

69   SELECTION 1

1   B   This is a good definition of opportunity cost.

2   C   The other options relate to movements *along* the supply curve.

3   C   Supply will extend and demand will contract.

4   A   The change in revenue is the same as the fall in price. Therefore there is no change in volume.

5   D   A rise in the exchange rate is effectively a reduction in price.

6   A   This is about substituting other factors for labour because its price has gone up. Options B and C encourage the substitution and option D makes it easy. Only option A makes substitution unlikely.

7   B   This is a classic example of the operation of diminishing returns.

8   D   Technical improvements could apply at any scale of operations.

9   B   Perfect competition requires a homogeneous product. Product differentiation is an important aspect of monopolistic competition.

10   D   Monopolistic competition involves a number of competing producers. A market with one dominant producer is somewhere between oligopoly and monopoly.

11   C   It is a peculiarity of terminology that the part of the economy owned by individual members of the public is called the private sector and not the public sector.

12   A   Fiscal policy is about government finance, that is, taxation, spending and borrowing.

13   A   Note that interest payments are current account items.

14   B   A and D are benefits of fixed exchange rates; C does not apply to any exchange rate system.

70   SELECTION 2

1   C   This is the signalling function of the price mechanisim.

2   B

3   D   Fixed costs are fixed and both marginal and average variable cost may fall before diminishing returns occur.

4   D   Do not confuse the long and short run effects: diseconomies of scale and diminishing returns respectively.

5   A   The other choices are external economies of scale: bulk buying is internal.

6   A   The other options are not always true.

7   C   Homogeneity means the producers are in competition with one another.

8   B   Only this factor necessarily leads to reduced consumer welfare.

9   C   Opportunity cost is the key to understanding comparative advantage.

10   D   Tariffs allow domestic producers to raise their prices.

71   SELECTION 3

    1   C
    2   B
    3   A
    4   B
    5   C
    6   B
    7   D
    8   C
    9   A
    10   A

72   SELECTION 4

    1   C
    2   A
    3   B
    4   B
    5   A
    6   B
    7   C
    8   D
    9   B
    10   D

73   SELECTION 5

    1   B
    2   C
    3   D
    4   A
    5   A
    6   B
    7   D
    8   C
    9   D
    10   A

74   **SELECTION 6**

1	A
2	B
3	D
4	B
5	C
6	A
7	D
8	C
9	B
10	A

75   **SELECTION 7**

1	D
2	A
3	D
4	B
5	C
6	B
7	C
8	A
9	A
10	C

76   **SELECTION 8**

1	D
2	B
3	D
4	D
5	C
6	B
7	C
8	C
9	D
10	A
11	D
12	D
13	B
14	A

3

MOCK EXAM

Stage 1

November 1999

Economic Environment

ECN

INSTRUCTIONS TO CANDIDATES

Read this page before you look at the questions

You are allowed three hours to answer this question paper.
Answer the ONE question in section A (consisting of ten sub-questions). *Answer ONE question ONLY from section B.* *Answer TWO questions ONLY from section C.*

Turn over

**DO NOT OPEN THIS PAPER UNTIL YOU ARE READY
TO START UNDER EXAMINATION CONDITIONS**

SECTION A - 28 MARKS

ANSWER **ALL** FOURTEEN SUB-QUESTIONS

Each of the sub-questions numbered from 1.1 to 1.14 inclusive, given below, has only ONE *right answer.*

REQUIREMENT:

On the SPECIAL ANSWER SHEET *provided at the end of this question paper, place a circle 'O' around the letter (***A***,* ***B***,* ***C***, or* ***D***) that gives the right answer to each sub-question.*

If you wish to change your mind about an answer, block out your first attempt and then encircle another letter. If you do not indicate clearly your final choice, or if you encircle more than one letter, no marks will be awarded for the sub-question concerned.

1.1   In all economies, the fundamental economic problem is that

    A   consumers never have as much money as they would wish

    B   resources are scarce relative to human wants

    C   there is always some unemployment of resources

    D   the supply of resources is always less than the demand for them

1.2   Which ONE of the following is NOT a cost of production for a firm?

    A   Salaries of senior managers

    B   Normal profit

    C   Interest payable on loans

    D   Corporation tax

1.3   If the demand for a good is *price inelastic*, then the total expenditure on the good

    A   will fall if the price rises

    B   will be constant if the price rises

    C   will rise if the price rises

    D   will rise if the price falls

1.4   All of the following would lead firms in an industry to locate close together in one area EXCEPT which ONE?

    A   A local supply of raw materials

    B   Specialist training facilities located in the area

    C   The opportunity for external economies of scale

    D   The existence of a cartel in the industry

1.5   A profit-maximising firm will attempt to produce where

    A   marginal cost is equal to marginal revenue

    B   average costs of production are lowest

    C   marginal cost equals average cost

    D   marginal cost is equal to average revenue

1.6   Which ONE of the following is an example of price discrimination?

   A   A bus company charging a lower price than a railway company for the same distance travelled

   B   A telecommunications company charging reduced rates for telephone calls made by government bodies

   C   Supermarkets charging different prices for fruit in different regions because local supply costs vary

   D   Petrol stations charging lower prices for unleaded petrol than for leaded petrol

1.7   All of the following are characteristics of oligopolies EXCEPT which ONE?

   A   There is a small number of firms in the industry
   B   There is a preference for non-price competition
   C   There is very little product differentiation
   D   There are entry barriers to the industry

1.8   Monopolies are undesirable because they

   A   control most of the market
   B   maximise profits
   C   do not pass on to consumers the benefits of economies of scale
   D   do not produce where average costs are lowest

1.9   Many building societies are now performing functions which are increasingly similar to commercial banks because they

   A   pay interest on all their deposit accounts
   B   have more branches than many banks
   C   provide full cheque accounts and money transfer services
   D   have a significantly greater level of deposits than banks

1.10   Which ONE of the following is the most *profitable* to a commercial bank?

   A   Advances to customers
   B   Balances with the central bank
   C   Money at call
   D   Treasury Bills

1.11   Which of the following are functions of money?

   (i)   A medium of exchange
   (ii)   A store of value
   (iii)   A unit of account
   (iv)   A measure of liquidity

   A   (i) and (ii) only
   B   (i), (ii) and (iii) only
   C   (ii), (iii) and (iv) only
   D   All of them

1.12   Which ONE of the following is a transfer payment in national income accounting?

   A   Educational scholarships
   B   Salaries of lecturers
   C   Payments for textbooks
   D   Payments of examination entry fees

1.13   Which of the following would increase the potential benefits from international trade?

    (i)   The existence of economies of scale in production
    (ii)   A high mobility of capital and labour between economies
    (iii)   Large differences in the opportunity costs of production between countries
    (iv)   Low international transport costs

    A   (i), (ii) and (iii) only
    B   (ii), (iii) and (iv) only
    C   (i), (iii) and (iv) only
    D   All of them

1.14   All of the following would raise the demand for imports in a country EXCEPT which ONE?

    A   A rise in consumer incomes
    B   A reduction in tariffs
    C   A rise in the domestic price level
    D   A devaluation of the exchange rate

Total Marks = 28

SECTION B – 24 MARKS

ANSWER **ONE** QUESTION **ONLY** - **EITHER 2 OR 3**

EITHER

2.   The following is based on a newspaper extract and refers to competition in a retail petrol market.

> The government department responsible for competition and fair trading has cleared supermarkets (which sell many goods as well as petrol) and leading oil companies of unfairly low pricing. But petrol retailers, who fear the closure of smaller petrol stations, reacted angrily. The retailers' spokesman said the competition regulator had failed to protect consumers, who would have to pay higher prices in the future.
>
> The Director of the government department said its investigation had found no evidence of unfair competition despite the rapid decline in the numbers of independent petrol stations. Although there have been major changes in the industry since 1990, with supermarkets taking more than 20% of the £20 billion market and the number of smaller retailers falling to less than 10,000 compared to 40,000 in the mid 1960s, he insisted that competition between the supermarkets and major oil companies had been in the interest of consumers.
>
> He pointed to a fall of one third in the real selling price of petrol received by retailers. In 1990 a retailer would receive 15p for a litre of petrol, after handing over tax to the government. The equivalent now is just 10p. This had led to a drop of a third in the profit margin, from 6p to 4p a litre, and reflects what the Director described as 'a vigorous struggle between the supermarkets and the major petrol retailers'.
>
> The battle for market share saw a fierce price war two years ago, initiated by Esso. But prices have recovered and independent retailers warned that they would continue to rise as more small retailers were forced out of business. But the Director insisted that there was still hope for small retailers. A study by his department had shown that smaller petrol stations could charge higher prices to offset lower sales volume and could survive by being innovative.

REQUIREMENTS:

Using BOTH your knowledge of economics AND material contained in the extract,

(a)   describe the changes which have occurred in the structure of the petrol retailing industry in recent years;   **4 Marks**

(b)   explain what is meant by the term *economies of scale.* What form might they take in the retail petrol industry?   **4 Marks**

(c)   use the concept of economies of scale to explain the changes in the structure of this industry which you have identified;   **4 Marks**

(d)   identify and explain TWO items of evidence that would support the claim that the industry is very competitive;   **4 Marks**

(e)   identify the benefits that consumers might be expected to get from competition in the retail petrol industry AND explain how this may change in the long run;   **4 Marks**

(f)   explain the claim that small petrol retailers could still be profitable despite competition from larger retailers.   **4 Marks**

Total Marks = 24

OR

3.   The following data refer to an economy between 1987 and 1997:

	Real gross domestic product (GDP) £ billion	Inflation [Increase in the retail price index] %	Consumer credit [Increase in lending to consumers] £ billion	Interest rate [Bank base rate] %	Sales of cars million
1987	515	4.2	6.3	8.9	2.184
1988	542	4.6	6.9	8.9	2.403
1989	552	8.3	6.8	14.2	2.494
1990	552	9.8	4.6	15.0	2.179
1991	540	5.8	2.3	11.2	1.708
1992	540	3.9	0.5	10.0	1.694
1993	548	1.2	2.6	5.9	1.853
1994	572	2.6	5.7	5.2	1.991
1995	587	3.5	8.2	6.7	2.024
1996	601	2.1	11.2	5.9	2.093
1997	620	3.1	12.1	6.9	2.157

REQUIREMENTS:

Using BOTH your knowledge of economic theory AND the data given,

(a)   identify THREE data series which indicate that this economy experienced a recession during the period. Explain each of your choices.   **9 Marks**

(b)   explain how the level of *consumer expenditure* and the *rate of interest* are linked;   **3 Marks**

identify and discuss evidence from the data which supports this link;   **2 Marks**

(c)   explain the monetarist model of inflation using the quantity theory of money;   **7 Marks**

(d)   using the data given, identify and explain EITHER

one piece of evidence which supports the monetarist model;

OR

one piece of evidence which contradicts the monetarist model.   **3 Marks**

Total Marks = 24

SECTION C - 60 MARKS

ANSWER **TWO** QUESTIONS ONLY - 24 MARKS EACH

---

4. **(a)** Explain how the price mechanism operates to allocate resources in a market economy.

    6 Marks

    (b) Show what is meant by the terms *public goods* and *merit goods,* AND explain why the price mechanism might not be an effective one for allocating resources in these cases.   **10 Marks**

    (c) Using appropriate diagrams, explain how governments may use *indirect taxes* and *subsidiaries* to alter the consumption and output of particular goods.   **8 Marks**

    Total Marks = 24

---

5. **(a)** Explain what is meant by the term *financial intermediation.*   **4 Marks**

    (b) Describe the economic functions of stock markets and their role in the process of financial intermediation.   **10 Marks**

    (c) Explain how share prices are determined, AND identify and explain TWO factors that would lead to a rise in the general level of share prices.   **10 Marks**

    Total Marks = 24

---

6. **(a)** Explain what is meant by *monetary policy,* AND discuss the circumstances under which a government might wish to adopt a *restrictive (contractionary)* monetary policy.   **8 Marks**

    (b) Explain the methods by which a central bank might conduct a restrictive monetary policy.

    8 Marks

    (c) Explain the probable effects of a restrictive monetary policy on

    (i)   business profits,   **4 Marks**
    (ii) business investment.   **4 Marks**

    Total Marks = 24

---

7. **(a)** Distinguish between *structural unemployment* and *cyclical (demand deficient) unemployment.*

    8 Marks

    (b) Explain how governments could use fiscal policy to reduce unemployment.   **8 Marks**

    (c) Explain why fiscal policy may not always be effective in reducing unemployment.   **8 Marks**

    Total Marks = 24

---

8. **(a)** Explain how exchange rates are determined in the foreign exchange markets, AND identify the main factors involved.   **6 Marks**

    (b) Describe the economic effects of an *appreciation (rise)* in a country's exchange rate on

    (i)   the terms of trade,   **5 Marks**
    (ii) the balance of trade.   **5 Marks**

    (c) Identify and explain TWO benefits for the business sector of a country which joins with other countries in adopting a single, common currency (eg the European Union).   **8 Marks**

    Total Marks = 24

SPECIAL ANSWER SHEET FOR SECTION A

1.1   A   B   C   D

1.2   A   B   C   D

1.3   A   B   C   D

1.4   A   B   C   D

1.5   A   B   C   D

1.6   A   B   C   D

1.7   A   B   C   D

1.8   A   B   C   D

1.9   A   B   C   D

1.10   A   B   C   D

1.11   A   B   C   D

1.12   A   B   C   D

1.13   A   B   C   D

1.14   A   B   C   D

ANSWERS

DO NOT TURN THIS PAGE UNTIL YOU HAVE COMPLETED THE MOCK EXAM

1.1	B	D looks tempting, but it is not as precise as B

1.2	D	Tax depends upon tax computations, not economic reality. Don't forget that normal profit is the opportunity cost of enterprise.

1.3	C	A and D = elastic demand, B = unit elasticity.

1.4	D	Members of a cartel can locate anywhere.

1.5	A	This is a point of definition.

1.6	B	A relates to two different firms and D relates to two different products. C is tempting, but it is the different conditions of supply which lead to the price difference.

1.7	C	Product differentiation is an important example of non-price competition.

1.8	D	A and B are not **in themselves** undesirable. C is a political point rather than an economic one.

1.9	C	This is a badly worded question. It appears to be asking for a point of definition of the difference between banks and building societies as they used to be. It would be clearer if the words 'in that' were substituted for 'because'.

1.10	A	The higher the risk, the higher the return.

1.11	B	Different types of money have differing degrees of liquidity.

1.12	A	A transfer payment is one not made in return for a productive service.

1.13	C	Highly mobile capital and labour could themselves move to wherever they were most efficiently employed.

1.14	D	This would make imports more expensive.

2

> **Pass marks.** This question revolves around the growth in petrol retailing by the supermarkets and the decline of the independent retailers. Barriers to entry are a major point of theory, with oligopoly a subsidiary one. In part (b), the CIMA suggested solution gave a fairly standard list of economies of scale without relating them to petrol retailing.

(a) Since 1990, the supermarkets have built up a 20% share of the £20 billion petrol market, competing principally on price. Their willingness to do this has forced prices down quite significantly, resulting in a one-third cut in profit per litre.

The major oil companies, led by Esso, responded with a major price war two years ago. Petrol retailing is largely **oligopolistic** and a price war would not be expected to produce much change in market share. It is no surprise that prices have recovered.

The reduction in after-tax revenue per litre has affected smaller independent retailers badly. They do not enjoy the same economies of scale as the large operators and cannot cover their costs at the reduced prices. Partly as a result of this, their numbers have fallen to less than 10,000, though the supermarkets are not entirely responsible; the decline in their numbers actually started in the 1960s.

(b) Economies of scale are factors that cause average cost to decline in the long run as output volume increases. They must not be confused with the **short run cost reductions** associated with the **division of labour**.

Internal economies of scale arise from the more effective use of resources by the firm, while **external economies** of scale arise because of the growth of the industry as a whole. An example of the former is the utilisation of indivisibilities, such as being able to run a large machine at its maximum capacity; the **fixed cost is the same whatever the throughput**, so fixed cost per unit declines as volume increases. An example of an external economy of scale is the creation of a large pool of skilled labour which individual firms can draw on.

Working forwards through the supply chain, economies in the petrol industry would include those discussed below. *(Note that the first item does not strictly relate to petrol **retailing**, but we have included it since the oil majors are involved at all stages of the industry.)*

- The ability to build larger storage facilities and to ship larger quantities in larger tankers would give advantage, as would the use of larger oil refineries. These are examples of **dimensional economies of scale** where capacity expands as the cube of the linear dimension but the increase in costs of construction and operation are much lower.

- Where crude oil and refined products are bought on the international markets, **purchasing economies** would occur: higher volumes could be purchased at lower prices.

- **Marketing expenditure would be more economic** as the number of outlets grew: the same corporate image designs would be used, the brand name would gain increased exposure and advertising campaigns would reach more motorists who had access to the product.

- **Stockholding would become more efficient**. The most economic quantities of inventory to hold increase with the scale of operations, but at a lower proportionate rate of increase.

(c) **Economies of scale make larger operations more profitable than small ones**. In this industry, the supermarkets have achieved a market share of over 20%. This implies a very large scale of operations and the enjoyment of the economies of scale outlined above. As a result, they have been able to make an acceptable level of profit and have continued in petrol retailing, even during a price war. The independent retailers, on the other hand, operating on a smaller scale, have not achieved the same economies. At the same time, their margins have been squeezed by falling prices. As a result, many of them have left the industry.

(d) After-tax revenues have fallen by one third since 1990, the time of the entry of the supermarkets into petrol retailing. This indicates **that the retailers are competing on price**, quite apart from the price war of two years ago. The reduction in the numbers of independent retailers is, to some extent, also a symptom of competition on price. The **less efficient** retailers were unable to make satisfactory levels of profit and so they left the industry.

(e) Competition makes it more difficult to sell since the consumer has **choice** and must be **persuaded to buy**. This means that suppliers must offer greater benefits. These may take the form of enhanced product features, reduced price, or more intangible factors such as the perceived security of buying an established brand.

Petrol is a commodity, **with little scope for product enhancement**, so it is likely that the chief inducement to buy will be reduced price. However, the increasingly oligopolistic nature of the industry will probably limit competition on price. There is scope for extending the opening hours of filling stations and extending the range of goods and facilities they offer. Filling stations themselves can be built in convenient locations and provided with canopies to keep the weather at bay. There will also be loyalty schemes of various types, most largely worthless in economic terms, but providing some innocent amusement.

(f) The Director said that smaller filling stations could charge higher prices to offset lower volumes and survive by being innovative. The aim for the smaller retailer would be to justify higher prices by providing some element of service or convenience that the larger operators did not. Some customers might value such services as pump attendants, having windscreens cleaned and oil and screenwash topped up. Also, there may be some local markets in areas of sparse population where the volume of sales is not great enough to interest the larger operators. A small retailer could enjoy a local monopoly under such conditions.

3

Pass marks. Note that the consumer credit series gives the *increase* in lending, not the absolute value. This is a common source of misunderstanding in data response questions. Make absolutely certain you understand the nature of the data presented in time series.

In part (d) you are given a choice; we have considered both options for completeness. Do not be tempted to do this in the exam – you will not score extra marks!

(a) Real gross domestic product (GDP) is a major component of national income, adjusted to remove the effect of inflation on the value of money. The **GDP series** indicates that there was **growth in the economy from 1987 to 1990**, albeit at a reducing rate. The economy shrank in 1991 and did not begin to expand again until 1993. It was not until 1994 that GDP exceeded the value for 1990. This indicates that **productive potential was underemployed** and output less than it could have been between 1990 and 1994.

A similar picture emerges from the consumer credit series. Growth in lending collapsed over the three years 1990-1992, though there was never an actual reduction in the total amount lent compared with the previous year. **Consumer credit is closely linked to the level of consumption** in the economy and these figures indicate that the level of consumption stagnated between 1991 and 1993. **Confidence** in the their own economic prospects is necessary before consumers commit themselves to borrowing in order to finance consumption. Growth in lending did not recover significantly until 1994.

The series on sales of cars confirms the indications given by the first two series selected. Sales grew steadily during the first three years of the period and then declined rapidly to a low in 1992. There was some recovery during the remainder of the period, but by 1997, the level of sales was still lower than in 1987. A car is a major purchase for most households, usually requiring finance over several years, so this decline emphasises the loss of economic confidence mentioned above. We are not told which country these figures refer to, but in the UK, most new car purchases are made by companies. A cut in the company car budget is a very common way for UK companies to reduce costs, which would be a standard reaction to recession.

(b) Interest rates affect consumer expenditure in three ways.

   • When a household has **variable rate loan commitments**, such as most mortgages in the UK, its **disposable income** depends on the interest rate. If interest rates go up, its disposable income and hence its consumption fall and vice-versa.

- Interest rates affect to some extent the willingness of households to finance consumption by borrowing. If interest rates are very low, borrowing and consumption are likely to boom, while very high rates will have the opposite effect.

- Households with surplus funds have to decide what to do with the money. High interest rates may encourage prosperous households to save more and consume less. However, poorer households may well prefer to improve their material standard of living.

(c) Irving Fisher first formulated the quantity theory of money in 1911, in the form of the identity

$$MV \equiv PT$$

Where M is the money supply, V is the velocity of circulation, P is the general level of prices and T is the number of transactions. MV and PT are, effectively, two different ways of measuring the level of activity in the economy. T was believed to be constant and V to change only very slowly, if at all. With these assumptions, the theory predicts that **inflation is directly related to increases in the money supply.**

Milton Friedman re-stated the quantity theory of money, as follows.

$$MV \equiv PQ$$

Where Q is the quantity of national output per period, and PQ is the money value of national income at current prices.

Monetarists argue that V and Q are independent of M. Therefore, an increase in money supply M will tend to raise prices P, by the following process.

- Individuals will have more money than they want.

- They will spend this excess money, buying not just bonds (as Keynes believed) but also equities and physical goods.

- The greater demand for physical goods will boost expenditure in the economy and hence the money value of national income.

- However, a rapid increase in the money supply will increase spending at a faster rate than the economy will be able to produce more physical output.

- A rapid increase in the money supply will therefore inevitably be inflationary.

For monetarists, **changes in the money supply cause changes in the money value of national income.** This contrasts with the Keynesian view that changes in the money supply are caused by changes in national income, not vice versa.

(d) Let us assume that the consumer credit series gives a rough indication of the growth of the money supply. We can then see that the fall in the annual rate of growth from £6.8bn in 1989 to £0.5bn in 1992 was accompanied, with a lag of one year, by a fall in inflation from 9.8% to 1.2% over the period 1990 to 1993. This would tend to support the monetarist view that the rate of inflation depends on the growth of the money supply, since falls in the one were followed by falls in the other.

However, between 1994 and 1997, the annual growth of the money supply accelerated from £5.7bn to £12.1bn. During this period, inflation remained more or less constant at about 3%, and, if we assume the same one year lag and consider the three years 1995 – 7, it actually declined slightly. This contradicts the prediction of the monetarist view.

4

> **Pass marks.** Part(a) of this question is a most fundamental part of economic theory. You absolutely must be able to explain it. Parts(b) and (c) are also basic topics you should be familiar with; standard diagrams are the key to the answers.

(a) The basic economic problem is that **resources** are finite but people's **wants** have no limit. In a market economy, the price mechanism operates to achieve the most satisfactory possible allocation of scarce resources.

A good's **equilibrium price is set automatically by the interaction of supply and demand**. If supply exceeds demand at a given price, the price will fall, and vice versa, until equilibrium is reached. At the equilibrium price the quantities supplied and demanded are equal. There are no shortages and no surpluses. The price mechanism thus automatically accounts for both customers' preferences for consumption and firms' capacity to produce.

When excess demand causes the price of a good to rise, the producers make **supernormal profit**. This encourages them to increase production and attracts other firms to enter the market. Extra resources are thus automatically allocated to production of the good and supply increases. As supply increases, the price falls until the equilibrium price is reached; supernormal profit disappears and supply and demand are equal.

A similar process reduces the consumption of resources for the production of a good in surplus. If **supply exceeds demand, the equilibrium price falls** and producers make less profit. They discount existing stocks and cut back production. Some firms may leave the industry. There is thus an automatic reduction in the quantity of resources devoted to the good. Supply falls until it matches demand at a new equilibrium price.

(b) The consumption of a **public good** by one individual or group does not significantly reduce the amount available for others. Furthermore, it is often difficult or impossible to exclude anyone from enjoying the benefits of such a good, once it has been produced. The classic example of a public good is a lighthouse: its light cannot be affected by mariners' observing it, nor can they be prevented from doing so. As a result of these characteristics, **individuals benefiting from a public good have no economic incentive to pay for it**, since they might as well be **free riders** if they can, enjoying the good while others pay for it. The provision of public goods therefore tends to be undertaken by governments and paid for from public funds.

As explained above, the price mechanism incorporates people's preferences into the allocation of resources, and those preferences vary from person to person. Also, inequalities of income constrain the consumption patterns of poorer households. Both these factors tend to reduce the resources allocated in a free market to the production of certain **goods whose consumption could be objectively considered to be beneficial to all**. Such goods are called **merit goods**; they are considered to be worth providing in greater volume than would be purchased in a free market, because **higher consumption is in the long-term public interest**. Education is one of the chief examples of a merit good. A high standard of general education is without doubt an important pre-requisite for economic growth. However, it is quite costly to provide and there are many parents who could not afford to provide it for their children and some who would choose not to do so. Education is thus provided by government throughout the developed world and in many less developed countries as well.

(c) An **indirect tax** is imposed on expenditure on goods and services. A **selective indirect tax** is one imposed on some goods and services but not on others (or which is imposed at a higher rate).

If an indirect tax is imposed on a good, the tax will shift the supply curve upward by the amount the tax adds to the price of each item. This is because the price to consumers includes the tax, but the suppliers still only receive the net-of-tax price. In the diagram:

- the supply curve net of tax is S_0
- the supply curve including the cost of the tax is S_1
- the tax is equal to $P_1 - P_2$ or the distance A - B.

So if demand is for X_1 units, say, the price received by suppliers will be P_2 but the price with tax to the consumer would be P_1 - and the tax would be $(P_1 - P_2)$ or distance AB.

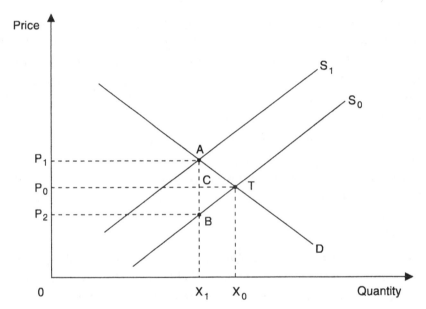

An indirect tax

Without the tax, output would be X_0 and price P_0. Total expenditure is shown by the rectangle OP_0TX_0. After the tax has been imposed, a new equilibrium arises at point A; output falls to X_1 and price with tax rises to P_1. Total expenditure is OP_1AX_1, of which P_2P_1AB is tax revenue and OP_2BX_1 is producers' total revenue.

The effect of the tax is to reduce both output and consumption of the good.

A **subsidy** is a payment to the supplier of a good by the government. It is rather like indirect taxation in reverse. It shifts the supply curve downward by the amount of the subsidy.

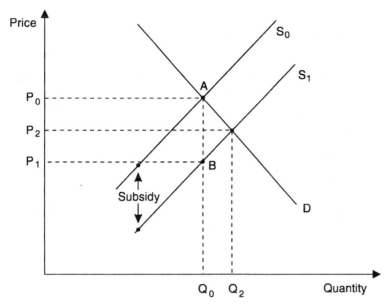

Subsidy

In the diagram:

(i)   supply curve S_0 is what the supply curve would be if no subsidy existed

(ii)   supply curve S_1, to the right of S_0, is the supply curve making allowance for the subsidy.

For example, if output is Q_0, the price to consumers is P_1, but the price to the suppliers is P_0, because suppliers receive the subsidy AB or $(P_0 - P_1)$ on top of the market price paid by consumers.

If there were no subsidy, the free market equilibrium price would be P_0, and output Q_0.

A subsidy per unit equivalent to AB is introduced so that suppliers would now be willing to produce Q_0 at a lower price (P_1 rather than at P_0). In other words, the supply curve shifts from S_0 to S_1. But there will be a shift in the equilibrium quantity produced to Q_2, which can be sold on the market for P_2. Thus the effect of the subsidy will be:

(i)   to increase the amount supplied in equilibrium; and

(ii)   to decrease the price, but the decrease in price will be less than the value of the subsidy itself.

5

Pass marks. In part (c) we have provided several examples of factors which affect share prices.

(a) **Financial intermediation** comprises the processes involved in channelling funds from lenders to borrowers. **Financial intermediaries** provide important services.

- Their **expertise** allows them to advise their clients on where to invest funds for the best return and on ways of raising finance. It also enables them to use money deposited with them in the most profitable way. This **encourages saving** and **provides finance for potentially profitable projects**. They enhance **allocative efficiency**.

- They undertake **maturity transformation**. Depositors generally wish their funds to be reasonably liquid, while borrowers wish to be sure that their finance is secure and will not be suddenly withdrawn. Financial intermediaries can **lend for longer periods of time than they borrow** because they have a **continuing stream of short-term depositors**. The total of money deposited remains high enough to finance long term loans even though on any given day many short-term deposits are repaid. This is profitable for the intermediaries as they receive higher rates of interest from long-term borrowers than they have to pay to short term-depositors.

- Financial intermediaries also perform **risk transformation**. Any individual borrower may fail to pay back a loan. Risk-averse savers would thus be unlikely to lend directly to borrowers. The financial intermediary spreads the risk across many loans and factors it into the interest charged. Even though some of the money deposited collectively by savers may be lost, the intermediary is able to guarantee the repayment of any individual deposit.

(b) **Stock markets** are markets where financial instruments issued by commercial organisations are traded. These financial instruments are of two principal types: **shares**, which represent an element of **ownership** of the company, and **bonds** or **debentures**, which represent a **loan** to the company.

A **stock** market has two main components: the **primary** market and the **secondary** market.

The primary market is concerned with new issues. This is the process by which capital is raised for new companies and to invest in new projects.

The secondary market is where existing shares and bonds are bought and sold. This market does not provide capital for companies; its function is to **provide liquidity for investors** by enabling them to realise their assets. This makes investment in new issues more attractive, since investors are not locked in to their investments.

An important aspect of a stock market is the **degree of security it gives to investors**. It should regulate the process of financial intermediation to prevent fraud and sharp practice and should ensure that investors receive sufficient information to make informed investment decisions. Stock market regulations should **enhance the efficiency of resource allocation**.

A stock market also contributes to the **public finances** by facilitating trade in government debt; this provides liquidity for investors and for the government.

(c) The market in shares is not controlled in any way, so the price of shares is determined by **the interaction of supply and demand**. An equilibrium price is reached in the normal way. While the total number of shares in a given company is finite, the amount available for purchase will tend to increase as their price goes up and shareholders are tempted to sell by the prospect of a capital gain. Demand for a share is affected by a number of factors, which are dealt with below.

A major influence on demand for a given share is the market's **perception of its likely future profitability**. A company which is trading successfully, or which has announced an advantageous new product or appointed a respected chief executive, will find demand for its shares rising.

Sometimes **fashion** will create demand, occasionally to a seemingly irrational extent. An excellent example of this is the current enthusiasm for any company which proposes to exploit the Internet.

The **trade cycle** and the state of the economy affect demand for shares: during a boom most share prices will rise, but if **interest rates** are raised to combat inflation, companies will be less profitable and prices will fall.

There are also **longer-term effects** such as the growing prosperity of the post-war 'boomer' generation which has contributed to the sustained rise in US share prices. The growth of personal pensions in the UK has had a similar effect.

6

> **Passmarks.** There are other monetary policy controls which you could mention in part (b), including hire-purchase controls and special deposits by banks at the Central Bank.

(a)   A government's monetary policy is concerned with the money supply, interest rates and the exchange rate of its currency. It is a fundamental area of macroeconomic management, with particular relevance to inflation.

Monetary policy is often used to **influence aggregate demand downwards when prices are rising**. This typically occurs when the trade cycle is in the **boom phase** and shortages are appearing, particularly of skilled labour. The overall aim is to reduce growth in the money supply. This is often achieved by raising interest rates, which has the effect of reducing disposable incomes and making new borrowing less attractive.

(b)   Governments have several monetary policy techniques.

- **Open market operations.** The Central Bank can influence both interest rates and the money supply by dealing in **bills**, which are short term financial instruments. Bills are issued by companies, by local government and by central government itself. Interest rates can be raised and the money supply reduced **by increasing the supply of government bills**; the greater the supply, the lower will be the price, which equates to a higher rate of interest. The increasing discount on the government bills will attract funds, thus **reducing liquidity**. It will also make other investments less attractive, thus **forcing interest rates up**.

- **The statutory reserve ratio.** The regulator of a country's banking system will normally require clearing banks to maintain a certain minimum percentage of their assets in the form of **liquid funds**. The money supply can be controlled by altering this percentage, since **the funds are not available for lending**.

- Controls on lending. **The Central Bank may impose** direct controls **on lending by the banks. These may be** quantitative, **as when a percentage limit is placed on growth in lending, or** qualitative, **as when the banks are asked to lend only for industrial investment rather than consumption or speculation.**

(c)   A restrictive monetary policy will both reduce the availability of credit and raise interest rates. Businesses will therefore find it difficult to finance their operations and will have to pay more for their borrowing. At the same time, customers will have less disposable income and be less inclined to finance purchases by borrowing.

The increased cost of borrowing will tend to reduce businesses' profits. The reduced demand will force them to cut back the scale of their operations, possibly moving them to a higher point on their average cost curves as they lose **economies of scale**.

It has been argued that since business investment tends to be long term, it is not very sensitive to increases in interest rates. An alternative view was outlined by Keynes in the concept of the **marginal efficiency of capital**. All funds for investment have an opportunity cost: either the **interest charged for borrowing,** or the **interest that could have been earned** by investing internally generated funds elsewhere. Clearly, a business will not invest in a project if its anticipated returns are less than the cost of the capital required. **As interest rates rise, the number of projects worth investing in reduces** and hence the total value of investment may be expected to fall.

7

> **Passmarks.** The first two parts of this question are quite straightforward, but part (c) is more demanding. You may have a difficult choice to make in the exam when deciding which questions to do. Do not rush into a question unless you are reasonably sure you can tackle all the parts. On the other hand, if you are scratching around for your last question, one like this might be a good choice, since you can almost certainly get good marks on the first two parts, even if you do badly on the third.
>
> *Prize winner point.* The **balanced budget multiplier,** mentioned in part (b) is a simple but impressive point to make in any discussion of fiscal policy.

(a) **Demand deficient unemployment** occurs when the level of aggregate demand in the economy falls below the level necessary to maintain full employment. In other words, there is a **deflationary gap**. Aggregate demand is made up of a number of elements so, for instance, a reduction in government expenditure can lead to demand deficient unemployment, as can a high exchange rate if it reduces export demand. The alternative name for this type of unemployment, **cyclical unemployment**, emphasises that it is associated with the recession phase of the economic cycle, when domestic demand of all kinds is likely to fall.

Demand deficient unemployment is likely to affect all parts of the economy simultaneously, but **structural unemployment** tends to be concentrated by region or industrial sector. It arises because of **developments that change the structure of the economy, causing industries to decline.** Such developments are often associated with **technological developments,** as when robots replace labour (productivity increases, but workers are made redundant) or the development of new **substitutes** for older products, as when the availability of powerful PCs reduced the demand for mainframe computers.

Structural unemployment often affects **specific regions,** since many industries develop in tight clusters, usually to take advantage of some local advantage. The UK cotton industry had a heavy concentration in Lancashire, so when cheaper foreign cotton products captured the market, Lancashire suffered heavy unemployment.

(b) **Fiscal policy** is that part of government policy that deals with **taxation,** and the government's own **spending** and **borrowing**. Government spending is an important **injection** into the national circular flow of income and thus an important part of **aggregate demand** (AD). If a government's spending is greater than its tax revenues, it must make up the difference by borrowing. This will expand AD and the money supply, increasing economic activity and creating more demand for labour. Even a balanced budget, where spending is paid for entirely by taxation, will have an expansionary effect. This is because taxpayers would have saved some of the money paid in tax, if they had been able to keep it, but the **government spends it all**; this is called the **balanced budget multiplier.**

Such an expansionary policy is only appropriate if there is an **inflationary gap,** that is to say, national income is below the full employment level. If full employment already exists, such a policy will merely lead to shortages of labour, rising wages costs and cost-push inflation.

(c) There are a number of reasons why an **expansionary fiscal policy** may not succeed in reducing unemployment.

Welfare benefits tend to rise when a government commits itself to increased spending, for political reasons. This has two negative effects on unemployment.

- A **poverty trap** may arise, in which the unemployed are worse off in low-paid employment than not working at all.

- High benefits can make people **more selective in the work they will consider doing**; the ensuing longer period of job search is an increase in **frictional unemployment**.

Fiscal policy measures are subject to **significant and unpredictable time lags** before they take effect, particularly because of the interaction of the accelerator and the multiplier. As a result, an expansionary policy measure undertaken during a recession may not produce results until the recovery is already under way, it then merely adds to inflationary pressures.

Expansionary fiscal policies are widely believed to increase the rate of **inflation**. Government borrowing in the form of short-dated bills merely replaces one form of liquidity in the banking system with another; the **banks can continue to create credit** at the former rate and the government spends the funds it has borrowed. The result is **an increase in the money supply**.

Heavy government borrowing will inevitably force interest rates **up. As a result, customers will have less** disposable income **and they will be less inclined to finance purchases by** borrowing. **AD will thus tend to fall. Also, businesses will have to pay more for their borrowing; a business will not invest in a project if its anticipated returns are less than the cost of the capital required. As interest rates rise, the number of projects worth investing in reduces and hence the total of investment may be expected to fall.**

8

> **Passmarks.** This is a question which can be answered in fairly simple terms; the danger with such a question lies in going over the top and answering at too much length. You must allocate your time carefully with questions like this so that you achieve a balanced answer, with all parts treated fairly.

(a) Fundamentally, exchange rates are determined by the **relative supply of and demand for the two currencies concerned** on the international currency markets. If residents of the US wish to buy UK goods they must exchange dollars for sterling to do so. Similarly, UK residents wishing to buy US goods must obtain dollars by exchanging sterling. The relative volumes of dollars and sterling being traded determine the dollar/sterling exchange rate.

Demand for goods is not the only factor determining demand for currency. A more important factor is **the demand for financial instruments**; the current **high price of sterling** is a result of **overseas demand for UK securities**, which is itself the result of the relatively **high level of UK interest rates**.

While free-floating exchange rates, determined as explained above, are now usual in the developed world, for many years exchange rates were fixed and maintained at set values by **central bank intervention** in the foreign exchange markets, creating demand or supply as required.

(b) (i) A country's **terms of trade relate the average price level of its exports to that of its imports**. Thus, if a country's exports are largely agricultural produce and its imports are mostly **machinery**; and the price of foodstuffs falls on world markets but the price of tractors remains the same: then that country's terms of trade have deteriorated. Notice that the terms of trade relate to prices only; actual volumes of imports and exports have nothing to do with determining them, though a change in the **terms of trade** may affect the **quantity of trade**

Terms of trade are usually measured by establishing index numbers for the prices of imports and exports. These are related by this formula:

$$\text{Index of export prices} \frac{\text{Index of export prices}}{\text{Index of import prices}} \times 100$$

A rise in a country's exchange rate will mean that its exports are worth more foreign currency, while the cost of its imports in foreign currency will not have changed. As a result, its terms of trade have improved.

(ii) A country's **balance of trade** accounts for the **total values of its imports and exports of** physical **goods**. It thus differs from the terms of trade since it encompasses **volumes** as well as **prices**.

If a country's exchange rate appreciates, **imports become cheaper** when valued in the home **currency**; if demand for imports is price-elastic, the total value of imports will increase. At the same time, **exports will become more expensive** in **foreign currency**; if demand for them is also elastic, their total value will go down. As a result, it is likely that **the balance of trade will deteriorate**; the greater the combined price elasticities of imports and exports, the greater the deterioration is likely to be.

(c) The main advantage for business of international currencies such as the Euro is reduction in the costs associated with transactions involving two currencies.

- The **transaction costs** associated with buying and selling foreign currency will be avoided.

- **Hedging** against future exchange rate movements, with its associated costs, will no longer be necessary.

There will be other **general economic advantages**. Provision of **international finance** would become easier, since the values of the assets and liabilities involved would not be subject to the fluctuations of exchange rates. Similarly, possible exchange rate movements could be eliminated from considerations of **price**. This should make international business more attractive. International business generally should become more attractive, providing greater opportunities for growth in sales and sources of supply. The consequent **expansion** should tend to increase **economies of scale**.

See overleaf for information on other
BPP products and how to order

CIMA Order

To BPP Publishing Ltd, Aldine Place, London W12 8AA

Tel: 020 8740 2211. Fax: 020 8740 1184

Mr/Mrs/Ms (Full name) _____

Daytime delivery address _____

Postcode _____

Daytime Tel _____

Date of exam (month/year) _____

	7/99 Texts	1/2000 Kits	1/2000 Psscrds	1999 Tapes	1999 Videos	1999 CDs
STAGE 1						
1 Financial Accounting Fundamentals	£18.95 ☐	£9.95 ☐	£5.95 ☐	£12.95 ☐	£25.00 ☐	£34.95 ☐
2 Cost Accounting and Quantitative Methods	£18.95 ☐	£9.95 ☐	£5.95 ☐	£12.95 ☐	£25.00 ☐	£34.95 ☐
3 Economic Environment	£18.95 ☐	£9.95 ☐	£5.95 ☐	£12.95 ☐	£25.00 ☐	£34.95 ☐
4 Business Environment & Information Technology	£18.95 ☐	£9.95 ☐	£5.95 ☐	£12.95 ☐	£25.00 ☐	£34.95 ☐
STAGE 2						
5 Financial Accounting	£18.95 ☐	£9.95 ☐	£5.95 ☐	£12.95 ☐	£25.00 ☐	£34.95 ☐
6 Operational Cost Accounting	£18.95 ☐	£9.95 ☐	£5.95 ☐	£12.95 ☐	£25.00 ☐	£34.95 ☐
7 Management Science Applications	£18.95 ☐	£9.95 ☐	£5.95 ☐	£12.95 ☐	£25.00 ☐	£34.95 ☐
8 Business and Company Law	£18.95 ☐	£9.95 ☐	£5.95 ☐	£12.95 ☐	£25.00 ☐	£34.95 ☐
STAGE 3						
9 Financial Reporting	£19.95 ☐	£10.95 ☐	£5.95 ☐	£12.95 ☐	£25.00 ☐	£34.95 ☐
10 Management Accounting Applications	£19.95 ☐	£10.95 ☐	£5.95 ☐	£12.95 ☐	£25.00 ☐	
11 Organisational Management & Development	£19.95 ☐	£10.95 ☐	£5.95 ☐	£12.95 ☐	£25.00 ☐	
12 Business Taxation (FA 99)	£19.95 ☐	£10.95 ☐	£5.95 ☐	£12.95 ☐	£25.00 ☐	
STAGE 4						
13 Strategic Financial Management	£20.95 ☐	£10.95 ☐	£5.95 ☐	£12.95 ☐	£25.00 ☐	
14 Strategic Management Accountancy & Mktg	£20.95 ☐	£10.95 ☐	£5.95 ☐	£12.95 ☐	£25.00 ☐	
15 Information Management	£20.95 ☐	£10.95 ☐	£5.95 ☐	£12.95 ☐	£25.00 ☐	
16 Management Accounting Control Systems	£20.95 ☐	£10.95 ☐	£5.95 ☐	£12.95 ☐	£25.00 ☐	

£ ☐

POSTAGE & PACKING

Study Texts

	First	Each extra	
UK	£3.00	£2.00	£ ☐
Europe*	£5.00	£4.00	£ ☐
Rest of world	£20.00	£10.00	£ ☐

Kits/Passcards/Success Tapes

	First	Each extra	
UK	£2.00	£1.00	£ ☐
Europe*	£2.50	£1.00	£ ☐
Rest of world	£15.00	£8.00	£ ☐

Master CDs/Breakthrough Videos

	First	Each extra	
UK	£2.00	£2.00	£ ☐
Europe*	£2.00	£2.00	£ ☐
Rest of world	£20.00	£10.00	£ ☐

Grand Total (Cheques to *BPP Publishing*) I enclose a cheque for (incl. Postage) £ ☐☐☐☐

Or charge to Access/Visa/Switch

Card Number ☐☐☐☐ ☐☐☐☐ ☐☐☐☐ ☐☐☐☐

Expiry date ☐☐☐☐   Start Date ☐☐☐☐

Issue Number (Switch Only) ☐☐

Signature _____

We aim to deliver to all UK addresses inside 5 working days. Orders to all EU addresses should be delivered within 6 working days. All other orders to overseas addresses should be delivered within 8 working days.

* Europe includes the Republic of Ireland and the Channel Islands.